Praise for
DROWNING IN ADDICTION

"Whether you are struggling with addiction, or have a loved one struggling with addiction, this book is an amazing resource! There are so many lessons that will help you rise above your struggles. This book provides tools to cultivate faith that everybody can join the movement and RECOVER OUT LOUD!"

—Carey Peters, Co-Founder of the Health Coach Institute

"If you're struggling or know someone who is struggling with an addiction, read this book. The authors offer a diverse array of paths to recovery. Through their courageous stories, they offer new hope. They prove their thesis: EVERYONE can recover. This book could change your life. In fact, **this book could save your life.**"

—Sara Connell, author *Bringing In Finn*

"As someone whose lost a best friend to addiction, I can confidently say this is a must read for anyone who is looking for a way out, or any friend or family member supporting someone in the same."

—Zander Fryer, best-selling author and
world-renowned speaker

"Recovering out loud is what our world needs now. Through their vulnerable personal stories and hard won guidance, these authors represent the future of addiction recovery by recovering out loud versus in anonymity."

—Craig Ballantyne, author, *The Perfect Day Formula*

"This book was written by not just one, but three people who broke free from the ruthless chains of addiction that destroys relationships, and steals so many lives. They each have a unique, gripping story from the belly of the beast through withdrawal, relapse and finally recovery. A courageous, insightful book loaded with powerful questions and raw truths from three survivors undeniably committed to helping others. They are the real deal."

—Stacey Morgenstern, Co-Founder, Health Coach Institute

"The authors share their experience, wisdom and hope with open, courageous hearts. I love seeing powerful leaders coming together to vulnerably share themselves for the benefit of others."

—Eric Neuner, CEO, Health Coach Institute

DROWNING IN ADDICTION

DROWNING IN
ADDICTION
SINK OR SWIM
A PERSONAL GUIDE FOR CHOOSING
YOUR LEGIT PATH TO RECOVERY

SCOTT LEEPER
MICHAEL ARNOLD
ANDREA CARR

gatekeeper press

Columbus, Ohio

Drowning in Addiction: Sink or Swim

Published by Gatekeeper Press
2167 Stringtown Rd, Suite 109
Columbus, OH 43123-2989
www.GatekeeperPress.com

ISBN (hardcover): 9781642374629
ISBN (paperback): 9781642374612
eISBN: 9781642374605

Printed in the United States of America

Dedication

For Scott's father.

For those who sunk and taught us the ways
in which not to live.

For those who continue to swim and win their battles
against addiction.

For the families who had to grow and continue to learn
through the adversity of addiction.

Acknowledgements

The authors would like to collectively thank:

- The Health Coach Institute, Carey Peters, and Stacey Morgenstern (co-founders of HCI), and Eric Neuner (CEO of HCI)—for bringing light to the world, instilling belief in ourselves, letting us know that change is possible, and ultimately bringing us together to create a powerful book.

- Sara Connell—For being an amazing person and writing coach, and for calling us thought leaders from the beginning before we saw it in ourselves. You were instrumental in bringing our personal power out.

- Those who allowed us to tell your story—Your story is more powerful than you know and will reach people that need to hear your story specifically. Your challenges, tragedies, and successes will impact lives throughout the world!

- Our endorsers—Your belief in us and our message is unparalleled. We greatly appreciate you sharing our message within your spheres of influence.

Michael would like also to acknowledge:

Dad: You are my hero. You are my saving grace. I love you.

Mom: You are the definition of unconditional love. I love you to the moon and back and beyond the stars.

Ann: Thank you for your love and support.

Twinney: We shared an egg. You are my right hand man. My best friend. You are my savior. Thank you for always pushing me to never settle. Thank you for seeing what I am capable of before I could see it. #5 and #11 forever.

CT: Thank you for believing in me and for ALWAYS being there for me without any judgment. You are the most selfless person I know. CT, I love you so much.

To my Sponsor Robin Miller: Words do not do justice for what you mean to me. You were the first one to tell me that my past is my greatest asset. I love you so much.

Dave-O Whitelaw: For always telling me to not just carry the message but to BE the message.

Marcy Pickering: You saw me in the dark and stayed until I found the light. You have never left my side. Your friendship and love is unconditional. Thank you for not giving up on me.

Zander Fryer: You helped me to believe that anything I want to do is possible. ANYTHING. You gave me permission to fly.

To My Mentors: To those of you who have mentored me at some point during this journey I am on: THANK YOU. Thank you for giving me love, advice, and insights so I can continue to grow into the coach, author, speaker, and person that I have become. Words do not do justice for what you have given me and continue to give me. I am eternally grateful.

Andrea would also like to acknowledge:

Dad: I miss you every day. In a lot of ways, I saw myself in you. Our battle was the same—and even though you left us the way you did, I have found light in that darkness. I continue to fight for myself and my recovery largely because of you, your choices, and your death. I know you fought long and hard, and that you did the best you could. I love you, I miss you, and I forgive you.

Mom: You have always supported me, been there for me, and helped me find the way the many times I was lost. I could not ask for a better mom. You are grace incarnate. I love you so much.

Roger: Thank you for stepping into the role of being the kind of father figure that I always wish I'd had. Your unwavering love, faith, and dedication has been instrumental in how close and how strong our family bond is. I know I can always depend on you, and that means the world to me.

My siblings and my friends: You guys are the best friends I'll ever have. All of you have witnessed me go through the deepest lows and the highest highs, and each of you continue to cheer me on in my recovery journey. You are the best team I could have. I am incredibly proud of all of you, and I love you guys to the moon and back.

Scott would also like to acknowledge:

Dad: Through your death, you taught me the ways in which not to live. In death, you continue to teach me how to live life to the fullest, reach those struggling with inner demons, and never compromise my dreams and ambitions. I love you. I miss you.

Ashley: You have been with me through the roughest of times and the best of times. Thank you for seeing the good in me, even after my mistakes. Thank you for making me feel on cloud nine while keeping me grounded! You continue to be my rock, and this journey is sweeter with you on it with me! I love you.

Jaxson: Thank you for being an amazing son! You are full of life and personality. It is the greatest honor of my life to be your dad. I will always love you and will always be proud of the amazing person you are becoming. I love you, son.

Serio Pensa: Our conversations have furthered my resolve to become the best entrepreneur that I know how to be. You have instilled a higher level of belief in me that I didn't see, even a year ago.

My mentors: Those of you who have mentored me at some point during this journey I am on, I couldn't be more grateful for the advice and insights you have provided so I can grow into the coach, author, speaker, and person that I have become.

Our service members and first responders: My brothers and sisters, I couldn't be prouder of the work you do for our communities and our nation. Thank you for standing guard and keeping a watchful, protective eye over us. I trust you will find insights in this book that will help you grow from all that you have experienced.

My growing support system: My family, friends, and acquaintances, your growing support has been amazing! I cannot begin to express how much your words throughout this process and my journey have meant to me. With each positive word and phrase, you add fuel to the inferno that burns inside me!

Dr. Sean Stephenson: It was your words in Phoenix that taught me "not to throw the shoe back." This simple insight has provided me the tools to see past the negative actions people take and see a person who may be struggling with something I will never understand. You continue to be my mentor, even though you weren't aware.

Contents

Introduction 1

CHAPTER 1: Michael - Part 1 11

CHAPTER 2: Andrea - Part 1 27

CHAPTER 3: Scott's Dad - Part 1 41

CHAPTER 4: Shining The Light 65

CHAPTER 5: Consequences 93

CHAPTER 6: Michael- Part 2 131

CHAPTER 7: Andrea - Part 2 159

CHAPTER 8: Scott- Part 2 173

CHAPTER 9: The Many Paths To Recovery 193

CHAPTER 10: Part 3 - Living Sober: Michael, Scott, Andrea........ 227

CHAPTER 11: The Ripple Effect.. 251

Sources For The Book.. 263

Introduction

THERE IS A young, vivacious woman in Telluride, Colorado, who goes to sleep at night with a bottle of Evan Williams Whiskey under her bed. Every few hours, she wakes up and sips on the glass lip to avoid the shakes. What little is left of her life is consumed with making sure that she is never without a drink.

A Marine stationed at Camp Lejeune, North Carolina, is about to cheat on his wife after taking his alcoholic father off life support. Every day, even months later, he hears the wheeze of his father's last breath and is consumed with rage that his father chose alcohol over life.

A young woman in Georgia with a bright future ahead of her goes into seizures from alcohol withdrawals. She doesn't know what's wrong with her at first, but she eventually realizes that, if she doesn't quit drinking, she will be dead within six months.

Addiction doesn't care who you are or where you live. It doesn't matter your race, religion, sexual orientation, or education level. A mom in the North Shore of Chicago does cocaine while her kids are at school. An African-American corporate vice president in Florida drinks his dinner. A CEO in downtown Portland hides a flask and a bottle of Xanax in his desk drawer at work. A valedictorian at an Alabama high school fills her water bottle with vodka every morning before going to school. A middle-aged gas station clerk on the outskirts of Oakland, California, gets high on meth every break. No one is free from this.

ADDICTION DOES NOT DISCRIMINATE

Our book is for the person who thinks they might have a problem, the person who knows they have a problem but has not found a way to stop, and the person who has tried AA or therapy or rehab and has not found a way to maintain sobriety. Also, it is for the friends, family, and loved ones of the addict/alcoholic.

To the addict/alcoholic:

This book is here to give you hope. This book is here as a resource for you to know that there is more than one way to recovery. This book is here to show you just how bad your life can get and also how beautiful your life can get.

To the family members/friends/loved ones:

This book is here to show you that you have no control over what the person in trouble is going to do. This book is here to give you relief from any shame or guilt you are carrying because you can't save the one in trouble. We are also here to give you hope- that there are more ways than ever for an addict to recover.

Our book is unique in several ways. First, it is written by three individuals. Second, two of the authors are addicts who found and maintain sobriety in very different ways; the other author is an individual who is not an addict but almost had his life destroyed by the addiction of a family member. Lastly, because of our individual experiences and recovery, we do not offer just one path to sobriety and healing. We believe that, just as addiction doesn't discriminate, recovery does not discriminate, either. We believe that you just have to pick a path- any path- and stick to it.

We do not sugar-coat or hand hold in this book. Denial of the harsh reality of addiction only prolongs the addiction and unhelpfully inhibits the inevitable emotions that an addict or family member must feel to recover. We want to be transparent so that you can recover. If you are in the grip of alcohol or drugs or any addiction, you are in a fight for your life. We are going to give you everything we've got so that you do not become another tragic story but instead triumph, recover, inspire others, and ultimately, heal and uplift our planet.

How This Book Came to Be

SCOTT:

In April 2018, I attended an event hosted by the Health Coach Institute. The Health Coach Institute was founded by Carey Peters and Stacey Morgenstern. During this event, a young woman stepped on stage for a coaching demonstration. The woman's name was Michael. She started to describe a person who blamed others for her wrong-doings, who made excuses for many things, etc.

"Who are you describing?" Carey asked.

With tears starting to stream down her face, Michael responded, "Myself. The person I used to be. Now, I'm in recovery. I had an addiction to alcohol for many years, and that was the way I lived my life—like a victim."

Tears filled my eyes. Not tears of sadness, but tears of pride for this young woman, whom I had never met. I honestly don't remember much of the rest of the demonstration because I was in awe over this amazing person, who was willing to share her story of addiction on stage in front of 800 strangers!

As I witnessed Michael's story, I heard the mentality of my father, especially when she described this person making excuses for everything. My dad, especially in his last year or two of life, made excuses every day for why he continued to drink.

As soon as the coaching demonstration finished, everyone in attendance had the opportunity to practice the coaching exercise with a partner. I completed the exercise but was too distracted. I had to meet Michael. I had to tell her how much I appreciated her and how proud I was of her for beating insurmountable odds! After the practice session, I waded through the crowd of coaching dyads to reach her. As I introduced myself, I felt this aura of power surrounding us.

"I'm Scott Leeper," I told her. "I just wanted to give you a hug and tell you how proud I am of you for getting sober. So many people are not with us today because they couldn't beat this, like my dad." My throat tightened and my voice cracked as I looked at this strong, healthy woman. "So thank you!"

July 16, 2018

Mishawaka, Indiana

Back home after the conference, I received a Facebook message from Andrea:

> *Hi, Scott!! I'm so inspired by all the work you are doing* (Andrea was referring to me sharing my father's story to inspire addicts and family members of addicts to seek help) *and I wanted to see if you would be interested in coming on my podcast as a guest. Thank you either way!!*

I was stunned! I knew I'd been putting my message about my dad out there, but to actually be invited onto a podcast? Of course! Admittedly, I just learned what a podcast was a few short months prior to this. If you are interested in the episode, check out her website at www.andreaecarr.com.

July 17, 2018

It's 7:00 p.m., and I am getting ready to do a podcast with Andrea to discuss the topic of emotions and addiction in the male, first responder, military, and post-traumatic stress disorder (PTSD) survivor populations.

The flow was perfect! With each question Andrea asked, I was able to articulate my answers easily, describing how addiction is tied to first responders and military with mental struggles. She asked me questions about my dad and how I was able to pull myself out of my pit of misery after his death. And what should have been about a forty-minute podcast turned into almost an hour and a half! The energy was so high, I could have talked for another four hours.

During our conversation, I couldn't help but wonder if my father had utilized the tools Andrea and I discussed- such as sobriety podcasts and a recovery coach, he would still be here today.

July 24, 2018

Not a cloud in the sky. It was a beautiful, summer day, and I was sitting in the upstairs, open area of 101Co3 (my shared workspace for entrepreneurs, small business owners, and remote employees). I was a newly certified Health and Life Coach working on building a coaching practice and fulfilling my dream of helping people on the deepest level possible, the mind. Mindset coaching can be used in many different areas of life, including addiction. Everything we do, every habit we have, and every thought we think (negative or positive) begins in the mind. While I had imagined coaching regular people to achieve greater health and success, since Andrea's podcast, I found myself thinking more and more about how addicts and families of addicts could greatly benefit from mindset coaching.

A thought popped into my head.

"I need to write a book!"

Even a year earlier, I would have laughed off the idea. I'd tried to write a book when I was a young kid, but I lost the notebook and never tried again. For the last couple of months, I had a thought growing in the back of my mind to write a book about addiction and to share my dad's story so that others didn't have to go what I went through. I didn't give it any energy until now.

I wanted to write a book. I could feel the idea burning in my chest. But the project sounded daunting. I didn't want to do it alone.

Within minutes, I was typing a message to Michael and Andrea:

Good morning, ladies! What do you think about collaborating to author a book about addiction?

On July 30, 2018, we held our first video call, and the three of us agreed to co-author a book with a big mission: to save lives, to show the many roads to recovery, and to provide hope to addicts, alcoholics, and loved ones of addicts and alcoholics. During our call, Michael told us about a writing coach who just happened to have trained with Health Coach Institute!

On August 6, 2018, we met with phenomenal writing coach, Sara Connell, for the first time. During out initial talk, one thing stuck out in my mind. Sara asked us to close our eyes and visualize the day we would receive our published book. I almost couldn't control my emotions. I had a hard time speaking. My eyes became waterfalls, and I visualized myself kneeling in the middle of an office space in a new home, hugging our new book. I saw myself speaking at community groups, treatment centers, schools, universities, organizations big and small, and conferences with Andrea and Michael. I saw people freeing themselves from addiction. I saw families healing and releasing guilt, shame, and fear of judgment. I saw a new era of addiction recovery.

RECOVER OUT LOUD

For too long—too many decades—too many people have dedicated themselves to overcoming addiction and have hidden their recovery in silence. People don't like to talk about it because they still have too much shame, guilt, and embarrassment over their past actions. We have found that there is still a lot of fear of acceptance and judgment for people being "found out" for having an addiction. We have found that people hide because of fear of relapse, fear of employers, or fear of relationship judgment; fear of self-doubt made the urge to hide worse. For all its positive benefits, social media has created even more pressure for addicts to hide. Not only do those struggling or those close to someone struggling must deal with some of these issues in a public setting, now on social media platforms, a person connected to these struggles sees countless others pointing the finger, shouting that "ADDICTION ISN'T A DISEASE, IT'S A CHOICE!"

These accusations only exacerbate the problem and drive the person further into addiction. However, for every person who may be pointing the finger, ten more people will welcome the addict, alcoholic, or loved one with open arms. Societal norms have changed, and we are beginning to understand that putting a label on this problem does not matter. What matters is that people need help. Recovering in silence robs the addict of the support and accountability that much of the public would offer if they choose to recover out loud. Not only will recovering out loud provide support and accountability, but it may help active addicts know how *not* alone they are and encourage more people to recover. Recovering out loud creates a ripple effect.

BE THE CHANGE

As a team, we take Gandhi's words to heart. If we want others to recover out loud, we knew we'd need to walk our talk. So now, every day, we choose to recover out loud. The three of us choose to be the beacon of light that we wish we had when we were in the dark. We choose to own our personal histories. There is power and value in vulnerability. We are driven to share our experiences, strength, and hope so that people in our shoes know that they have a chance. Change is possible.

We will show you a host of paths that you can take in order to recover. We understand from our own experiences that one path does not fit all. We will share stories of success from the different paths people took to recover. This book is a CALL TO ACTION. We pose questions at the end of each chapter for you to take a moment to answer and GET REAL with where you currently stand so that you can make a choice to take action or stay stagnant. Furthermore, this book serves as a resource for you to decide which path you desire to take: the path to healing or the path to continued destruction.

You didn't pick up this book up on accident. Something in you wants to change, to free yourself, to create a healthy, awesome, radiant life beyond your wildest dreams. It could be your own addiction that you are battling. It could be your friend/significant other/family member who is suffering. You picked this book up because you want this change. You deserve this change. You are curious about what it means to SINK or SWIM. This book is not just something to read, it's an invitation. It's a mandate. We believe that everyone can recover. You just have to be willing. Willing to try. Willing to take a chance on you. So: Will you SINK or will you SWIM?

*Some names and identifying details have been changed to protect the privacy of some individuals and/or organizations.

SINK

CHAPTER 1

Michael

September 2015:

SWEATY. I CAN barely catch my breath. My heart feels like it's going to come out of my chest. I roll over and grab my cell phone off the nightstand to check the time: 1:30 a.m. I lean over the side of the bed, reach my hand to the side, and grab the bottle. Evan Williams Green Label 750ML to be exact. I take a swig. Instant satisfaction. I take another swig. Whew. Just breathe, Michael. I stay sitting up in bed until the anxiety begins to subside. I look at my phone to double check that I set my alarm to wake up in an hour. I lay back down; my heartbeat starts to slow. I feel relief for a brief moment. I close my eyes and fall back to sleep. An hour later, my alarm goes off. I can barely breathe. Sweaty, shaking, I grab the bottle and do it all over again until 6:30 a.m. when the last alarm goes off.

"Max, Max, it's time to get up."

I wake my fiancé, Max. Max is 5'8" with a short beard, short black hair, and incredibly beautiful hazel eyes. He is the kindest man I have ever been with. I call him "Mr. Soccer" because he is wicked awesome at the sport. Max works construction, so his days are long and hard. Some days, I pray for rain because when it rains, Max gets to come home early.

I grab the bottle of Evan Williams that is in the kitchen, line up two shot glasses, and throw them back to start my day. I grab my miniature dachshunds- the weenies- out of bed and take them outside to pee. While outside, I look up at the sky. I look up and just breathe.

God, get me through another day and I'll never drink again.

Get me through this day, look over the weenies, and I will get better—I promise. I said this prayer every single day. I remember this vividly because it was in these moments that I felt that I would have a chance. It was in these moments that I actually thought I would be okay. Well, that bull crap prayer went right out the window the moment my body started to shake, and I reached for the bottle.

Walking back upstairs, something hurts . . . I look down and notice several more bruises on my legs, and I lift up my shirt and see bruises on my hips. Absolutely NO IDEA how I got them. I must've fallen into something. I grab the dog food and feed the weenies, then I look at my phone. I see texts from my mom and Catherine and Twinney, my sisters. I feel annoyed but I respond with love to get it out of the way.

"Goooooood Morning Catherine! I love you bunches and bunches and I hope you have a super awesome day! Me and the weenies love you bunches and bunches."

"Twinney!! Good morning! I love you so, so much and I hope you have an awesome day. Me and the weenies love you bunches and bunches."

"Good Morning Mom! I hope you have an awesome day. It's a beautiful day here today. Me and the weenies love you so much!"

So much enthusiasm. So much acting. So many lies.

Catherine, Twinney, and Mom worry about me, but as long as they hear from me, they are okay. They worry a lot about me because I don't talk to them the way that I used to, which was multiple times a day! Now, I have nothing to say. I have slowly started to become a shadow of what I once was. Mom and Catherine live in Chicago, and Twinney lives in Dallas, so they depend on me to text them. I feel obligated to calm them down and the daily texts keep them off my back. They also depend on my dad to check on me since he splits his time between Telluride and Denver with his wife. Dad is really the family's rock at this point.

I scroll through all of my texts to see who I texted, what I said-no recollection. Every thirty minutes, I take a pull from the Evan Williams bottle. Some pulls were bigger than others but the point is . . . I never stopped. Sometimes in my blackout phases I would just go crazy with texting. Especially people I used to date- seeking comfort and attention because I was not getting any of that from Max. Max is always too drunk to be able to be intimate with me. Or maybe it's my fault, too. I honestly just want to feel wanted. I smack my head. Feelings of embarrassment and anger fill me up and I immediately delete everything. I wish I could turn back time and not send those messages. Did I actually see my dealer last night? I stand there in the kitchen trying really hard to remember, but I can't. I get extremely sweaty and nervous. *Does Max know?* Max hasn't said anything yet. I immediately start to fret. I look around, check my pockets for a bag or two of cocaine. Can't find it anywhere. Whew. I guess I didn't see him last night.

I wouldn't wish this feeling on anyone. This feeling of the unknown and not knowing what I said, what I did, is awful.

I pour coffee for Max and bring it to him in bed as he watches SportsCenter before showering. I go back out to the living room and pour myself a cup of coffee. I add a shot of whiskey and turn on the living room TV. I immediately put on the movie *Titanic*. I do this every morning, but as soon as Max gets out of bed and comes into the living room, I turn the movie off because I am embarrassed to be obsessed with Leo and Kate and the sinking ship.

I start to get ready for the day. I grab my eight-ounce stainless steel flask and fill it up as a backup in case I leave the house. I can't be without. I inventory how much whiskey I have left. I look at the bottle in the bedroom and the bottle in the kitchen. I make sure I have enough to get me through until the liquor store opens at 10:00 a.m.

In Telluride we have three liquor stores. I make sure to rotate where I go so that the same cashier doesn't see me multiple times a day. Honestly, this is one of the most embarrassing parts about my problem: having to see the cashiers. I tell myself that they have no idea to make myself feel better, but I know that they know. I just black that out. Anyway, having to analyze this drives me crazy, but it's necessary because if I don't have enough my anxiety will spike and I will tell myself I might die. And I can't die. I am 29 years old.

I try to think of how I got here. I remember when my days were not all like this. But where did I go wrong? What happened?

There were no signs in my family that I was doomed to be an alcoholic. Yes, we were of Irish descent, but my mom and dad never talked about anyone being a massive alcoholic or drug addict, except for just one of my cousins on my dad's side who was addicted to cocaine and drinking. I thought I was safe. Being an alcoholic would never happen to me. I had a total stigma on addicts and alcoholics: they were people who lived in the city, the homeless, the dead beats.

MY FIRST DRINK

I remember my entire seventh-grade class had a party at a classmate's house. I was nervous going to the party with my twin sister, Casey, and a few of our friends because I knew we were doing something that we were not supposed to be doing. Casey and I lied to our dad and mom about our plans for the evening, and so did the rest of our friends. All I knew is that there was going to be alcohol and drinking involved. Was I going to kiss a boy? Were we going to be dancing? When we walked in the door to this giant home up on the ski area, the main level of the house was dark. We heard music thumping, so we walked down the stairs to where the lights were on and the music was going. Pretty much my whole class was there. That calmed my nerves. We all walked over to the fridge where the beer was, and to the right on the counter, there was liquor with red Solo cups and mixers such as OJ, ginger ale, Coca-Cola, Sprite, and cranberry juice. I can honestly say I don't remember what liquor I drank, but I just remember grabbing one of the bottles and taking a massive swig of it and almost puking! Then I had a few Heineken beers. It was fun- new and exciting. It was exciting until we had to call 911 because one of our classmates passed out and wasn't waking up and almost died from alcohol poisoning. We were thirteen years old. We were all scared. The police showed up to the house and took down all of our names. We all had to do community service and go to alcohol classes, but that didn't stop us. Well, it didn't stop me, at least. I continued to party on the weekends throughout the rest of middle school and high school even though I was a athlete who lettered in all of my sports (volleyball, basketball, and track) and graduated with honors. I just drank on the weekends—the same as all my friends. I drank hard and fast and always blacked out.

I thought I was normal. I would drink whatever was in front of me: beer, wine, liquor. It was all the same to me. In college, things stayed the same: I drank all of the time, but so did most people. I think a part of me knew that my drinking had a different tone. I always had to take it farther: drinking before meeting up with everyone, sneaking it so I got a head start. Why did I do that? I don't know. I honestly don't know.

After college, I moved back to Telluride and there was ALWAYS a reason to drink and everyone DID! Festivals, summer softball, powder day on the ski hill, celebrating summiting a peak, you name it. So I never had to drink alone. I could manage it. I thought I was managing it.

When I would think about how much I drank, I'd get upset and drink more. My drink of choice became specific: Evan Williams Green Label Whiskey. Ask me how Evan Williams became my best friend, and I couldn't tell you. One day Max brought home a bottle of it and I realized I really liked it and didn't want anything else. No more beer, no more wine- just me and Evan Williams.

*   *   *

It's 7:45 a.m. and Max is leaving for work. I beg him, ask him if he can have the day off and stay home because I do not want to be alone.

"Max, do you think you'll get off early?"

"I don't know, babe. Call your friends," he says.

"Well, what about lunch time? Can you come home around lunchtime and see me?"

Max rolls his eyes. I can see the frustration in his face, as this is something I do every morning expecting a different result.

"I'll text you. Have a good day. I love you."

"Love you, too, babe."

He walks out. There I stand, my anxiety pulsing like a current. My heart is beating so fast. I can't even pinpoint thoughts because I am just so focused on my breathing. My hands get clammy. A massive wave of fatigue sets in. It's hard to keep my eyes open, but I start to gain control of my thoughts. I just keep asking God to let me be okay.

I walk into the bathroom, open the medicine cabinet, and grab the bottle of Xanax. I look at it, pondering whether or not taking one of these will make me feel better or if I should just go for the whiskey.

"I should just take one and be done with the whiskey."

"Xanax will have the same effects! Just go with the Xanax."

"WAIT! Maybe I shouldn't mix it. Maybe I'll wait until tomorrow to just take Xanax and not drink anymore. Yeah . . . that's what I will do. I will wait until tomorrow."

It's always tomorrow.

I start to think more about maybe texting my dealer. I don't need any more cocaine. I'm not going out in public to be around people. (That was when I did it the most, when I was going to be around people. I couldn't be drunk and risk blacking out in public so I used cocaine to stay alert). My dealer and I formed a great relationship. I'll never forget the first night, over a year ago, when I was strapped for cash going to his house to get my gram, telling him I didn't have the money for it. He gave me a look I'll never forget. He didn't need to say the words. Sex for drugs. I was desperate. The thought of having sex with him to get my gram or even eight ball sometimes made me cringe. But I did it. It had gotten to the point where if I didn't want to pay for it, I could just sleep with him. No brainer, right? Save money, have sex, and get my drugs. PERFECT! This became a routine. I couldn't believe how easy it was. Some days, going over there was absolutely embarrassing, though, because the place was packed with people and we just went into the bedroom to have sex, get the drugs, and I was on my way. Even when I did have the money, I just started opting for sex.

No one knew this secret. No one. It was my burden to bear. I was safe about it, so I wasn't hurting Max, right? No need to say a word.

I stare at myself in the mirror in the bathroom. I feel gross. I feel just awful having these thoughts. This has been going on for far too long. My eyes start to water.

I leave the bathroom and walk back into the kitchen to pour a shot and call my mom. By this time, I know that Mom can talk because she is off of the train and at her office. The conversation is pretty much the same every morning:

"Hey, Mom!"

"Hi, Michael!"

"How is your morning, Mom?"

"I am just getting into work. Can I call you tonight?"

"Just shoot me a text."

I never answered the phone at night. I couldn't risk my mom finding out how bad it was.

Then, I call Catherine and then Twinney and have the same conversations.

I must be honest and tell you that what happened throughout my days after about 8:00 a.m. is rather blurry because by this time I was in a constant state of being drunk. It was brutal. I was stuck. Deep down, I knew that I had to get it together. Deep down, every day, I truly hated myself. Hated that I felt I had to live this way. I was stuck. I was at the mercy of the bottle. Evan Williams was a colossal anchor keeping me in the middle of the ocean; I was unable to swim to shore. I could not get out of it. This had been going on for far too long. By this time, I had lost all of my jobs due to my drinking. It was no one's fault but my own and my addiction. Here is a sampling of what I lost during that time:

The first job I lost was working at an office. I thought working at this place I could get it together because I had responsibility and I had to show up. That didn't happen. I brought my flask with me to work to drink every time I went to the bathroom. The tipping point was when I went home on my lunch hour, had too many pulls of Evan Williams, and passed out on my front lawn on the way back to work.

The next job after that was at a hotel working the front desk. I fired myself from this one. I couldn't make it through an eight-hour shift. My anxiety was through the roof and I panicked. I called my boss and said I was sorry but I could no longer work for him and couldn't even give two weeks notice because I was in such a bad way.

In my last job, I just stopped showing up. My friend owned the company and had put me in charge. She trusted me. It was fine for a while, until it wasn't. I started using the company card for personal purchases because I was so broke, and then I just simply ignored all of her calls because I knew she wanted to talk about it and I didn't. I put her in a bad place and we parted ways.

Still, that wasn't enough. I had my ego. My pride. My ego was still too big to get help. I stayed quiet about what was going on in my life because I didn't want anyone to know. Everyone knew me as happy, bubbly, energetic, always smiling, always hugging, and just a beaming ray of sunshine. People lit up when they saw me walking down the street because everyone knew they could count on me to lift them up.

I was a hurricane of happiness. No one ever saw me down. No one ever saw me less than high energy. So, when the drinking got bad, I stayed in. I drank at home by myself or just with Max as we had that in common. I could no longer socially drink with friends. A few glasses of wine or a cocktail wasn't enough.

Then . . . FINALLY- I had hope! My older sister announced that she was getting married in Chicago on November 6, 2015. To me, this was my chance to prove to my family that I could get it together- that what was going on with me was just a horrible phase.

I had the perfect plan to sober up. Max and I would drive from Telluride to Chicago and make it a road trip and see family along the way. We couldn't drive and be drunk. The driving would keep us in check. The first part of the drive was going to be the longest, to my grandparents' house in Topeka, Kansas (fourteen hours from Telluride), and then the next day, we would make it up to Chicago to be with the family (eight hours from Topeka).

Once we committed, the plan frightened me. It scared the crap out of me. I didn't want to fail, and yet I had no idea how we were going to pull off this feat. Deep down, I knew I was in more trouble than I wanted to admit to anyone or myself. I just kept praying for a miracle. The closer the trip came, the more the plan began to reveal its frayed edges. Neither Max nor I went a day without whiskey. Which one of us would drive? Never mind the drive, how was I going to pack for this trip? We also had to watch our money, as it was tight due to me not working. It made me so nauseous thinking about how we were going to do this.

I couldn't disappoint my sister. I knew I had been disappointing my entire family up until this point. Lord knows if they actually thought I would be there. I wanted to show them that this was just a horrible phase even though my outer appearance showed otherwise. I started to retain water in my face. I was swollen. I honestly looked like a battered housewife because of all the bumps and bruises on my body from falling and running into things. I tried to not think about that and simply focused on the fact that my family was counting on me. I was counting on me.

Somehow, we got all packed and loaded in the car without getting drunk. Max, the weenies, and I started driving from Telluride. By the time we passed Denver, the weather was horrendous. It was tornado-like rain and so we had to pull over in Limon, Colorado, for the night. We just couldn't keep continuing down the road with the weather the way it was. I called my grandparents to let them know that we were not going to make it until the next day and that we would get up super early to make it by lunchtime. A seven-hour drive. Max and I found a hotel and started drinking the minute we checked in.

*　*　*

I woke up on the hotel bed sweating. Nauseous. Confused. Delirious.

"Michael! Wake up. You had a seizure."

"I what?"

"You had a seizure, babe. Right when we walked into the room. I called your sister."

I was confused. I was scared. None of this made sense to me.

A seizure? How did that happen? I was confused. I didn't know what to think. My mind was racing. I just wanted this whole experience to go away. I calmed down and just sat on the bed, emotionless.

Now, a normal person after a seizure would probably stay off the booze. A normal person would probably call an ambulance, go to the hospital, and get a CAT scan.

Well, I am not "normal"- I am clearly an alcoholic. I just asked Max for the Evan Williams bottle that we brought with us. There wasn't much left. I sent Max to go around this tiny town and find a liquor store to get more so that we could make it to my grandparents' the next day. Max left the room, found the liquor store, and picked up some burgers. He returned, and I just drank a little more and ate the burgers Max had ordered for us and fell asleep. All I could think about was surviving this. I just wanted to survive and wake up feeling normal and not the way that I was.

Throughout the night, I had nightmares. Terrors. Shaking. My anxiety again was awful. I would just take little sips off the bottle to try and calm down. I didn't take big swigs so I could be okay when I saw my grandparents.

The next thing I knew, it was morning. We again got the car packed. Max decided to drive first as it was raining but not that bad, and I was still not in the best shape. I got in the passenger seat. My body felt weak. I was out of it. I couldn't focus on anything. Max started to drive.

October 29th- The Darkest Hour

Bright lights. I start to wake up. Where am I? I look around. The first thing that I notice is that I am in a hospital bed. I look to the left and there is an IV in my left arm. My mouth is so dry. My tongue and mouth hurt. My jaw is throbbing. My head is pounding.

Something is wrong. I see Max in the corner in a chair. I can barely keep my eyes open. It hurts to talk.

"Max. MAX! What's going on?"

Max's eyes are swollen wet. He gets up from the chair and comes to my bedside and holds my hand.

"Max, what is going on? What happened?"

"You had another seizure in the car, babe. I had to call 911."

"Where are we, Max?"

"We are in Burlington, Colorado."

"Burlington?"

"Burlington. We were driving in the worst rainstorm, and before I knew it, Sampson (one of my weenies) flew out of your lap into the back seat. Michael, he flew across the car to the back."

I looked at him confused. I couldn't wrap my head around it.

"You started foaming at the mouth, and then your jaw froze and you almost bit your tongue in half. I was driving and trying to stay calm. I called 911, and they said to take the next exit and so I did. I pulled over at the McDonald's here in Burlington and the ambulance came accompanied by two cop cars. It was hailing."

Max started crying. He was holding my hand. I was emotionless. I was in disbelief. I was seriously confused.

"Max, what's wrong? Max, I am so sorry."

"MICHAEL, YOU FLAT LINED IN THE AMBULANCE. They had to RESUSCITATE you."

At this point, I couldn't comprehend those words. I can honestly say looking back I just didn't know what to say. My body was numb. I was numb. I flat lined?

The doctor and nurses came in with a cart with instruments to take my vitals. I don't remember exactly what anyone said to me. I was in an awful state. I had no focus. What I really remember is trying to eat ice chips, but my tongue and jaw were in so much pain that I just couldn't muster up the strength. I just sucked on the ice and couldn't chew.

I begged to be released. I said that Max and I were fine. We would be fine. I needed to get out of there. I was pissed. I was embarrassed.

I just wanted it all to go away. I wanted to snap my fingers and be in Chicago.

We left the hospital and Burlington. I was not okay. My tongue was swollen; my head was pounding like a jackhammer. My body made it very clear to me that I probably shouldn't have left the hospital so soon.

Max is on the phone. I hear my dad's voice through the Bluetooth speaker. "We don't want her grandparents to see her this way."

I HAD MISSED MY SISTER'S WEDDING.

After the hospital, we turned around. We had to. I was too sick to make it. What did I have Max do as soon as we left the hospital? Find a liquor store.

I thought I was invincible. I really thought that I could figure it out. I thought that maybe, just maybe, there would be a day, an AHA moment that I would come to my senses and be able to get control.

Have you said that to yourself? I was the furthest thing from in control. What I didn't understand then is that there was no chance left I could manage my addiction on my own.

In the last year of my addiction, I:

- Lost two jobs

- Ran my entrepreneur business into the ground because I was too drunk to run it—Ruined relationship with my business partner

- Managed another good friend's business and ran that business in to the ground

- Let myself go from work because I needed to go home and drink

- Carried whiskey with me to all of these jobs to get me through the day

- Passed out on my front lawn during lunch from one of these jobs because I drank so much on my lunch break (Awesome, let me tell you.)

- Drank through every game of my rec league soccer league, never finishing a game completely coherent
- Passed out on the softball field playing rec league softball. My best friend's husband had to carry me out of the park over his shoulder.
- Had countless affairs while engaged to be married

But, hey! I totally had this! These instances were just a phase, right? I was in total denial. I was in such denial and deceit with my family that I even lied to them about having Max take me to detox. I wanted my family off of my back and to let me be.

I cut everyone out. I blocked them on social media and wouldn't respond to their calls and texts. I was mad that they kept pressuring me to do something that I clearly was not ready to do. Didn't they get the point after I relapsed back in February after trying to get sober? (I started AA on February 14. I only went to appease my family. I wasn't ready. I got through 37 days on will power alone and then I left).

Some Point in Early December 2015

My dad had been begging me to get help. My family and friends were depending on him to be the one to get through to me.

Dad presented me the options to go away for treatment but I couldn't fathom it.

I offered every excuse in the book until Chase, one of my best friends since childhood, came to my house.

"We both know you can't do this on your own, Michael."

I was a blubbering mess. I was angry.

"Chase, I can't go. I don't want to go."

"You have to go- and we both know I am right behind you." He laughed to ease the moment. Chase was also an alcoholic and in a bad way himself.

"I can't go away for Christmas, my thirtieth birthday, and New Years. No way. I'll go after."

Chase just shook his head. He knew right then and there that he couldn't get through to me. No one could. He got up and walked out of my house.

I drank more. I resented my family and friends. I wasn't supposed to be THAT person who throws her life away and goes to rehab. That was not going to be my reality.

Every time I got angry, passed out, drank myself to sleep, I would tell myself lies. Lie to myself that it would be okay. That I could get back to being a normal drinker.

December 8th

Shallow breaths. Weak muscles, lower backache. Delirious. Every movement hurts. Do you know what this is? Do you know that feeling? You know . . . that feeling of your body shutting down on you? Every step up my stairs back from the liquor store this day for some reason was completely unbearable. I was walking back in the alley to my house from the liquor store. It was mid morning. Just another day in my messed-up world. I had been contemplating everything that my family, Chase, and Marcy (another good friend) had been saying to me. It was the first time that I came to the realization that I was at the end. I was knocking on death's door.

I opened the door to my house and tripped and fell to the floor. The whiskey bottle and my cell phone went sliding across the floor. I lay on the cold hardwood floor. I could literally feel my heart struggling to beat. I could feel my muscles cramping and not being able to function. My body was shutting down on me. I really thought that was it. It was in this moment I rolled over and looked up at the ceiling. I am not joking when I say I saw white light and I also saw my Grandma Margaret and Aunt Mary Michael (they are dead). They asked me a simple question:

"Are you going to come join us up here, or are you going to live, Michael?"

I started crying. I looked at them and then I saw my phone across the floor. I inched forward and grabbed my phone and called my dad.

"Dad. Get me out of here. Let's go."

I had just purchased what I now know was my last bottle of Evan Williams Green Label Whiskey.

DECEMBER 10th

Chase came back to the house and packed my bags with me to go to Serenity Treatment Center. I couldn't believe this was actually happening. I had no idea what to expect. What I did know was that I was scared to death but I was also so incredibly done with my life as I knew it. I also knew that I had a good chance of not making it to Serenity because it was located on the other side of Colorado from Telluride. My dad knew that I was in critical condition. He had spoken with a doctor about the proper way to get me there safely.

The most important thing the doctor said to my dad: **LET MICHAEL KEEP DRINKING THE WHOLE WAY.**

I was so bad that they could not risk me seizing in the car.

Dad pulled up in his black Acura Sport Wagon. He looked relieved and ready to get me out of Telluride. Chase gave my bag to my dad. Max hugged me goodbye. He said I was doing the right thing. I made sure that when I got in the car, there was whiskey on hand.

I got in the car. I was shaking. I was scared. And deep down this time around . . . I knew I was ready.

LET'S GET REAL

1. Are you at the point where you have to drink all of the time because you don't want to feel the shakes?

2. Have you experienced seizures due to drinking too much?

3. Have you missed important life events because you were too drunk or high to participate?

4. Have you lost a job/passed out in public/or simply don't remember conversations you had because of drinking or using?

5. Do you tell yourself that your addiction is just a phase, that you can manage it? That you're in control?

CHAPTER 2
Andrea

August 2012

I AM SITTING IN my parked car talking to my mom on the phone. It's late, almost midnight, but the grocery store parking lot I'm sitting in is lit up with at least two dozen streetlights. Still, I am suddenly and inexplicably unable to read the large posters in the windows of the store. The neon signs hurt to look at. I rub my eyes and blink a couple of times.

My mom finishes the story she was telling me, and that's my cue to wrap up our conversation. I'm only parked here because it's the last place on my way home that my phone gets service.

"Okay, Mom. Okay, I love you, too. Yes. Good night!"

We hang up. Immediately, panic hits me. My chest and throat contract, and I gasp for air. Terror.

Wait, no, no, no. What? Why now, why me?

Whatever it is, *the thing* is happening again, harder and faster than it ever has before. My hands start shaking, so much so that my phone slips from my grasp and lands somewhere on the floorboard.

Breathing hard through my nose, I double check that my emergency brake is on, and I reach down to the floor, desperately trying to find my phone, but I can't feel it or see it.

I can't see anything.

This is not the what I thought it was. This is not anxiety. This is something new. I have no idea what is happening to me, and I am terrified.

Just have to get home. It's okay. It's okay. I'm okay. It's okay. I'm okay.

I fumble with my keys until I get my car started. The engine roars to life and the sound is deafening.

What is wrong with my car? It's okay. Just get home. It's okay. I'm okay. It's okay. Just get home.

I turn off my emergency brake and put my car in gear. I grip my steering wheel and gear shift tightly in each hand to try to keep myself from shaking. My legs feel weak, and I accidentally let up on the clutch too quickly. My car stalls. I can barely breathe now. I clench my teeth and start my car again.

Using all my strength, I keep my limbs rigid enough to get my car into first and pull out of the parking lot. I manage to drive the quarter-mile to my apartment and pull into a parking space.

I grab my purse from the backseat and fish my phone out from under the driver's seat. Getting out of my car feels more like climbing than just standing up.

What is wrong with me? I haven't had a drink since last night. I'm not drunk, I'm not even hungover.

My entire body is shaking now. There doesn't seem to be anyone around, but I get the sudden feeling that *I am in danger.* Wildly, nearing panic, I spin around. The dark street, the trees, the buildings glow neon—everything around me looks and feels like I've been dropped into the absolute worst kind of acid trip.

The stairs that lead down to my apartment look a million miles long. I cling to the wooden railing. I manage to stumble down the dark stairwell to the door of the basement apartment that I share with my roommate.

As I turn the key, I'm half hoping and half dreading that she'll be there and be awake. I can't remember if I saw her car on the street. As the door swings open, I notice that her dogs aren't there, meaning she must be out of town.

Did she tell me she was going anywhere?

The kitchen is dark, only the hall light is on, and the whole place feels menacing. I still have the unnerving feeling that I am in danger, but less so than when I was still outside.

I force myself to walk into the dark living room, one hand clutching the wall to keep myself upright. I don't know where the light switches are right now, and I can hardly see anyway.

When I make it to the couch, I collapse onto it. My purse falls to the floor. Lying down is so much worse than standing. My already blurred vision goes almost completely dark.

I reach into my purse for my cell phone to try call for help. When I find it, squinting hard, I can see that I have zero signal. We never get reception in this place. I give up on calling for help and pull the couch blankets over myself. Now I'm freezing and drenched in sweat. Whatever is happening to me, it is serious.

Breathing is harder than ever. My ribcage feels like it's going to literally break inwards and crush all my organs. My entire body is shaking violently. The realization that I am desperately thirsty washes over me, but I know I can't make it fifteen feet to the kitchen sink.

The thing I've been fighting is winning. I can't move. I can't breathe. I can't see. I can't call for help. I am convulsing. I am freezing. I am thirsty. I am terrified. I am alone. I give up.

I am not okay.

Then everything goes black.

One Year Earlier

August 2011

I was twenty-two when my first long-term relationship ended. We'd dated for four years. The break-up was mutual, and I had been feeling in my gut that it had been over for a long time. We weren't right for each other. We had a lot in common on the surface, but our personalities started to clash. As we grew as individuals, we grew apart as a couple.

The first few days following the break-up, I felt free, elated, and excited about all the new possibilities that were now open to me. However, I did not take any time to look inward and really check in with myself. If I had, I would have realized that internally, I was mourning the loss of my future that I had created in my mind during our early years together.

Stephen and I had been together since I was eighteen. He was my first love. I initially thought that it would last forever. There were many things I admired about him. He was creative and talented; he was genuinely a good person. But our fundamental values were different. Our communication had never been strong, and it only deteriorated with time.

We both drank, but my drinking was far more destructive than his, and it did play a role in our relationship ending. By this time in my life, I was already *almost* a daily drinker. My ex had little tolerance for how I acted when I binge drank to the point of blacking out, which happened at least three times a month by the time we broke up. I felt enough shame to curb my intake just enough to not yet fall off the deep end.

After we broke up, I was completely free to do anything I wanted. Unfortunately, I chose to self-destruct almost immediately. After crashing at my mom's house for two weeks, a friend invited me to go up to Asheville, North Carolina for the weekend. We stayed her cousin's house and drank the whole weekend with friends; some I already knew, and some I met for the first time.

These were people that could keep up with my level of drinking. We took shots of top-shelf tequila back to back, tore through several six packs of craft beers, and chain-smoked organic cigarettes. The first night alone, we polished off a handle of tequila between four people. We must have had ten to twelve beers each, and we were up until dawn.

After crashing for a couple hours, we went out and got Bloody Marys for brunch to curb our hangovers. I ended up puking in the bathroom of the quaint café, trying to be quiet about it. I remember feeling embarrassed and anxious. I thought the staff knew and were judging me. This was one of the first times I really noticed anxiety as part of a hangover, but I brushed it off and quickly forgot about it. I preferred to think about how much fun we had had the night before-something I would learn later is called euphoric recall. It's what helps alcoholics keep drinking.

The rest of the weekend was the same. At night, we would bar hop for a while, then head back to the house and get absolutely smashed. I didn't get sick the next two days, and I had so much fun. I felt like these friends, and new ones I had just met, were my people. I did not feel judged for my drinking around them. This should have been a red flag.

Along with my new friends being heavy drinkers, Asheville is also home to an enormous number of microbreweries. I was in love with the hippie culture of the city, and it didn't hurt that craft beer was my favorite thing to drink.

On Sunday, when it was time for my friend and I to go back to Georgia, I didn't want to leave. I felt like my life in Georgia was over; many of my friends sided with my ex, and I didn't have my own place anymore. I was ready to make a change. My family all lived in Georgia, but Asheville was only a four-hour drive away. I had no reason to go home except for my job, and I was ready to leave that, too.

The entire ride home, I brainstormed not only on how to make it happen, but *how quickly* I could make it happen. At the time, it felt like my life was on the verge of being *amazing*. I was going to live where I wanted to live. I was finally going to be happy. In hindsight, I was running away. At the time, Ashville was my ultimate geographical goal.

I simply didn't think that I had a drinking problem. Yes, some people got annoyed with me when I drank, but that was their problem, not mine. I told myself that my drinking had not caused any serious damage. I saw zero problems with moving to a town that had been named the official "Beer City USA" more than once.

Only a few days later, I packed everything I owned into my tiny two-door Ford Focus hatchback and drove four hours to my new life. One of my new friends was looking for a roommate, and I made the jump. I was finally moving to Asheville, all the best things were yet to come, and there was no reason to think that I was running away from anything.

September 2011—July 2012

It took me nearly two weeks to find a job in Asheville. My savings were running out very quickly. I was spending money as if I had more than I did to keep up appearances with my new friends and especially with my new roommate, April.

April was someone I hardly knew when I moved in with her. I had a lot in common with her on the surface. The main thing we had in common was binge drinking, which we did every night. Every night at our house was a party. On nights when it was just the two of us at home, we still drank almost as heavily. At first, this was a lot of fun, but of course, it was toxic from the beginning.

When I started my job search, I was hoping to work somewhere like a cool, hip little café. After weeks of applying everywhere, I finally got a job at a sports bar. It was my least favorite of all the places that I had applied at, and it's the only place I got a call back from. I went in for an interview, got hired, and started working right away.

I made new friends within the large staff. Nearly all of them drank as much as me. That was our only way of connection, and for most of me and my friends, it was all we had in common. In Asheville, I had the largest group of friends of perhaps my entire life, and three of them were genuine, lasting friendships.

For months, nothing really changed, but bit by bit, everything in my life began showing cracks. I worked extremely long hours for low pay, I blacked out nearly every night, and I spent my days apologizing to everyone around me. My roommate and I started getting in arguments over the smallest things, and that escalated into drunken fights almost every night.

I didn't check in with my family back home in Georgia often. Only April and a couple of friends really knew how I was living. I kept saying to myself, *'Next month, I'll have enough money, and I'll get my own place,"* and every month, I didn't have enough money. Surprise, surprise.

I drank because I missed my family. I drank because I hated my job. I drank because I felt trapped. I drank because I was depressed. I drank for any reason and for no reason. I drank because somehow, over the last year, alcohol had wormed itself deep into not only my life, but also into who I was as a person.

My drinking had been problematic for years, which I can define with this simple statement, "Every time I drank, it/I caused or experienced problems." But somewhere in the first six months of 2012, at twenty-three years old, I became 100 percent, without a doubt, a full-blown alcoholic.

I blacked out every single night, and I really, really don't want to admit this publicly, but not only did I black out every night, I drove home or elsewhere wasted nearly every night of the week.

I stopped getting hangovers. Instead, I awoke every morning with such severe anxiety that my hands visibly shook, I had difficulty breathing, and I experienced chest/ribcage tension and pain that lasted almost all day.

I didn't tell *anyone* how miserable I was or how much pain I was in. To me, I had developed what I believed was "severe anxiety," due to ongoing stress in my life.

This was another thing I felt I was strong enough to face alone. But no matter what I was telling myself, it was getting worse. Every day, I was afraid to look at my phone, afraid to see my coworkers' reactions, afraid of other people, and afraid of myself. The only relationship I was not afraid of was my relationship with alcohol.

One night, April and I got into a knock-down, drag-out fight over something stupid. I don't remember what started the fight, more than likely something she or I did while drinking. It was bad enough that I packed my stuff and loaded up my car. No plan; I just got out of there.

I started driving towards another friend's apartment. She was out of town, and I had been stopping by to feed her cat for the last several days. It was perfect, and I couldn't believe I hadn't thought of going there earlier. It was three or four in the morning, and I was extremely grateful that I had somewhere to go where I could be alone. I was grateful that I didn't have to wake anyone up and explain anything. I was exhausted but relieved. Yes, I was technically homeless, but that was better than staying where I had been, and I knew I'd find a new place.

I felt hopeful for the first time in almost a year. I was so sure that *everything in my life was about to get better.* Unfortunately, I was dead wrong. The worst was yet to come.

* * *

The next morning, I woke up in the sunny living room of my friend's apartment. Her cat was snuggled up to me, fast asleep. I felt more rested than I had in months.

My mind felt bright and clear for the first time in a long time. I did not consider that maybe I didn't wake up in a fog of panic and dread like usual because I had gone to sleep sober. I'd only had two beers before the fight with my roommate.

I wish so badly that I could reach through time and tell twenty-three-year-old me to listen to her body, to slow down, to pay attention, and show her the obvious connection between her alcohol intake and her wellbeing. But I can't.

Back then, as I've said before, I thought that *facing difficult or painful things on my own, without asking for help, meant that I was strong.*

So, on that sunny morning, I pulled out my journal, and I began to formulate a plan and got to work. I texted all my friends who lived locally, seeing if they knew anyone needing a roommate. Luckily, I immediately found a place to live. Another one of my coworkers was looking for a roommate; she said that I could move in that same day.

I went shopping for new work clothes, a few storage bins, and a bunch of things I didn't have time to grab from my apartment with April. Before the sun set, I was already moved into my new apartment. I had all my necessities hung up, put away, and organized.

That night, I went out and drank with a bunch of my coworkers to celebrate. I was relieved to have a new place to live where my home was not a battlefield. I was momentarily happy. For the first time in years, drinking felt fun again.

August 2012

My "morning anxiety" became exponentially worse once I had almost no one monitoring me. I say "almost" because I did have at least three very good friends in my life at the time who tried to help me, who tried to make me see that my drinking had gotten out of control, who continued to be there for me even when I acted abhorrently. They were not the friends I hung out with the most because they didn't drink like my other friends and I did—and drinking is all I wanted to do.

Every single morning, I woke up feeling worse than the day before. My hands shook for the first couple of hours every day at first, but quickly it began to be all day long. My chest muscles and my rib cage itself began to hurt at some point, and that too just kept getting worse. I had difficulty breathing all the time. My eyes were incredibly sensitive to light, and loud noises would startle me out of my skin.

I was anxious all the time, and that too increased in intensity until I was always in a state of near-panic—about everything and about nothing, day in and day out.

I didn't know this at the time, but I was putting my body through alcohol withdrawal every single day. Everyone I knew drank as much as I did, and *they* didn't seem to be addicted, so why would I be? Clearly, I was under the impression that I would be able to tell if they were going through the physical and mental agony that I was. How? How did I know that they weren't? I knew my behavior when I drank was far more extreme than most of my friends, but I'm an intense person. I told myself, and this was just part of my personality.

One rule that I had was that I would not drink before work. I don't remember exactly how or why I kept myself from doing this. It's possible that I subconsciously already knew that once I had one drink, I wouldn't be able to stop, and I'd lose my job. Maybe it came from society's picture of an alcoholic being someone who drank from morning to night. Of course, this is not true for everyone addicted to alcohol. I didn't know that if I had drunk some alcohol in the morning, my symptoms would lessen. I never tried it.

I had no idea what the actual symptoms of alcohol withdrawal were, and I had no idea that I was a candidate. I had looked up all my symptoms, but I didn't admit to myself the likelihood that alcohol was part of the problem. I didn't look up anything about alcoholism. I couldn't see the truth right in front of me.

Here is what my day would look like. Starting when I got off work, usually around midnight, I would drink until I passed out, sleep for about five hours, wake up in near panic, hands shaking, heart racing, difficulty breathing—and get ready for work. The symptoms lasted all day until I got off work and had a few drinks.

Alcohol withdrawal happens when one's body is used to having a certain minimum amount of alcohol intake in order to function normally. This is physical dependency. When someone addicted to alcohol goes too long without drinking, they will experience withdrawal. The severity of withdrawal varies from person to person. Again, I knew none of this.

On the night of my first seizure, the opening scene of this chapter, I had to work a fifteen-hour double shift. I had slept maybe five hours the night before, so it had been around twenty hours since my last drink. That is what caused the first seizure, and I went on to have six more, for a total of seven seizures in only two weeks. The most severe results of alcohol withdrawal are seizure, coma, and death. I did not know that what I was experiencing was something that could have easily killed me.

After the seventh and last one seemed to last almost all night, I called one of my best, most supportive friends. It was 5:00 in the morning and I asked her to take me to the hospital. I had held off calling her for hours, literally waiting as long as I could stand it so that I wouldn't wake her up in the middle of the night.

I didn't feel like I could ask anyone else. I was scared, and I trusted her. She immediately came and picked me up and took me to the emergency room at the hospital downtown.

I didn't know what to say when I got there or how to fill out the forms. I thought I was having panic attacks, maybe mixed with something else I couldn't identify. My symptoms didn't quite fit the description of a panic attack, but it was the closest thing I could find to explain what I was experiencing.

At the hospital, I was told I was severely dehydrated and that I had a kidney infection. I'd had a kidney infection before, and this news surprised me because I felt no pain this time. The doctor said that could happen. It took three bags of saline (IV in each arm) to rehydrate me, and I was given a prescription for antibiotics to treat the infection.

I do not remember anyone at the ER asking me about alcohol consumption. I can only assume that they believed my dehydration was related to my kidney infection. When I talked to the doctor, I told him everything I had been experiencing. I said I thought I was having panic attacks, but that they were horrific and surreal. I remember thinking that I did not explain it very well. For that, the doctor gave me a prescription for Ativan (a drug that mimics the effects of alcohol). That was it. I was out the door. I left feeling confused and not understanding why they couldn't tell me what was wrong with me. I do give them some benefit of the doubt, though, as my memory of the hospital visit is admittedly hazy.

September 2012

At a house party with a bunch of friends one night, I burned some major bridges while I was blacked out. I hurt people that I cared about; I lost the respect of others. Of course, I don't remember anything from that night, but I was told that I was picking fights with everyone and spouting off secrets told to me in confidence. The next morning, I could no longer deny that alcohol was at the center of the problems in my life.

I admitted to myself, finally, that I had a problem. Once done, that could not be undone. I felt immense shame not only about being alcoholic, but for all of the things I did or didn't do while in active addiction.

I couldn't keep living the way I was living, and I mean that literally. I felt like I was dying, every single day. I swallowed my pride and made a phone call.

"Hey, Mom, I need to come home. I'm at work and I can explain later . . . Just, I need to know if you can come get me. I need to come home. I need help."

LET'S GET REAL

1. Do you drink to reduce social anxiety? Does drinking alcohol make you feel more comfortable around people?

2. Are you one of those people who can drink others "under the table?"

3. Has anyone close to you ever expressed concern about your drinking?

4. Have you stopped experiencing "regular" hangovers after binge drinking?

5. Have you noticed any physical or emotional symptoms that either become worse or better with alcohol?

6. Have you ever gone to the doctor or hospital for anxiety or other symptoms and not mentioned the amount you drink?

CHAPTER 3
Scott's Dad

ROWING UP, I looked at my dad as my hero.

My dad, Scott Leeper, Sr., had substance abuse issues for as long as I can remember. Unfortunately, it was early 1985 when I was first affected by his substance abuse problems. One early spring day, my mother, a young Janet Leeper, was emptying pockets and putting laundry in the washer when she picked up my dad's short-sleeved, button-up shirt. She emptied the front breast pocket and found a tin foil wrapper concealing about a dozen pills of all shapes and sizes—capsules, pills, and caplets. She immediately knew something was amiss.

Later that day, my dad came home.

"What are these and where did they come from?" my mom inquired.

"I'm, um, holding on to those for a friend," my dad stammered.

"I don't care if these are yours or a friend's, Scottie could have gotten a hold of these, and who knows what could have happened! I'm done!" she stated, clearly exhausted by many other bouts of illicit drug-fueled stand-offs with my dad. I was eighteen months old at the time, and my older sister was about six.

"I'm going to my mother's house. You have the weekend to pack your stuff and move out."

"Wha- why? You should have threatened me!"

"I shouldn't have to . . ." she ended. And with that, she did what was necessary to protect herself and her kids- and left him.

From 1988 to 1997, my dad seemed to clean up and worked as a medical tech for the South Bend Medical Foundation, where he would analyze patient specimens. My guess is that he probably had to stare at pee, poop, and other bodily fluids all day. Sometime in the mid-1990s, my dad was stuck with a dirty needle and contracted Hepatitis C. This would later be just one piece of the deadly concoction that would take his life in 2012, not to mention all the medications he was on to deal with the hepatitis. Already at this point, my dad's liver and kidneys were putting in as much time as a prisoner of war in a Japanese POW camp during World War II. Day in and day out, his organs were constantly working to metabolize all the medications that he was prescribed. Unfortunately, just like a POW, there's only so much work a person's liver and kidneys can put in before they shut down.

In 1997, he seemed to be living a clean life because I never really witnessed any substance abuse issues whenever I was around him. That year, Dad completed a computer science degree from Indiana University and transitioned from stool samples to working for a computer education company in Mishawaka. He taught for the company and became a phenomenal teacher. I heard stories from his friends and various colleagues that he would even take an entire computer apart, put it back together, but omit one little piece and challenge the students in his class to determine which tiny piece was missing from this 3D puzzle! I can still visualize the computer geniuses that came to my dad's memorial service.

During his memorial service, we had a table by the front door, displaying what seemed to be an endless amount of computer certifications that rivaled the thickness of a phone book.

Dad was doing well for himself even on a salary of less than $50,000 a year. He seemed happy, and things seemed to be clicking right along for him. He stayed in a decent apartment in Mishawaka and drove a hunter green Dodge Cirrus with leather interior, sunroof, and all the other bells and whistles. We lived together at the time. Things were good between us.

In 2006, the company that my dad was teaching computers for went out of business, and my dad had to hit the job-hunting trail. It wasn't long before he found another position teaching aspiring IT gurus about computers in another town nearby, Goshen. Although my dad found a job, this seemed to be the point that his life started to take a downward spiral like a pilot getting shot out of the sky. By this time, I was fighting a battle myself in the Middle East. I was a Marine on my second deployment to Iraq. Unfortunately, I wasn't able to be around to see some of the signs that his life was unraveling. Even if I was around, looking back, I don't know that my eyes would have been open enough to see anything amiss. I was in my early twenties at this point and loved being able to go to the beer store and buy a case of Miller Lite and hang out with the boys. Thinking about it now, I could have easily become a statistic of alcoholism. Addiction ran strong in my family. Just like my dad, my grandfather drank. He was successful in his recovery but had to go through dialysis three days a week for four hours at a time for about the last twelve years of his life as a result of his alcoholism. My aunt was also an addict. She died of throat cancer as a result of years of drug and alcohol abuse, along with smoking.

After his company in Mishawaka closed their doors in 2006, my dad had to move in with my sister, Jenny, and her family for a few weeks. By this time, creditors were chasing Dad like the CIA. I couldn't tell you how much debt he accrued from medical bills and student loans, but the estimate was in the millions. MILLIONS! He couldn't afford a place of his own because, even though he was working for another company, doing what he was doing before, he was making about half of what he had previously.

I asked my sister recently about this time with my dad. "He was happiest when he was drinking," she said. The one thing everybody remembered about Dad was that he was a "happy go-lucky guy" who always made people laugh. Unfortunately, like Robin Williams, this was my dad's way of dealing with his serious depression problems that he so successfully concealed. Budweiser and Bloody Marias were his drinks of choice at this point. My sister can see the Bloody Maria fixings on the counter still: tomato juice, tequila (Jose Cuervo in this case), and sometimes Tabasco with a celery stalk. I remember Dad would even trade out the tequila for a Corona beer occasionally. Other days, my sister reported that Dad drank Maker's Mark bourbon and Knob Creek. He always bought the expensive stuff, even though creditors continued to come after him like rats.

Although he only called my brother in-law, Ed, out to the front porch to drink with him a couple times a week, my dad would drink until his speech slurred every night. As if that weren't enough, most days Dad would stop at one of two of his favorite bars. He was like a country song—slave at work all day (only white collar in this case) until 4:00 or 5:00 p.m., then go to his favorite bar, with his favorite people, his favorite drink, and make himself and everybody around him happy. Because only alcohol can make things fun, right? These places would give my dad an open-ended tab each week. Then at the end of the week, he would pay his bar "bill" when he got paid at his $12-an-hour job.

Although he wasn't drunk leaving the establishment around 7:00 or 8:00 p.m. after drinking large quantities of beer and liquor, he would come home to my sister's house and continue to drink a combination of Budweiser and his Bloody Marias or whatever was on hand.

"Hey, can you switch my laundry?" he would ask her as he tipped the bottle of Budweiser back and took another liver-scarring swig.

Irritated, she would respond, "Yeah, sure . . ." while thinking to herself, "You have time to drink a beer, but you don't have time to do your laundry." While everybody else would sit on the front porch and hang out, Jenny went inside to clean up his messes. His pay-off was buying food or taking them to dinner, which always included alcohol, when he got paid. Meanwhile, the creditors continued to call.

One night as Dad drank himself into oblivion, he passed out and peed on their green couch in the living room. He left the drenched cushions for my sister to find and clean up.

Ed protested. They already had three young boys living at home—a fourth man-child was too much. My sister agreed that things were bad but didn't want to evict him. My father's behavior continued to drive a wedge between my sister and Ed, weakening their marriage.

"I go to work so that you can stay home and take care of the kids. I'm not going to support your dad too," Ed told Jenny. "Your dad is grown. He can figure it out on his own."

My dad had a friend in the next town over (Elkhart) who agreed to let my father move in. While living in Elkhart, Dad would bring his friend over to my sister's house and commence to drink on the weekends mostly. When Dad would drink at their house, he would empty a twelve-pack of beer and half a bottle of liquor. Even after all of this alcohol rushed into his bloodstream, he appeared sober as a judge. Dad stayed with his friend for about two years before he moved himself into a small, one-bedroom apartment just a few doors down from my sister.

While all of this took place, I was thousands of miles away. By this point, I had returned from Iraq and augmented to active duty when I received orders to Okinawa, Japan. While I was there, I discovered an issue with my credit report.

Before getting married to my wife, Ashley, my dad and I had a shared cell phone plan. Once Ashley and I got married, my dad and I decided to split the plan so that I could start a shared plan with Ashley. He was supposed to go into the cell phone store and give them his information to start his own plan. Shortly after getting to Okinawa, I found out that this never happened. My dad never provided them with his information therefore, there was a $250 delinquent bill on my credit report! I was angry. This debt was a representation of all the ways my dad had let me down.

Okinawa

After finding out about the cell phone delinquency, I did not speak to my dad for almost three years, almost the entire time I was stationed in Okinawa. I was just angry. My pride kept me away too long to make up for the lost memories with my childhood idol, my dad. Sometime in 2010, we spoke for the first time and decided to put the cell phone incident behind us. Even though some of the frustration was still there, I was elated to make amends with my dad. I had no idea at the time that I barely had two years left with my dad.

November 2010

I had just turned twenty-eight the month prior. It was cold out. The snow had already started to coat the houses, trees, and streets. You could see the snowflakes fall past the hue of the street lights. Fall was in full swing and winter was right around the corner. Notre Dame football (which is just across town) was on virtually every TV, and the stores were getting busier and busier with people buying all the turkey and cranberries for Thanksgiving. At the time, I was a Sergeant in the United States Marine Corps and home on leave for the holiday. This particular night, I was hanging out at Jenny's house, along with my other two sisters and their families. Every time I came home, I avoided much time with my dad. I was constantly busy visiting family and friends.

This visit was different. My dad was supposed to meet me at her house. It wasn't too difficult to meet me there since he lived on the same street, four houses down. I could hit his little shack with a baseball if I threw it. We agreed that he would meet me at my sister's house at 7:00. I was a little apprehensive about him coming over because this was only the second or third time we had spoken since mending our relationship. I looked down at my watch. 7:23 p.m. "Go figure, he didn't show," I said in my head.

"Hey, Ash!" I hollered through the house to my wife, Ashley. "I'm just going to walk down to his place!" I threw my coat on and walked down the street to his little apartment. My feet crunching in the snow and breath visible as I exhaled, I approached his door. The apartment was a two-apartment red brick building that typically had drug traffic in and out of the front door before my dad moved in. The windows were lined with white trim. There was a white awning over the two front apartment doors that seemed to suggest that this building was used for some sort of business decades ago. There were two white doors in the front. His was on the left, apartment 554B. The "front yard" was simply a concrete jungle of cracked, uneven sidewalk and the road.

I knocked harder than I thought I would on someone's door whom I just mended my relationship with. A minute later, Dad appeared.

"Hey," he mumbled as he was swaying in the doorway.

"Hi . . . did you forget to meet me at Jenny's house?" I asked impatiently.

"Ah, sorry! I was jusss. . . ."

"Dad, are you drunk?"

As he sat down in a tattered recliner in his living room, he said, "I had a couple," looking at me pitifully.

"I've heard that before," I thought as I shook my head, and I could feel myself getting angry. I started to look around during a brief period of awkward silence. The apartment was maybe 500 square feet. A recliner and beat-up couch were in the living room, surrounding an old box TV with an antenna sticking out of the top. His bedroom door was open, and the light was off. I walked into the kitchen. Covering every surface were PILES and PILES of empty beer cans, empty vodka bottles, and empty whiskey bottles. The whiskey and vodka bottles were plastic, which is typically a sign of a cheap liquor, the kind of liquor that alcoholics buy when they don't have money for the "good stuff." The kitchen looked like a recycling plant!

At this point, I became furious. "Dad, what are you doing?!"

Unable to contain his drunk emotions and now sobbing like a child, he answered, "Look at me. I'm fat. I'm nasty. Nobody loves me. Nobody wants me. This is what I have. What do you want from me?"

I froze. I may have seen my dad shed a few tears in the past, but I never saw him actually cry. This was my hero, my childhood idol. Sobbing like a little kid! Tears welled up in my eyes. I didn't know what to do. I didn't know what to say. My mind was racing a million miles a minute. I wanted to be mad at him, to yell back. I wanted to tell him to man up! At the same time, I wanted to give him a hug and tell him it was going to be okay. I wanted to take away his pain. But I couldn't. All I could do was sit there. At this point, I may have said something along the lines of, "Alcohol won't help you," or, "Why don't you talk to somebody?" Maybe I didn't say anything at all. The problem was . . . I didn't take any action. The rest of the night was a blur. All I could think about was my dad crying, drunk, and depressed.

Thanksgiving 2010

We all met at Jenny's. This was the first Thanksgiving in three years that I was in the United States and with family. Despite the previous evening, I woke up thankful that my dad and I were talking again. We had all the fixings and my dad never held back when it came to food, especially Thanksgiving! I still have a picture of me and my dad breaking bread together. But the one thing that glares at me in this picture is the bottles of beer that we had in front of us. Blue Moon. That I brought. I always bought the "good stuff" when I would drink with my dad. I didn't want to buy that pee water that he would drink. Although nothing out of the ordinary occurred on this occasion, I bring this up is because I KNEW dad had a SERIOUS problem and I Just. Added. To. His. Addiction. I saw the signs and did nothing. I turned a blind eye and acted like nothing was wrong because I wanted to drink, and how easy it was to just pop another top with Dad and act like everything was just fine.

Around the same time, still hiding his medical problems from years of alcohol abuse, Dad had another episode and had to go to the hospital. More unpaid hospital bills. This time, he tried to tell us that the doctors diagnosed him with diabetes.

My wife, Ashley, overheard this conversation that took place at my sister's dinner table, as Dad was actively checking his blood sugar with a needle prick and digital reading from a small computer telling him what his blood-sugar level was. "This doesn't sound like diabetes to me," she thought but didn't confront him. To this day, we are unaware of whether this was a misdiagnosis or his deception.

"I am writing in response to your posting on the Lakeland healthcare website for the position of LIS System Analyst. After reading your job description, I am confident that my skills and my passion for technology are a perfect match for this position." (November 19, 2010.)

These are the words typed by my dad for a position he applied for and received in St. Joseph, Michigan, his dream position. With his experience in the medical field and in the IT field, the job was a perfect fit for him!

"FINALLY! Dad is really starting to do better for himself! He's going to be making great money working in the IT department of a large hospital!"

These were some thoughts that went through my mind after hearing he landed the job. But this "fantasy" wouldn't last long. His need for alcohol far outweighed the prestige or income of any position he could possess as a computer guru. When moving day came, my sister and brother-in-law helped him move from Indiana to Michigan. There seemed to be more clean-up than packing. Trash bags of empty Budweiser cans and several different types of liquor bottles were cleaned up and thrown away. Tequila, vodka, whiskey, Jose Cuervo, Maker's Mark, Grey Goose, off brand, top shelf, plastic bottles, glass bottles, 750ml bottles (also known as a "fifth" in some settings), gallon handles. There seemed to be no end to the "variety" that was thrown away.

Maybe four or five months passed since Dad landed the job with the hospital. My dad found out that grandpa, who lived in Anderson, Indiana, had fallen and hurt himself. Grandpa Curt was in his late seventies and was still going through hours and hours of dialysis, in an attempt to put a Band-Aid on what he did to his liver and kidneys years before from his alcohol and drug use. Suddenly, dad "made the decision" to quit his job and move in with Grandpa Curt in Anderson, rather than grandpa moving in with him. At least that was the story Dad told us at the time. Jenny helped him move, but there was an awkwardness to this move. Dad seemed to just want to abandon all his belongings—pots, pans, furniture, etc. He just seemed to want to off-load it.

"Go through it and take what you want. Whatever you don't want, I'm going to throw away," he instructed her.

"Dad, you can't just throw away all of these papers. They have your name, address, and Social Security number on them. Somebody could steal your identity."

"Well, just take them with you and shred them."

Ed would later find a termination letter from the hospital where Dad was employed, dismissing him from his job for showing up to work intoxicated.

There had been some relational distance between my sister and my dad while he worked at the hospital in St. Joseph. Eventually, when it was time to move, Dad asked her to help him. "Sure," was her response, as it seemed to become her patented line with dad. This move seemed to be eerily similar to Dad's move from Mishawaka to St. Joseph. Another move, another clean-up that rivaled a miniature disaster relief effort. More alcohol. Beer cans. Unpaid medical bills. Old food in the refrigerator. "Like he just let himself go," my sister would later tell me. A typical red flag, food that was moldy and untouched in the refrigerator, but empty beer cans and empty liquor bottles everywhere. Just as others who dealt with alcohol dependency, most of his diet consisted of alcohol, rather than food. Also, amongst the miniature state-of-emergency area, six half-gallon bottles of Lactulose, untouched. Lactulose (drug class: laxative, osmotic: ammonium detoxicants) is a prescription medication used in the treatment or prevention of complications from liver disease, such as hepatic encephalopathy. Although this is not a cure, this medication can be used to improve mental state. It is a sugar solution made to decrease the amount of ammonia in the blood. Later in this chapter you will see how hepatic encephalopathy affects a person. At the time, nobody really knew what that was, so nobody paid any attention to it and moved on with the cleaning efforts.

Dad moved in with my grandfather around September 2011. He visited my sister numerous times, but something was different. He would drink while at her house, but not as much as he used to. Drinking too much would make him sick. Rather than his usual twelve-pack and two or three Bloody Marias within about a four-hour span, it would be a twelve-pack and two or three Bloody Marias within a twelve-hour span. Almost like a normal summer party in some households.

While living with Grandpa Curt, Dad would complain to my sister, "Your grandpa hates me. He is so mean to me." Eventually, Grandpa would open up to my sister about why he was portrayed as a hateful old man.

"You know, I gave your dad $10,000 and let him live here free! I don't have a clue what he did with my money!"

While living with Grandpa, Dad did not work. He always said he had to take care of Grandpa. However, eventually some truth was brought to light.

"I can't work," Dad finally told me at one point. "The Lactulose is some nasty stuff! Even though it's cleaning me out, I can't be away from the bathroom for more than ten minutes! I'm in the bathroom all day, every day! I can't get away from that toilet! I have even pooped my own pants several times! It's embarrassing!"

Early Spring 2012

Dad was on his way to my sister's house to visit for the weekend. I'm guessing by this point, he stopped using the Lactulose since he was driving to a location much further than ten minutes away. On his way, he was pulled over by police in a small town called Swayzee in the middle of Indiana. Just a cute little town in between where my sister lived and where my grandfather lived. Dad was pulled over because he was swerving and appeared to be driving under the influence of alcohol or drugs. To the police officers' surprise, he blew zeros on the breathalyzer! Dumbfounded, the officers followed protocol and let him drive away since they couldn't detain him or arrest him. He really didn't do anything wrong. Since I wasn't there, I could only deduce these were the reasons they let him go.

Even though this was only supposed to be a two-hour trip from Anderson to Mishawaka, FIVE HOURS LATER, Dad was pulled over again by the Rochester Police Department, about an hour northeast of Swayzee. This time, even though he still blew through the straw on the breathalyzer and the read-out showed zeros across the display, the police detained him. I'm not quite sure the difference between the two departments, but I can only imagine what could have happened if he wasn't detained.

9:00 p.m. My sister's phone rings. "Good evening ma'am, this is the Rochester Police Department. We have your dad, Scott Leeper, here. Due to his slurred speech and how he was driving, we gave him a breathalyzer test, and he clearly has not had anything to drink. He is telling us he is perfectly fine to drive, but clearly he is not. He is drooling and can't keep his own spit in his mouth. He's refused medical attention. He's still upright and coherent enough to make his own decisions, but we are not allowing him to drive. He also has some shotguns in the back of the van and told us he wanted to make sure his dad's shotguns were safe and taken care of. He was also pulled over in Swayzee hours ago."

"This is stupid. Your dad is an adult," my brother in-law said to my sister. "We shouldn't have to go pick him up like a teenager." My sister was torn. They left to get him.

On their way, they passed his gray Pontiac Montana minivan that was facing north on the side of U.S. Route 31, the main artery that connected South Bend and Indianapolis. On the other side of the highway sat a gas station that appeared to be a bit worn out from an outsider's perspective. Attached to it was an old highway diner that appeared to attract the occasional lone trucker who stopped in for a hot meal that would remind them of the meals they were missing at home while on the long road to their next destination. To this day, I feel a stab in my heart every time I pass this diner. This diner signifies the beginning of the end for my dad.

A slender officer with a military-style haircut released my father to my sister. "Your dad needs medical attention," he said. My dad got into the car, still drooling and slurring his words.

"Dad, I really think you need to be checked out. Do you want to go to the hospital?" Jenny asked.

"No, no, nope."

Jenny took him home. He passed out on the couch immediately. She decided to brainstorm ways to trick him into going to the hospital.

The next morning, Dad was sitting on the toilet in the bathroom but not going to the bathroom. Still clothed, he was leaning over, concentrating and scrubbing his nails, with his jaw jacked opened. He appeared to be drunk as he was scrubbing his already clean nails.

"Dad, you alright?" Jenny inquired.

"Yeah! Yeah, I'm fine," he slurred in an attempt to reassure her that nothing was wrong. She could tell that he thought it was obvious that he was "fine."

"Dad, your nails are already clean."

"I know, I'm just recleaning 'em. I just want to make sure my hands are clean," he continued in what seemed to be a drunken state.

Jenny made him eggs, bacon, and hash browns for breakfast and kept a close eye on him that day. Around noon, Jenny and Ed decided to run and get his van before it was towed.

On the way to the van, they racked their brains as to what could possibly be wrong with dad, since he was acting drunk, confused, and disoriented, but didn't have any alcohol in his system. When they returned with the van, Dad continued to slur his words and slowly walk through the house like he was drunk, even though he didn't have a lick of alcohol.

He needed medical attention.

Around 3:00 or 4:00 p.m., "Ed," Dad said confidently in his own mind, "you and I should go get a beer. Jenny, you should have a beer, too. But I can't drive because I don't have my van."

"Okay," Jenny said, seeing her chance to get him to the hospital. "I'll drive you. I'll go have a beer with you, ONLY if you have yourself checked out. You don't have to get checked into the hospital. Let's just have the nurse evaluate you to make sure you're okay."

"I'm fine," he reassured her.

"I'm not going to drive you until you get checked out. Come on, Dad. Please, for me. For your daughter? Come on."

"Okay, but I'm not staying there."

Jenny took Dad to a local hospital in Mishawaka, and it didn't take long for the emergency room staff to find my sister.

The doctor informed Jenny that my dad's liver was not functioning and that the toxins in his blood were extremely high. "If we don't do a detox, it is going to kill him," the staff member told them.

The medical staff began a detox with Dad and gave him a drink that he had to get down. "All I can remember is the smell of sulfur or rotten eggs! It was the nastiest stuff I've smelled in my life!" Jenny later told me. "The whole hospital room smelled of sulfur!" Dad started to fart the smell of sulfur, and his breath and belches smelled like sulfur, too. But he started to return to normal and talk normally the next day.

The doctor started Dad on the Lactulose again. By the next day, he was somehow able to drive himself back down to Grandpa Curt's house. "He seemed like the dad that I knew," Jenny told me.

April 2012

Jenny's phone rings. It's Dad, from a hospital room in Anderson. "I've been puking up a lot of blood. Grandpa had to call an ambulance and I've been in here for a few days. There's something wrong with my stomach."

This would be the last coherent conversation with Dad that either of us would ever have.

May 13, 2012 (Mother's Day)

Mother's Day morning. Jenny's phone rang. The voice on the other end of the phone told Jenny she was calling from a hospital in Indianapolis. "Mr. Leeper was airlifted here to our facility in

Indianapolis. I should tell you that Mr. Leeper is not doing good. You should come down here as soon as possible."

"Happy Mother's Day to me," Jenny told Ed when she hung up.

* * *

Sixteen hours away the same day. It was mid-afternoon. The sun was high in the sky, and the sky was polka-dotted with clouds. Spring was in full swing, and the anticipation for awesome weather and summer parties was so thick I could taste it. Harley riding season! I was stationed at Camp Lejeune and living in a nice neighborhood in a small town called Stella, North Carolina. I was home with Ashley, who was six months pregnant with our son, Jaxson. My cell phone rang. "Dad is in the hospital for internal bleeding again," Jenny said. Her voice cracked with concern. "It's not looking good. He was airlifted to the hospital in Indianapolis."

I immediately felt my adrenaline spike. My heart started to race, and I could feel my face flush and start to sweat.

"Well, I will let my command know just in case it gets worse. Call me tomorrow and let me know how he's doing."

"I really think you need to come up," she said anxiously.

I sighed deeply as a sense of fear overcame me. "We'll drive halfway today and finish the trip tomorrow morning."

May 14, 2012

We were somewhere in Virginia when we stopped to get some sleep. As we got back on the road to make the second leg of our trip, thoughts started to flood in. *Dad is in a coma. I've never known anybody to be in a coma. I've only heard of death coming from a coma, but Dad will pull through. He has to, right? How long will it take him to recover? Will he survive? Will he die? Oh my God! He could die!* The thoughts kept flooding in. There was a dark cloud coming, and I couldn't see the light behind it. My mind continued to race faster than an NHRA dragster. I couldn't keep up with my own thoughts! My mind was flying at the speed of light. I'm not even sure if I was speeding at that point. The trip seemed to take forever but also seemed extremely short at the same time. The time felt like there was a war of whiplash going on in the space between my ears.

At the same time, I made every possible attempt to hide my terror from my six-months pregnant wife. "She doesn't need this kind of stress," I thought to myself, shielding her and our growing baby from the sheer terror I was dealing with internally. I'd been to Iraq twice at this point, I had some compartmentalizing strategies, I'd had to face challenges, but nothing could have prepared me for what I was about to endure.

It was around 4:00 or 5:00 in the afternoon when we arrived at my grandfather's house in Anderson. My grandfather, an old, grumpy man with wisps of salt and pepper hair on his head, who stood about 5'5" tall, mad that he was old and admittedly was just awaiting his day to die, was not very mobile at the time due to his four-hour bouts of dialysis, three days a week. Even though he wasn't very mobile, we stopped at his house to pick him up and take him with us to Indianapolis.

Within an hour of getting to his house, we were back in the truck and making the sixty-minute trip to the hospital in Indianapolis. "We're coming, Dad. Stay strong." It seemed like this thought teleported us to the hospital.

Typically, I get lost in hospitals, but I found the ICU quickly. I was on a mission. Get to Dad and find out how to get him out of his coma. I'd seen it in the movies and on TV all the time. The loved one is out of town when somebody is in a coma. The person comes home and walks in the hospital room, and the coma patient wakes up.

The ICU was in an upside-down horseshoe shape, and we entered at what would be the right end of the horseshoe. My dad's room was the fourth room on the right of the first hallway. The curtain was opened. Lights flashed from the machines that lined the walls. The machines looked like something out of an airplane or spaceship, with all the buttons and levers and lights and beeping. Far too complicated for me to understand. In the midst of all the machines, Dad. His hospital bed was slightly propped up, and there he was.

My dad always had a weight problem for as long as I could remember. He stood about 5'7" and, although I never knew his actual weight, I would venture to guess that he was around 300 pounds. But as he lay in the hospital bed, I could tell that he was extremely bloated and was holding a lot of water. He looked to be around 400 pounds. Next to his bed, IV bags dripped clear fluids through tubes and into his arms. A large blue tube entered his mouth and went down his throat and into his lungs to assist his breathing. His chest would rise and fall with the beat of the ventilator. *Shhh-tshhh, shhh-tshhh, shhh-tshhh.* Three drips to keep his circulation moving and a ventilator to keep him breathing, otherwise . . . death.

"Hey, Dad!" I said with as much excitement in my voice as I could muster. Who am I kidding, there was no excitement. Somber was more like it. Afraid for his life was more like it. Besides that, the room was so silent. It was all like something out of a bad dream. I stood on the right side of the bed, Jenny on the left. Ed and Ashley were standing at the foot of his bed, and Grandpa was closer to the door in his wheelchair, and for some reason, studying Jenny's every move.

Since we couldn't do anything but sit with him, we decided to go back to Anderson to rest. That night, there wasn't a lot of sleep. Not just because of racing minds, but Grandpa liked his house hot. The thermostat read 81 degrees! Since Ashley was six-months pregnant, we decided to go get a hotel room in the middle of the night.

May 16, 2012

We all piled into the vehicles and left Anderson to go back up to Mishawaka, where we were from and had other family members. We decided it best to take Ashley north to our hometown in Mishawaka so that she could see family and they could coo over her pregnant belly! We also needed this to feel some sort of normalcy and visit family since we lived so far away.

May 17, 2012

Jenny and I left everybody else in Mishawaka and went back down to Indianapolis to visit Dad. When we were done at the hospital, we suffered the heat at Grandpa's house again.

May 18, 2012

The next day, we went back to the hospital in Indianapolis. Dad was awake. Just like the movies, we visited and he woke up out of his coma! His tube was out and everything. There was a sense of elation, unlike anything I've ever felt.

"How was your nap?" I tried to joke, not really expecting any kind of answer.

"Shhenny," he whispered as he tried to push out words, while calling Jenny's name. It was clear that he had a hard time talking due to just coming out of a coma.

"Hey, Dad, I'm here!" she said with excitement in her voice.

After her acknowledgement, he looked over at me and without any voice, his lips shaped, "Ashley."

"You want to see Ashley?" I asked earnestly.

He nodded his head and lipped, "Uh, yah" like he always did whenever I asked him a dumb question when I was younger.

"She's back up in Mishawaka, but I'll bring her down so you can say hi! We'll go up there today, and I'll bring her, Ed, and the boys back down tomorrow, okay?"

He nodded yes and seemed to relax a bit.

May 19, 2012

Ashley and I woke up at her parents' house early enough to get right back down to Indianapolis. We stopped at Jenny's house to pick her up and at the local pharmacy to fill one of my prescriptions.

While waiting for my prescription, my cell phone rang. The area code was 317. Indianapolis. Anxiety began to fill my lungs.

"This is Brian, one of the nurses at the facility your dad is at. I am calling you because your dad slipped back into his coma and started to bleed from his mouth and rectally. It is imperative that we take him into surgery to stop the bleeding, but we need your permission to do so."

"GO! Make it happen! Get it done!" I yelled at the faceless voice on the other end that had delayed in giving the care my dad so desperately needed.

"Right away, sir. We are prepping him for surgery now. It should only take about forty-five minutes."

"Fine! Get it done!"

I rushed out of the pharmacy and jumped in the truck with Jenny and Ashley inside.

We quickly stopped at my in-laws to pick up an overnight bag for Ashley, then to Jenny's house to pick up Ed and the boys. Both stops took less than five minutes each, and we were on our way back down south. One part of the trip that always took a while to get through was a town called Kokomo. Kokomo was halfway between South Bend and Indianapolis. There were traffic lights and bad traffic.

"Get out of my way!" I yelled every thirteen seconds. I picked up the phone and called the Indiana State Police.

"I'm calling to see if we can get a police escort through Kokomo. We are on our way down to Indianapolis because my dad is on his deathbed, and I don't know how much time he has left. This is extremely important and traffic seriously sucks right now!"

"I'm sorry, sir, but we can't authorize a police escort."

"Thanks for nothing!" I hung up.

I continued to weave in and out of traffic and to punch the gas pedal as often as I could. I think Dale Earnhardt would have been proud at my racing skills that day.

We arrived at the hospital in two hours, literally running into the ICU. "He's still not here!" I thought as we approached his room.

"He is still undergoing surgery. It has taken longer than expected," a nurse informed us from behind. "I can escort you to the waiting room closest to the OR."

Another hour passed as we sat in the waiting room. My mind continued to race. "This procedure was supposed to take less than an hour," I'd worry every ten seconds. The door opened and a team of five doctors walked in.

"Are you the family of Scott Leeper?"

"Yes," I replied.

"The first procedure we attempted didn't work. We tried a liver bypass so he wouldn't bleed internally, but his liver is so scarred, we couldn't get through. There is one other procedure we could try, but we have already given him eight units of blood, so his quality of life will be zero."

A lump settled in my throat and my eyes began to well up with tears. "Hang on, I need to make a phone call."

"Grandpa, it's me. The doctors are here. They just told me that the procedure they just tried on Dad didn't work. There is one other procedure they could try, but they already gave him eight units of blood, so his quality of life will be zero."

He responded with two words . . . "Handle it."

I hung up and looked at Jenny; she knew Grandpa had left the decision up to me.

"Scottie, I can't make this decision," she said with tears running down her face.

Suddenly, the weight of the world was crushing down on my shoulders. I've never felt a weight like this. I was given the obligation to take somebody's life, my dad's life. I fell in my chair and let my head fall into my hands. I was sobbing. Pools of tears filled my hands and landed on the floor like a waterfall fixture in a pond. I didn't want to respond. I had to respond. They were waiting for me to make a decision, and Dad was in the operating room awaiting his fate. This was an easy decision but the most difficult decision I will ever have to make. It felt like an eternity before I said anything.

Finally, without even raising my head to look at the team of doctors, "Don't do the other procedure," I agonizingly responded.

"We will make him comfortable and bring him back up to ICU so you can say your goodbyes."

The pain to sentence dad to death was unbearable. I was shaking. I went into an adjacent room by myself. I fell to the floor in a heap. I'd just made a decision that would stop my dad's beating heart. "GOD, WHY?" I asked through the tears. "THIS IS A NIGHTMARE, THIS ISN'T TRUE! WAKE ME UP! PINCH ME PLEASE!" I kept thinking.

I didn't wake up, though; I was already awake. Nobody was going to pinch me out of this nightmare. It was real.

We took the wrenching trip back up to the ICU and waited. Each step felt harder than the last. In my mind, I was the Roman Emperor who just made the decision for the gladiator, thumbs up or thumbs down. Thumbs down.

Dad was rolled back up to his room and reattached to his lifelines. Blood was on the floor still from when he was bleeding hours earlier. Ashley, Jenny, and I stood there in silence, knowing this would be the last time we ever saw our dad alive, even if it was with the assistance of machines.

Trying to find any way to lighten the mood, I tried to joke with Dad, "If the Bears win the Super Bowl this year, I will know you were cheating."

"Dad, if you ever come visit me, please come as a lady bug because I don't ever see them," my sister cried.

Soon after, Jenny said, "Are you guys ready to go to the waiting room?"

"You guys go ahead. I made the decision, I have to stay here with him."

They walked out slowly.

It was just me and my dad. Scott Leeper, Sr., and Scott Leeper, Jr. I sat there in silence. Tears were streaming down my face. A never-ending amount of snot running out of my nose. Amongst the beeps of the machines and arbitrary conversations throughout the ICU, there was an eerie sound coming from the depths of Dad's chest. The death rattle. I'd heard that's the sound made when a person is near death and has fluid stuck in their lungs as they attempt to breathe.

It was a little before 7:00 p.m. I stood up and set my chair to the side. It was time. I didn't want it to be, but I knew it had to be.

"I'm ready," I told the nurse at the nurse's station shaking in my voice.

"Okay, we will ask you to step out briefly as we take him off the ventilator. We will give him a shot to make him comfortable so he won't be in any pain."

I didn't know what to think about those words. It was almost like a consolation for the fact that my dad was about to die. There was no point in fighting it. I don't think I had the energy or will to fight it at that point. I felt an emotional exhaustion unlike anything I've ever felt, even after being in a war zone twice.

I stepped out of the room. They closed the curtain behind me. I felt I was abandoning him and the people walking in were now the executioners who took action. The Roman Emperor had given the thumbs down.

There was an opening in the curtain on the opposite side of where they'd tried to tug it closed. Although I didn't want to, I had to watch. Two female nurses, wearing blue scrubs, with pens in the blouse pockets and a stethoscope around one of their necks, were in his room, one on either side of his bed. Flipping switches, hitting buttons, then the removal of his breathing tube.

My father opened his eyes and looked up and to his right to the nurse by the monitor with his vital signs. I don't think he spoke any words, but he raised his right arm toward the nurse and seemed to lazily try to grab her arm. It didn't take long before he put his arm back down and closed his eyes for the last time. I'm not quite sure what he was trying to communicate to her, but I've concluded one of two things he was trying to say.

"It's okay, it's time for me to go."

OR

"What are you doing? Give me back my breathing tube!"

I could only hope it was the former. The other nurse to his left gave him the injection- the one that would make him drift off into his deathly sleep, never to wake again.

The nurses opened the curtain and walked out of the room. "You can go back in now," they said as they gave me apologetic looks.

"How can these nurses do this?" I wondered to myself as I slowly walked back into the ICU room.

Dad was still breathing. I could only tell because his death rattle was more pronounced. "Gurgle, exhale, gurgle, exhale." The room was quiet. The monitor with his vitals was off. The lights that were once vibrant and colorful no longer had life in them and they were dark. The ventilator was off and quiet. The only sound in that room was the rattling breath and a father's son sobbing.

"Dad!" I cried out. "Why did you have to do this? Why couldn't you get help? What was so bad that this had to be your outlet and death? We loved you!" Even when I thought I couldn't cry more, a faucet of tears turned on and I cried harder. Even a bit of anger, "HOW COULD YOU?! Okay, I'm not mad, please wake up, Dad!" My body was heavy, my eyes burned, my heart was in a million pieces, and my mind was exhausted and still running faster than a jet.

Three minutes went by. His breaths were getting shallower with each breath. A gurgle, followed by an exhale, then a ten-second pause. A gurgle, followed by an exhale, then a seventeen-second pause.

Five minutes later, a gurgle, an exhale, then silence.

At 7:08 p.m., my dad's spirit left his body. He was no longer a slave to the bottle. At the same time, in the waiting room, the rest of my family waited. My sister looked out the window and, there on the ledge, sat a ladybug. Through her tears, she saw the little creature spread its red and black polka-dot wings and fly away.

LET'S GET REAL

1. Have you had a similar conversation with a loved one, like I did with my dad? Do they feel that the bottle or the drug is their escape from not being good enough? Are these thoughts that go through your mind?

2. Are the signs that my dad had familiar to you? Are you or a loved one dealing with these signs? Do you feel powerless to stop or help the person with an addiction?

3. Are you afraid to approach your loved one about their addiction? Do you fear making the relationship worse if you confront them? Would you rather take them off life support like I did?

4. Have you lost a loved one to addiction? Have you faced these nightmarish memories or are they festering within you?

CHAPTER 4

Shining The Light

AMERICA LIKES TO drink.

According to the Centers for Disease Control and Prevention (CDC), more than 38 million adults in the United States reported binge drinking an average of four times per month and consume an average of eight drinks per binge. When it comes to our underage citizens, approximately 5.3 million people between the ages of twelve and 20 were considered binge drinkers, according to the 2014 National Survey on Drug Use and Health.

Binge drinking is defined as having four or more drinks within two hours for women and five or more drinks within two hours for men. In a country where drinking culture has transformed itself into binge culture, more and more people have accepted the social norm of drinking with the purpose of getting drunk as a staple of young life. For a lot people, going out with friends means, "we are going to tie one on" or "we are going out and getting so wasted." Going out drinking has taken on a whole new meaning of getting blasted, potentially puking your brains out, and possibly making the choice to add drugs to the mix. This has become a part of our American culture.

Alcohol shows up everywhere. Christmas parties, school functions, TV shows, movies, charity events, professional sporting events—it's everywhere. We live in a culture where alcohol floods our world. In all of these settings, heavy drinking has become extremely socially acceptable.

We put alcohol on a pedestal in the United States, but we do little to teach young people how to consume it responsibly. We model binge drinking and alcohol abuse. Kids rob their parents' liquor cabinets. They buy alcohol illegally and try to figure out how to get more. In America, we make alcohol A BIG DEAL.

Furthermore, drinking culture in the United States is popularized by comedy films such as *Neighbors* (and *Neighbors 2*), *The Hangover* trilogy, and *How to Be Single*. Our movies show us that drinking is a great way to celebrate and to mourn.

Popular culture movies don't show the dark side of this behavior, though. An estimated 88,000 people (approximately 62,000 men and 26,000 women) die from alcohol-related causes annually, making alcohol the third-leading preventable cause of death in the United States (after smoking and poor diet).

Alcohol consumption in wealthy, developed countries has declined over the past two decades, but dangerous binge drinking has increased among the young, according to a 2015 study published by the 34-nation Organization for Economic Co-operation and Development. The same study goes on to give these startling statistics: Among boys aged fifteen and younger, the proportion who have been drunk rose to 43 percent from 30 percent during the 2000s, while for girls the share rose to 41 percent from 26 percent. So, in the last decade and a half, the number of girls ages fifteen and younger who have been drunk has risen a whopping 15 percent. A 2016 study by the National Survey on Drug Use and Health Food found that "about two out of five young adults in 2016 were current binge alcohol users."

Binge drinking or drinking heavily during those college-age years can be the beginning of what is known as an alcohol use disorder (AUD). This condition is "a chronic relapsing brain disease characterized by compulsive alcohol use, loss of control over alcohol intake, and a negative emotional state when not using," as defined by the National Institute on Alcohol Abuse and Alcoholism (NIAAA).

The pressure and glorification of drinking affects women as well as men. While everything we share in this chapter can apply to any gender, we want to look at some aspects of female culture that we see affected by cultural attitudes to alcohol.

As we've seen, the "female drinking culture" in America has normalized heavy drinking for women of all ages. This includes college students who are barely (if even) twenty-one years old who are expected to be a part of the "college drinking culture," mothers who are encouraged to drink to reduce the stressors of motherhood in the "mommy drinking culture," and middle-aged and older women are perceived as being more fun by drinking as a central part of social activities (book clubs, girls weekends, family reunions).

College and young adulthood are where another consequence of binge drinking most commonly experienced by females emerges: sexual assault. While it is true that the perpetrator of these heinous acts is completely responsible for their actions, these situations are dramatically more common when the victim has either been drinking to excess, or drinking in an unsafe way, like accepting a drink from a stranger when there is a possibility the drink has been contaminated with a date rape drug.

According to WomensHealth.gov, the three most commons date rape drugs are:

- Rohypnol (commonly called "Roofies")
- GHB (short for gamma hydroxybutyric acid)
- Ketamine (a powerful animal tranquilizer)

While each of these drugs has its differences, all three have this in common—they make you feel weak and confused, or even cause you to pass out—so that you cannot consent to sex.

An article titled, "The Role Alcohol Plays in Sexual Assaults on College Campuses," from Alcohol.org gives these statistics:

- At least 50 percent of student sexual assaults involve alcohol.

- Approximately 90 percent of rapes perpetrated by an acquaintance of the victim involve alcohol.

- About 43 percent of sexual assault events involve alcohol use by the victim; 69 percent involve alcohol use by the perpetrator.

- In one-third of sexual assaults, the aggressor is intoxicated.

While it is extremely important that we do not place the blame on the victims of sexual assault and rape, the ugly fact remains that when women drink to the point of blacking out or making decisions that they would never make sober (such as leaving a bar with a stranger or passing out somewhere unsafe), they are more likely to get into dangerous situations.

*   *   *

When women move from college to the professional world, the drinking culture does not stop. Women and men may continue to drink to feel accepted, "a part of" the work place; there's pressure to drink or use drugs to impress, to fit in, to advance. Women with high-pressure jobs report several reasons for why they drink: keeping up with office drinking culture, cooling off after a stressful day at work, using their high-paying salaries to splurge on cocktail rounds, and taking opportunities to squeeze out career advice from their higher-ups or to bond with a boss.

Women with a master's degree or higher reported higher drinking rates than women without a diploma (74 percent to 34 percent), according to the CDC. Women with higher salaries and who worked longer hours in the office also reported drinking more.

Let's put some things in perspective on how our culture has changed. Generally speaking, in the 1950s, it was unheard of for a woman be part of the regular drinking crowd, but as more women enter the modern-day workforce, it's a part of the networking game.

To gain respect, women are meeting the standards men hold for themselves. They are trying to keep up to maintain respect. Why, though? Why does this have to happen? Typically, in the United States, the person in power knows how to drink.

This was the experience from one of our good friends at her first corporate job.

Sandra was recruited from a top midwestern university to work at what was considered the number-one advertising agency in Chicago, named "One of the Top 50 Companies in America for Women." Her father took her aside at Christmas and told her that she would be cut off from any financial support upon graduating from college. She aspired to move to London and work as a writer but took the advertising job instead, grateful that she would be able to use her creative talents and support herself with a salary.

The first day on the job, Sandra was assigned a mentor. He had gone to her university and gave her tips on how to navigate the highly political environment of the agency. "The perks make the job worth it," he said. "We fly first class, get tons of free food, the fridges and shelves are stocked with beer and vodka and single malt whiskey, and every December, there's this huge party. Ask anyone in Chicago- it's legendary. The drinking starts at 7:00 a.m. and doesn't stop until early the following morning. No spouses allowed. It's crazy," he finished and winked at Sandra.

Sandra's first year consisted of fifteen-hour workdays and flying back and forth from Chicago to New York. She was assigned to a brand that hosted evening events in bars, and part of her job was to attend these events on weekends and entertain the clients when they came into town. One of the senior creative directors on Sandra's account took a disliking to her. He would destroy her work and make blowjob gestures when she walked into rooms for meetings.

The harassment progressed. Soon, several of the senior creative directors made frequent comments about her appearance, rumored on who she might be sleeping with, and made sexual gestures when they encountered her in the hallway or even on airplanes when they flew back from meetings. Another person would have complained or demanded a transfer, but Sandra had a history of sexual abuse and came from an addictive family environment. The work environment mirrored what she knew in her family of origin. Many of these experiences took place in front of Sandra's female boss and other superiors who laughed at or ignored the behavior. She fantasized about quitting but did not know how she could support herself if she left. Her self-esteem was leveled. She felt paranoid and began to dread work. The experiences escalated. A fifty-year-old, married CEO of a vendor company stuck his hand up her dress at an event and suggested that she come to his hotel- that she ought to do what he said, him being in such a senior position. Sandra fled the bar where the event took place but still felt trapped.

Sandra became depressed and apathetic. She stopped drinking at work events, or at all. She was chastised at her review for not being "fun" or "a team player." One night, the majority of the people on her account were drinking in the senior VP's office. Sandra chose to stay in her office and work. The telephone rang, one ring, meaning that it was an internal call placed by someone in the agency. The person on the other end sounded familiar and told her he was giving a questionnaire for the company. He asked her questions that became increasingly personal and then sexual. Sandra felt her body grow cold as she asked the caller again to explain the nature of the survey. The caller moaned, coughed, and then moaned again, bringing himself to a sexual climax. Sandra finally went to Human Resources. The female HR director told her that because the call came from someone at the agency, they were unable to pursue the case. There would be no investigation.

The next week, Sandra was assigned to take a group of clients out to dinner with two other agency executives. After the dinner, the executives suggested that they all go to a strip club in the city. Sandra was appalled. She told her colleagues to choose another venue and made several suggestions of bars and restaurants nearby. The clients became excited about going to The Crazy Horse. Sandra ran across the street, signaled a taxi, and went home.

Monday morning, Sandra was called into the Executive VP's office. Her colleagues complained that she had left the evening early.

The VP lectured her on the importance of entertaining clients that her position demanded. Sandra felt as if she were in an upside-down world. She felt as if every day she became more a shadow of herself. "I felt unsafe going there as a woman," she said.

"We're disappointed in you," the VP said. Sandra resigned the following week.

Sandra escaped a terrible work environment, but some are not as lucky.

* * *

A friend of one of the authors was only eighteen years old when she was raped with the aid of a date rape drug.

One night after work, Amy attended a host party with a group of her coworkers. She knew and worked with everyone there, both men and women, and she felt safe around those people. Amy only remembers having one glass of wine, which the party's host had handed her shortly after she arrived. Ryan was a thirty-six-year-old man, whom she'd known for nearly a year. At the time, she didn't see any danger in accepting a drink from him, and the fact that he was pouring everyone's drinks just made it seem like he was being a good host.

The next thing Amy remembers, she was naked in a bed with a man on top of her. The apartment sounded empty, and it was almost completely dark. At first, she thought the man was her boyfriend, but that didn't make any sense—he was out of town.

Amy squinted up at the man's face, trying to figure out who he was, but his face, and everything else in the dark room, looked blurry. She had the strange feeling that time itself had slowed down. Her muscles felt heavy, and it was very difficult for her to even raise her head.

She slowly realized that the man on top of her, the man who was having sex with her, was not her boyfriend. It was Ryan.

Amy feebly tried to push him off her and to wriggle away, but he seemed impossibly huge, and she could barely move.

"No . . . no . . . no," she heard herself murmur.

Ryan grinned wickedly and just said, "Shhh . . ." and Amy lost consciousness again.

The next morning, she woke up naked in his bed, but she was completely alone. Ryan was not home. Her memory of the night before was completely erased. Amy did not remember any of the details above until two or three months later. At the time, she had zero knowledge of what had happened.

Amy had blacked out from drinking too much alcohol before, and that morning, she assumed that was what had happened. She blamed herself. She believed that she had too much to drink and that she'd had consensual sex with Ryan. She thought she had willingly cheated on her boyfriend. Amy was deeply ashamed of what she thought were her own actions.

She told no one what happened, and when she saw Ryan at work a day later, she acted like nothing had happened. For his own reasons, Ryan did the same.

Less than a week later, Ryan was busted at his home by the police and arrested on drug charges. Apparently, he already had a record, so he was sent to prison.

As mentioned above, Amy eventually remembered critical details regarding what had happened the night at his party. She researched date rape drugs after she realized that she could remember only one drink, and it usually took her seven or more drinks to black out.

Even though her recollection, her research, and Ryan's drug-related arrest all made it obvious to her what had happened, Amy didn't do anything about it at the time. She felt that there was no point, that she had no proof, and besides, he was already in prison. She buried it deep inside and got on with her life.

This happened almost ten years ago, and Amy never told anyone until very recently. She hopes that sharing her story might encourage other women to be more careful about who they accept a drink from and who they hang out with. Sharing her story was her way of healing a very old wound from a trauma that could have been avoided.

As we've seen, our society does a great job of rationalizing, encouraging, demanding, and even glorifying drinking. For the regular person, this may present social or professional challenges as we've described above. But Sandra and Amy's problem was the environment, not an addiction. What about potential or already active addicts who are not just drinking to "fit or join in" for fun, in a healthy way?

There is a progressive nature of alcoholism. It can start with just having a few drinks after work a couple days a week. Then, you drink on the weekends because everyone else is doing it. Before you know it, you are drinking every single day and not having just one. Then before you know it, drinking isn't enough, and you have to add in the drugs to keep you going so you don't pass out or black out.

Maybe you don't only drink when you are coping or when it feels healthy for you. Maybe you go straight to the pills or do a line of blow to drown out your sorrows or to celebrate a victory. Maybe you don't feel safe feeling your feelings or have learned to avoid or escape them.

* * *

"I didn't see my problem until I was in too deep." Jessica continues to explain the progressive nature of drinking that smacked her in the face.

"I drank a lot in college because that's what everyone did. Then I got a job in a rather large financial advisory/risk management firm after college, and I had to tone it back. I did for a while. Then I found guys at work who wanted to go out every night for happy hour, and I was stoked! We drank every night. I started coming in late. I was becoming disorganized with my daily routine, and I was forgetting to finish certain tasks for clients. So, what did I do to fix this? I started doing cocaine to take the edge off. It was $40 for one gram. I was told that would last me several days, so why not?! People told me that would help, and let me tell you, it did. I was so alert! I didn't black out anymore. It was awesome. Then, I wasn't just doing cocaine at night when we were drinking, I started bringing it to work and doing key bumps in the bathroom so that I would be alert and coherent at work. I thought it was helping. I was able to get a lot of work done, and then I couldn't wait to get out of there and go party. Everything was going so fast- I was out of control! I was doing cocaine in the morning before even leaving my house for work and slamming a screwdriver or two! I was doing a gram or more a day. I spent over $200 a week on cocaine. At first, it was awesome because I felt invincible and powerful. That slowly went away as it got to the point where even the cocaine wasn't helping. I was screwing up at work. I was forgetting client meetings. I was starting to mess up portfolios, and my boss pulled me aside and put me on probation and started having me do simple tasks every day to see if I could get my consistency back and not screw anything else up. It was so embarrassing. Anxiety was riddling my every move, and I became more concerned with my dealer and making sure I had enough to get through my days. Honestly, it's insane. It's totally insane. I went from having just a couple beers or cocktails every night to spending over $200 a week. I knew deep down that I needed to stop. I was about to lose my job, and the friends I was partying with slowly stopped hanging out with me because I was drunk or high all of the time. Always 'partying.'

I was lost. I didn't know what my next move was. I felt I was in too deep. I wasn't ready to give it up yet, so I managed to find other friends at the bars who wanted to drink and party like me. I didn't feel alone anymore. I was able to keep this routine up for awhile until it got the best of me. This routine cost me my job."

Jessica's story is quite normal. She went on to say that she knew so many people who were doing what she was doing. It was just what people did.

Look at the big picture. For many people, alcohol is how we cope. Drinking is what we do with feelings. When we get a job promotion, we drink. When your boyfriend or girlfriend breaks up with you, you drink. When your sports team wins the championship, you drink.

People may use alcohol to cope with:

- Difficult emotions
- Challenging life events, such as the death of a family member, a break-up, or an illness
- Boredom

- Stress
- Insomnia
- Trauma / PTSD symptoms
- Social Anxiety

College women and professional women are not the only ones encouraged to drink. Women of all ages have been particularly targeted by advertisers selling alcohol, with a heavy emphasis on wine.

There are drinking bracelets and necklace flasks, bras that fit an entire bottle of wine inside them, and "joke gifts" such as huge plastic wine glasses also made to fit an entire bottle of wine inside.

Online, you can find baby products like onesies and bibs with sayings like, "Mommy needs wine," and "Someone get my mom a glass of wine."

Sheri Fandrey of Addictions Foundation Manitoba says, "[Children] are picking up on the fact that their parents, especially their moms, have to be anaesthetized to deal with them, and I think that sends a subtle but dangerous message to our young people."

For shower gifts, women give each other sets of wine glasses with phrases that include, "Mommy's time-out," "Mommy Juice," or "Mama's turn to wine."

The messaging itself is not limited to products for sale. Memes are created and shared all over social media with the same messaging. There is even a Facebook page called, "Mommy Needs Vodka" with over three million followers, which is a lot of moms.

"Wine has become the code for 'I deserve it, parenting is hard, I need to decompress,'" says Ann Dowsett Johnston, the Toronto-based author of *Drink: The Intimate Relationship Between Women and Alcohol.*

JAMA Psychiatry published a study in 2017 which found that in the general population, problems with alcohol increased by nearly 50 percent from 2001 to 2013. Among women, alcohol abuse and dependence increased by 83.7 percent.

There are many facets to the female drinking culture, and they are complex issues, not easily distilled into black-and-white ideas. But the trends we are seeing here are certainly alarming, and the culture itself needs more attention if it is to be properly understood, and the problems therein dealt with. It is our responsibility as a society to try to understand all the dangers of alcohol normalization, binge-drinking, and possibility of addiction—and to work together to come up with solutions.

MILITARY AND FIRST RESPONDERS

SCOTT'S POV:

Not only are there societal and cultural norms surrounding female drinking, there are for male drinking as well. Again, everything we're speaking to here could apply to anyone, but this section comes from my personal experiences and what I have observed as a male in American culture today.

AddictionCenter.com, by Beach House Center for Recovery, states that young men in fraternities are more likely to drink in excess than young women in sororities are. These organizations might include a rite of passage or haze new members in ways that include alcohol. This may set up the young, prospective member to develop an alcohol dependency, or worse.

Another form of drinking culture may come from an individual's geography and sub-cultures. I love country music and have redneck roots, so it would be normal for me to enjoy songs about drinking in country music. Now, don't get me wrong, country music isn't all about just drinking songs, but there are a lot of them. Before working in this field, I've even thrown redneck parties, where everybody had to dress up as a redneck. Then as an added touch, I'd throw about three cases of empty beer cans in the front yard, then put another four or five cases of beer in a kiddie pool with ice.

Another arena for heavy or binge drinking is our military and first responders. Now, before you assume that all of our troops and first responders are alcoholics or abusing some sort of substance, think again. It is not all people in these demographics. However, these sub-cultures, by nature, could easily lead one to have some sort of substance dependency. I've witnessed and been a part of numerous experiences with heavy or binge drinking amongst my public service counterparts.

Day of Liberty—South Korea

One of my first experiences occurred in Pohang, South Korea, in 2002. I was a young Private First Class (E-2) in the Marines. My unit went to Camp Mujuk for some training. While we were there, we were given a day of liberty in a town close to Camp Mujuk, called Pohang. Day of liberty meant day of drinking. As we were starting our day of liberty, we stopped at a little shop that had arcades inside and a juice bar on the outside. Now, picture a bunch of tough Marines drinking smoothies in the middle of South Korea. We probably weren't the most intimidating bunch at that time, but rather a pretty comical sight! We quickly found booze and began partying.

During the day, my friend Kevin, who was supposed to stay sober, was more drunk than we were! It was all a result of drinking with the Republic of Korea Marines, which included pitcher-chugging contests and countless shots. On the way back, Kevin, who was drunk, got sentimental and wrapped his arm around my shoulder. "I love you, bro!" he exclaimed.

"Dude! Get off me!" I yelled as I pushed him away. I pushed him so hard that he flew across a car parked on the side of the road, leaving a dent on the hood. I had thought I only gave him a light shove.

We got back in a cab and headed back to base. The cab driver seemed to be driving at 90 miles an hour, when Kevin decided to roll the window down and lean out of the window from the waist up. He started to puke, but he wasn't facing where we came from, but was facing where we were going! The cab driver started yelling. We didn't speak Korean, but we were pretty sure he was yelling at Kevin for being halfway out of the window and puking all over the side of his car. We pulled him back in, but he wasn't done getting sick. We handed him a bag. The problem was, there was a gaping hole in the bag. The smell was rancid, and I felt myself starting to get sick. I made myself pass out and before I knew it, I woke up as we pulled up next to the base. I looked over and Kevin, who was also passed out, had puke running down his chest and puke oozing out of the bag. I kicked my other friend, Ryan, out of the car and ran to a nearby barrier so I could lose my dinner as well. The next day, we laughed about the night and thought of it only as a great party night.

Day of Liberty—Panama

My reserve unit conducted humanitarian missions in Panama. On Good Friday 2004, we were given a day of liberty there to check out the sights and sounds of Panama. Our first stop was the Panama Canal. It was quite the sight to be seen! Our next focus was to find alcohol. It wasn't quite as simple on this trip. Panama was a dry country on this day due to the overwhelming Catholic beliefs in South America. To buy alcohol on Good Friday was a crime. We didn't care.

We walked down to the row of cabs and found two drivers who knew where we could find beer. They drove us to a very poor part of town. When we stopped in front of this dilapidated house, we all started to pile out (six or seven guys piled in each of the older Toyota Corollas). As soon as we started to get out, the cab drivers became very worried.

"You stay! You stay! Get back in car!" they exclaimed in broken English.

After piling back into the cars, we saw them sneak out two giant coolers into the two cabs. I felt like we were transporting organs!

We drove to a deserted beach and opened the coolers. Luckily, it was just a lot of beer and no organs! We cracked open the bottles and began to drink. The cab drivers were drinking with us as well. Through conversation with the drivers, they told us that they were also off-duty police officers for the local community! At the time, we thought this was a pretty cool notion, not realizing that we were breaking the local law in a foreign country with local police officers. This could have ended much worse than it did.

In the military, people move from base to base constantly. It always appeared that we needed to size the "new blood" up before accepting them into the unit, even though we were all Marines and cut from the same cloth. Occasionally, we would be faced with a "unique" Marine.

June 6, 2008

After switching from reserves to active duty, I was a Sergeant (E-5) stationed on Camp Schwab, Okinawa, Japan, as a Heavy Equipment Operator.

"Bro, did you hear about the new guy in our unit?"

"Yeah. I heard he doesn't drink."

"Well, we can't trust this dude then."

This is a conversation I heard many times during my thirteen years in the United States Marine Corps. As a matter of fact, I was a part of these conversations numerous times as well, outside of this instance. To give you a little bit of history, the Marine Corps was founded on November 10, 1775, in Tun Tavern, Philadelphia. Tun Tavern was a bar. Therefore, most Marines pride their drinking "skills" and view their high tolerance for alcohol as a rite of passage. Again, these were some of my own views as well. The young Marines who entered the Fleet Marine Force didn't already have a high tolerance for alcohol (in most cases); it was built over time as a result of constant drinking outside of work hours. A study cited by the National Institute on Alcohol Abuse and Alcoholism (NIAAA) revealed the highest levels of negative effects, such as trouble with the command, missing duty due to alcohol-related illness, trouble with the law, or dependency, typically occurred amongst the lowest ranks of E1—E3. Although this study spoke on behalf of all branches of service, I personally viewed these issues in the Marine Corps, in my own command, and on duty as a Criminal Investigator.

One such case included a young Lance Corporal (E3), who was found facedown on the pavement on a base in Japan. When he was found, he appeared to have been assaulted. Unfortunately, this young individual's injuries came from drinking. He was too drunk to even understand (or feel) that his bottom jaw was split in half, with the right side of his bottom jaw pushed back into his head. I don't know how long he took to recover, but I would assume he had to have his jaw wired shut for no less than six months.

While I was stationed in Japan, curfews and restricted off-base activities were set in place for all troops after a young Marine became highly intoxicated and broke into a local Okinawan's home. Unknowingly, this Marine passed out on the couch, only to be awakened by the owner of the house screaming in fear and anger.

Another situation I witnessed was much deadlier. A young Marine was drinking with a few others. At one point, they all fell asleep, except for this Marine. He climbed up on the roof of his barracks, which was about seven stories high. It is unclear if this young man meant to or not, but he fell from the roof.

There was information that this person was missing all weekend. Nobody saw him or heard from him, and his friends became worried. All they remembered was drinking with him. His vehicle was still in the parking lot, but he was nowhere to be found. After a search party was sent out to look for him, he was found, almost folded in half, behind the A/C system on the back side of the barracks.

As you can see, some of the consequences come from the command if the alcohol-related incident is bad enough. In other cases, the consequences are permanent, creating a ripple-effect that will leave questions in the minds of the family, friends, and command of individuals who die in these incidents. However, if the young servicemember becomes overly intoxicated, but no serious incident arises, typically, the command will not enforce any adjudication on the servicemember. In some cases, troops will conceal the incident, and the command will have no knowledge of the situation.

From my experiences, the majority of higher-ranking officials in the military make the attempt to promote responsible drinking (if they condone drinking at all). However, an overwhelming majority of young servicemembers between eighteen and twenty-five years of age, utilize heavy and binge drinking to cope with being away from family for the first time, boredom, stress, PTSD, cultural traditions, or as a way to fit in.

Servicemembers deal with a lot of stress, especially when in a combat environment. Therefore, when the servicemembers return from combat deployments, they typically turn to alcohol as a relief and to reconnect with their fallen brothers. Many times, the servicemember will not stop at alcohol. After seeking counseling from psychologists and psychiatrists, a servicemember may also be prescribed different types of anti-depressants.

According to an article in *The Military Times*, dated March 29, 2013, at least one in six military personnel is prescribed some form of a psychiatric medication. Furthermore, cocktails are prescribed, such as an antidepressant along with an antipsychotic for nightmares, plus an anti-epileptic medication for headaches. Although these medications may be very necessary for some, most individuals will ignore the directions of their doctor and drink heavy amounts of alcohol in conjunction with taking these medications.

I was personally on a cocktail of medications for pain from bulging discs in my neck, PTSD, depression, anxiety, headaches, not sleeping at night, not staying awake during the day, Restless Legs Syndrome, and the list goes on! These medications included, but were not limited to: Adderall, Darvocet, Neurontin, Tramadol, Mirapex, Celebrex, Depakote, Ritalin, Naproxen, Metoprolol, and Provigil.

To make this even worse, I was drinking while on all these medications.

FIRST RESPONDERS

Another demographic that deals with a great deal of stressors and alcohol abuse are first responders. Police, firefighters, and EMTs see people on their worst days, almost every day, whereas the typical civilian may only see a person's worst day maybe once in their lifetime. This bombardment of crisis, life, death, and trauma can result in heavy drinking or binge drinking by first responders as a way to cope with daily stresses of the job. More first responders than general population members suffer from alcohol or opiate (antidepressants) dependency. According to www.alcohol.org, 15 to 30 percent of first responders suffer from PTSD, and around 20 percent of those diagnosed are also dealing with some form of substance abuse. Unfortunately, it can prove very difficult for the first responder to be open enough to get the necessary help to enter recovery, for fear of repercussions or a stigma by their command, peers, and community.

Today, there is a great deal of stress put on our law enforcement community. The daily reality of getting shot at, or having to shoot another human, witnessing the aftermath of a fatal accident, or being present for an autopsy of a child, can lead a police officer to use alcohol as a way of self-medication. According to Detox.net, a study revealed that the television depiction of police officers going to the bar nightly to unwind was common. The study suggests that some officers will enter periods of heavy drinking (fifteen or more drinks in a week for men and eight or more drinks in a week for women) or binge drinking (drinking to get drunk). In some cases, just like the military, these behaviors are deemed socially acceptable.

Just as police officers shy away from seeking treatment, Emergency Medical Technicians also fear damage to their reputation or careers and/or societal slander. EMTs also deal with stressors that most of the general population in the United States will not typically deal with. They are all but guaranteed to be exposed to traumatic events, such as those previously listed for police officers, irregular shifts, and risk of injury or death. EMTs will also attempt to self-medicate utilizing alcohol or antidepressants after being insulted by somebody they are trying to save, being unable to save a patient, and permanent images in their mind from a horrific crash site or crime scene, or even a brutal scene of an abuse case that turned to the murder of a child. There have even been whispers of EMTs who would go for an all-night alcohol bender, then hook themselves up to an IV to cure their hangover before starting the next day's shift. Our EMTs continue to battle various mental disorders due to these exposures, but many are fearful to seek proper help or don't feel that a counselor can help them, if the counselor has never dealt with what they are dealing with.

Firefighters deal with many of the same issues discussed for law enforcement officers and EMTs, as well as dealing with various electrical, structural, and vehicle fires. In an article published by www.firerescue1.com, dated April 7, 2015, 656 male firefighters participated in a study, funded by FEMA's Research and Development, on firefighters and alcoholism. Close to 85 percent of career firefighters and 71 percent of volunteer firefighters reported drinking alcohol in the last month. Approximately half of career and volunteer firefighters reported a binge drinking session in the past month. Compared to the general male population in the U.S. (62 percent of males in a study in 2013 by the National Survey on Drug Use and Health), this is a staggering statistic. Furthermore, the Centers for Disease Control and Prevention reported that out of 176,000 males, 23 percent reported binge drinking in the prior month, which is half of the percentage the firefighters reported.

This is not about stating an opinion on how our troops and first responders should not ever drink alcohol; however, it becomes a problem when using alcohol to simply unwind after a hard day turns into a need to use alcohol to escape reality. Although the general population might witness a tragedy or horrific event occasionally, public servants, such as military and first responders, deal with such horrors on a day-to-day basis. Due to the images that are seared into their minds and the memories of loss and tragedy, it is very easy to understand why our public servants feel the need to use whatever means possible to escape their reality. Unfortunately, adding a depressant such as alcohol usually only exacerbates their problems and often creates addiction.

Mack Thomlinson (Retired Police Chief)

Mack Thomlinson is a Navy veteran and retired police chief in Indiana. Although Mack has served his country and his community for his entire adult life, he, too, struggled with alcohol addiction.

"I started drinking in high school, maybe even before that," he stated as he discussed the beginning of a long fight with alcohol addiction.

Mack entered the Navy in 1978 after graduating high school at seventeen years old. Thinking back to his military days, he quantified those days as a free-for-all for drinking "because you could." Mack recounted those days as a lot of partying when they were done doing their jobs. He served for 4 years.

Upon leaving the military, Mack joined a police department in Indiana. He remembered the beginning of his law enforcement career in 1982 as starting with a bunch of old police officers from the 1960s era who had a "suck it up" mentality. After dealing with tough, stressful calls, the older officers would tell Mack, "You don't have stress in your life. Let's go outside and have choir practice." Choir practice is a term used amongst some police departments that signifies a group of officers going out to drink after a tough shift. I heard this term used when I was in the Marine Corps, as a leader, heavy equipment operator, and when I became a Marine CID Agent (Criminal Investigation Division).

Within five years, Mack was promoted to sergeant on the afternoon shift, which was the busiest. "We had choir practice all the time. We would sit out back of the police station and drink until 2:00 in the morning. Then go back to work the next day and do it all over again," he reminisced. "If I wasn't hanging out with the guys, I'd go home and drink. I don't remember a night where I didn't go home and have at least a few cocktails. It would either be beer with a shot of Jack (Daniels), or a half pint of Jack, because you wanted to get that feeling right away. Beer took too long. I had to have the buzzed or drunk feeling immediately."

Mack would admit that he would get buzzed or drunk, then drink beer until he passed out in bed. This would go on for years.

Shortly after joining the police force, Mack was married and had two children. At the time, he was working long hours and wouldn't get home until the children were in bed; therefore, he never felt his drinking had a negative impact on them.

Mack told stories about how he would drink even more after dealing with a traumatic event as a police officer. More specifically, the calls he responded to for fatalities were the biggest factors for heavy drinking after his shift.

"I remember responding to a call for a baby that died of SIDS (Sudden Infant Death Syndrome) and just watching the parents and what they were going through. Seeing deaths from people that committed suicide. The suicides that stuck with me the most were when somebody would blow their head off with a shotgun, or the person that stepped in front of a train. Another scenario is seeing a mangled body in a car accident. It's the death. Seeing children get hit by cars. The way I dealt with it was to go home and drink. You think it's going to take the pain away, but it doesn't. It will never go away. It's always going to be there. Drinking just made the pain worse. I was so desperate for someone to help me. The bottle was my substitute for that need."

I asked Mack about the worst call he dealt with during his career. The details were grim. Mack remembered, "This one sticks in my head because I only had about five years on the department. Two kids, about seventeen years old, were sitting on the train tracks facing each other. I'll never forget, they were drinking Budweiser. One of them had a Budweiser can sticking out of his blue jean jacket breast pocket. There was a freight train on the next set of tracks passing by them as they were drinking. They didn't hear the Amtrak coming at them until it was too late.

One fell back to get out of the way and the other one tried to dive out of the way. Both of them were cut in half. One was cut in half at the point of his lower stomach and the other kid was cut in half just under his sternum. Both of their upper bodies were just laying next to each other on the side of the track, right where they were sitting. The full Budweiser can, still in the jean jacket pocket. You could look up inside the torso of the kid that fell back and see nothing there. The kid that dove also had everything removed from his torso, but the train hit the top of his head and his brain was knocked out of his skull. You could look right down his skull and see out of his eye holes. Their legs stayed under the train and were found a couple blocks down the tracks.

I was twenty-eight or twenty-nine at the time, and we were out there for hours. We had to wait on the coroner, take pictures of the bodies and the scene, and back then we had to clean up the scene. I remember having to pick up legs that were just completely twisted and putting them in plastic bags. When you go home after that; what could possibly take that out of your head?"

Mack was drinking clear liquor at the time, so he drank himself to sleep with vodka and lemonade that night. Mack remembered drinking about a half a "handle" of vodka. He couldn't quite remember because he just drank himself to sleep.

Mack remembered another scenario where a lady was worried about her boyfriend, who was suicidal. When Mack and his partner conducted a wellness check on her boyfriend, Mack took two steps up the stairs and saw the top of this man's head laying on the stairwell with hair still stuck to the skull fragment. The man was lying on his bed with his head facing the wall and pulled the trigger of his shotgun. The skull fragment bounced around the room and landed outside of his bedroom on the stairs. His teeth were on his chest. The concussion of skull fragment hitting the wall cracked the drywall and his face was no longer there. This was the first call of the day at 8:00 in the morning.

"How do you go about the rest of your day when you see something like that?" Mack asked himself.

One other scenario Mack recounted was of a guy who walked out of a bar on a rainy night, walked across the street, and was hit by a vehicle. The next vehicle didn't see him and ran him over as well.

The second vehicle was a Toyota car that had a tie-down hook on the front. The hook caught the man's lower abdomen and eviscerated him from the lower abdomen to his neck. All of his organs were laid out underneath the car that he was trapped under.

Eventually, Mack would make Captain with his department and would serve in that role for twelve years. Mack recounted how stressful being a Captain on this force was due to the growth of the community but lack of growth of personnel numbers within the police department.

"I loved being a Captain, but it was stressful. You don't just have your beat (area of patrol), you have an entire city to run, make sure the guys are okay, doing the scheduling. You're doing everything, so the drinking never stopped. I'd go home and drink. Every night."

Even on his days off, Mack would drink with his dad and his brothers. "We'd watch our favorite sports teams, so there was always a reason to drink with them back then." Mack's brother was close to the same schedule on the police force as he was, so they would drink together most of the time. When they were drinking together, they would drink beer all day long, but Mack would have to sneak Scotch because he would get accosted by his dad and brothers. "Quit drinking that brown poison," they would always say to him. Mack remembered that his brothers could drink beer and stop. His own drinking increased. He needed the Scotch—more and more of it. His family continued to confront him about it.

"It was never them pushing me away," Mack recounted. "They were tired of my drinking problem, but it was me that pushed them away."

This confrontation was his first realization that he may have a drinking problem. In his mind, he began to play back the fact that he had to hide booze. Unfortunately, Mack just continued to let it go for years after the realization. "There were days I couldn't write out a report because my hands were shaking so bad."

In 2001, Mack was promoted to Police Chief and served for two years. The end of his tenure as Chief was not what he pictured. After the department suffered the loss of two officers gunned down while responding to a call, Mack was fired on a golf course by his superiors. Mack recounted, "I would hear later- in AA- that when you have resentments, alcoholics go drink. That's what I did. Right after he fired me, I walked right to the bar and drank three shots of Jack Daniels."

At fifty-six years old, Mack was ready to retire from the police department. One month before retirement, he suffered a severe knee injury that put him on crutches for the last month of his illustrious career. "I didn't want to go out like that. I wanted to finish the job, you know," he said, expressing his disappointment. "I felt sorry for myself. I continued to drink." Even this late in his career, Mack would wake up at 6:00 a.m. and think to himself, "Okay, I have an hour before I can buy a bottle of Scotch." Mack would sit in the parking lot of the grocery store and wait for 7:00 a.m. to roll around. "I would give it a couple minutes, so I didn't make it look as obvious. I would shake so bad that I could barely swipe the bottle across the counter of the self-checkout lane, at seven in the morning." Mack would walk to his car and drink three glasses of Scotch before even leaving the store parking lot. "This was when I was off shift and in my own car. I never drank on the job, but I probably smelled like booze at six in the morning before going to work. Sometimes, I don't even know how I got up or made it to the station."

In approximately 1998, when he was assistant Chief, Mack and his wife divorced. At times, Mack felt a lack of support from his wife but admitted he was the one who pushed her away. Close to the end of his career, Mack began a new relationship and got engaged. Around the time of his knee injury, Mack and his fiancé split up. Due to the loss of love, end of a long career, and a blown-out knee, Mack saw this as a green light to drink even more.

Four months before Mack retired, his dad died. "He didn't get to see me retire. So, my dad's gone. It was an ugly death. Cancer. Then a few months later, I retired and felt like I lost my identity. I felt like a nobody. I was a cop for 34 years and I get out, now who am I? So drinking just drowned these issues."

By this point, Mack's sister expressed concern because she would see him passed out, blackout drunk. After pleading with him, Mack agreed to go to a local rehab center. He only stayed there for one night. The next morning, his shakes were so bad, he just signed himself out. "You couldn't even read my initials, that's how bad I was shaking." Mack walked close to ten miles to get home from the rehab center. His first stop after going home,—the liquor store. He bought Doer's Scotch Whisky and a pack of cigarettes.

Approximately six months later, Mack and his fiancé worked things out and started seeing each other again. Stephanie was a nurse and worked long hours. Even though he loved her presence, he couldn't wait for her to go to work, so that he could start drinking. By the time Stephanie got home from work, Mack was already passed out drunk.

Stephanie applied and was hired for a travel nursing job, where she would travel to another town in Indiana for days at a time. Mack encouraged her to take the job, so he could continue to drink more at home.

In June 2018, Mack found himself drinking to the point where he couldn't even remember his name. "Thank God, Stephanie didn't leave me. I pushed other family members away and they walked, but she stuck by my side." As Mack drank to the point of forgetting the most basic of things, his name, Stephanie tirelessly called various treatment facilities to find Mack help. She contacted the Hazelden Betty Ford Foundation, an addiction treatment and advocacy organization. Finally, she received some information for Mack that was beneficial!

The staff at Hazelden Betty Ford Foundation informed Stephanie of a rehabilitation facility in Florida that specializes in the care of prior military and first responders. Unfortunately for Mack, the facility was full. As Stephanie battled to find an opening for Mack to undergo treatment at this facility, Mack attempted suicide four times. On three occasions, he used a pistol.

"I wasn't sure if I couldn't handle the gun because of how shaky my hands were, or if I just didn't want to die. Although I don't remember much, I do remember I didn't see a light at the end of the tunnel. I just thought this was never going to stop. I can't stop it on my own and there is nobody that can help."

The fourth attempt, Mack tried to hang himself with an extension cord tied to the rafters in his garage.

At last, Mack got a place at the facility in Florida. The staff was very explicit in their instructions to Stephanie.

"Do NOT let him stop drinking. If he sobers up now, he will have a seizure on your living room floor and die," a staff member instructed Stephanie. "Don't take him to the hospital. If you take him to the emergency room, they will try to detox him, and they will not do it the right way. The ER doctors don't know what they're dealing with, as far as his situation is concerned."

On Thursday morning, Mack woke up from being blackout drunk the night before. Stephanie helped him pack a bag and he boarded a plane for Florida. Mack was accompanied by his daughter in-law, Breanne.

Upon arrival, Mack was in detox for five days, where he was slowly weaned off the alcohol. Then for the next thirty days, Mack underwent rehabilitation treatment.

Since his completion, Mack has found religion as his anchor to maintain his sobriety. For the first time in his adult life, Mack feels he has his life back. He admitted that no form of self-help would have helped him into recovery. Even though some people find programs such as Alcoholics Anonymous (AA) helpful as the launch for their recovery, Mack believes that for him, those programs are more of a continuation of sobriety and recovery, rather than the start.

This life brought Mack and many of his fellow officers to a place where drinking became the go-to for any event. They drank after traumatic events and celebratory events as well. They would drink when somebody was promoted and they celebrated, they would drink when somebody got promoted but they didn't, they would drink at gatherings such as Christmas parties, when somebody had a baby, or when somebody got married. If there was an event big or small, tragic or exciting, alcohol was involved. Mack's highest blood alcohol content he can remember was 0.408.

"Police departments need to do better about counseling or debriefing. You can't just go to a bad call and just go home. You need to talk it out. I wish every officer had a coach or counselor to help them deal with these traumatic events."

Mack utilizes meditation and prayer as his anchors to maintain his sobriety. He feels that he does not have any days where temptation is high because he sticks with his routine of meditation and prayer.

"Every morning, I go out to the garage, read from my meditation book, and meditate for up to an hour, depending on how much time I have. Whenever there's a problem, I just give my problems to God and he takes care of them."

*   *   *

The stories we've shared in this chapter show that societal problems rise exponentially when any demographic makes heavy or binge drinking an integral part of their cultural fabric. Fortunately, we all have the power of choice. As individuals, if we feel we can drink in moderation, then so be it, if that is reality and not a lie. If our drinking has become a dependency and a way to escape reality, it is our responsibility to seek help. Collectively, we may want to review our social, work, and cultural groups and take a stand for healthy attitudes and behavior around alcohol. In the next chapter, we will share even more of the life-threatening and destructive effects of addiction. We've done this not to depress you, but because we needed to recognize the severity of these addictions before we could change. But stick with us- in the second half of this book, we will show you some alternatives to dependency and addiction- a few roadmaps for creating a happy, healthy life regardless of your gender, vocation, or lifestyle- corporate, parenthood, college, military, or the service of a first responder and more.

LET'S GET REAL

1. Did you ever sneak alcohol before you were twenty-one? Do you feel pressured to drink?

2. Do you cope with your emotions by drinking or using?

3. Do you feel that in order to "fit in" in any of the social/ work groups that you are a part of that you must drink in order to be accepted or to avoid feeling ostracized?

4. Since our society has normalized excessive drinking, how has this affected your personal drinking habits?

5. Have you experienced the drinking culture in the military? Do you have distrust in a person, just because they don't drink? Does this describe a loved one of yours?

6. Are there demons that are stuck within you that you can't let go? Is there something that you witnessed or experienced in your past that you are trying to escape through drugs or alcohol, just as Mack did? Is your loved one dealing with these demons?

CHAPTER 5

Consequences

ALCOHOLISM AND DRUG addiction are quiet and stealthy thieves. They arrive without warning. They sneak inside of you and take everything away, everything you value before you realize it's too late to stop them.

In a society where we rationalize and justify drinking and drugging, it's hard for people to see what actually happens when you take it too far. We see famous people like Elvis, Jim Morrison, Amy Winehouse, Mac Miller, Chris Farley, and Joni Mitchell die in front of our eyes all of the time. Families lose loved ones from drunk drivers and being high all of the time. Families lose loved ones from drug overdoses all of the time. It's almost as if we expect it. A DUI is a headline on *US Weekly* magazine; rehab becomes a punchline on late night TV. When we are in collective denial, we tend to brush the consequences under the rug. But as you've seen already, denial is insidious and even deadly.

MICHAEL:

When I was chugging Evan Williams every day and night, I was in extreme denial of my disease. Because I was in denial, I was unable to fully see the consequences of my behavior. I mentioned some of these already, but here are more of the consequences that I created when I was drinking and drugging:

- Lost three jobs
- Was in so much debt that I had to borrow money from my mother and father
- Lost the trust of others
- Friends slowly stopped returning my phone calls
- My family didn't believe me
- My health declined
- I was prescribed Xanax and Paxil to try to balance myself out
- Bruised easily from my blood being so thin and so malnourished
- Lack of focus due to being always drunk or high
- Esophageal rupture from throwing up so much
- Liver was failing, causing appetite loss and constant diarrhea
- Loss of my integrity
- Haunted by having sex for drugs
- Blacking out and not remembering conversations when the other person involved remembered
- My relationships with my family deteriorated
- They never wanted to talk to me, but they did to make sure I was alive
- Broke and in debt
- Several thousand dollars loaned to me between my dad and mom to help pay my bills

This is real. These things happen when you decide to keep going down the path of drinking and drugging. Only after I was sober could I hear how much I'd hurt my friends and family.

Here is what my best friend Marcy had to say:

"I watched Michael crumble right in front of me. It was awful. I tried to help her. I tried so hard. She was in such denial of her condition until one day she decided to give it a shot and detox for a night with me and try and get on the right path. I had hope. I would do anything to keep Michael safe. Keep her from continuing to ruin her life. It didn't work. She lasted a night with me not drinking, and it was one of the worst things I had to witness. I saw her dry-heaving, shaking, being in such paranoia from anxiety- I can barely talk about it without crying."

Marcy saw the consequences first hand. She loved me enough to try.

"I finally realized I couldn't fix her until she wanted to fix herself. It's not fun watching your best friend lie all the time. Say that everything was okay. Lie and say that she was done and that she was going to get better. I would listen. But I stopped believing. I watched Michael's health decline right in front of my eyes. Her face slowly started to swell and always had a red tint to it. Michael became weak, and her skin was dull and pale and ashy. It was ugly. Yet Michael just wasn't ready. I had to step away. I would always be there for Michael, but I was emotionally drained. I had to wait for her to actually save herself.

These are the things Michael did while drinking and on drugs:

- Made empty promises. Michael would say she would come and hang out with me at my house and she never did.

- Passing out or just blacking out at our softball games. It was hard to watch Michael decline that way and she still think she was fine. She thought she had her life together

- Conversations lost over the phone. I wouldn't know that Michael was as drunk as she was when I would be telling her really private things about my life. When I would revisit it with her, she had no idea what I was talking about. It was so disheartening.

- The constant lies. Michael would lie about going to work when, in fact, she was jobless but just didn't want to tell me. Michael would lie all the time about how much she had drank. She couldn't keep her stories straight.

I don't know why sometimes I stuck around. I think I stuck around because I knew Michael before it go so bad. I knew Michael had it in her to get out of this mess she had created. I wanted so badly to help her. I just decided to be there for her because no one else was. I can totally understand why people weren't. But I just wanted to believe someday she would overcome this thing- that I'd have my friend back.

ANDREA:

Alcohol abuse and addiction is not typically an overnight ordeal. One can spend years abusing alcohol before physical dependence or true addiction becomes their reality. Because alcohol addiction is degenerative, as one's addiction worsens, so do the consequences. For me, they started relatively small—hangovers and blurred memory—but eventually progressed into life-threatening situations.

My denial started long before Asheville. I first started drinking near-daily right after I turned twenty-one. It was the summer of 2010, and I was incredibly unhappy with my life. My long-term boyfriend and I were hardly communicating, even though we lived in the same house. I had zero goals in my life or plans for my future. I was working in a job that was increasingly stressful, and I was broke most of the time. Though I did drink alcohol before turning twenty-one, getting drunk wasn't even a *weekly* occurrence for me until that summer.

I had become fast friends with a group of girls around my age who had been "partying hard" for years already. Up until that point in my life, I had always kept more male friends than female—I felt uncomfortable in a group of women. I always felt like the black sheep, a tomboy among "more feminine" girlfriends. My social anxiety and low self-esteem both skyrocketed whenever I hung out with women.

At the same time, I craved the female friendship that was nearly absent from my life ever since high school. So, when I started hanging out with these "party girls," I really did want to create true friendships, and I wanted them to accept me. To clarify, I never felt pressured to drink around them, even in the beginning. In fact, it was quite the opposite. I welcomed heavy drinking into my life just as much as I welcomed my new friends.

Alcohol quickly became my *new best friend*. It completely erased the anxiety I felt when going out with my new friends because we would start drinking *quite literally* the moment we got to wherever we were going—and if it was a long drive, we'd "pregame" and hope someone in the group volunteered to be the designated driver. When I was drinking with the girls, I felt so cool. I felt like I belonged, like we were always having a blast.

I naturally could hold my liquor quite a bit better than most of the other girls, and I'd often be the last one still standing after a long night of drinking. It was in those early morning hours where I really started to experience the consequences of drinking so heavily. I began to blackout around halfway through the night.

Through blurred recollections and accounts from friends, I started having to piece together what I had done the night before up to three nights a week. The decisions I made while blackout drunk, even in the very early days of my drinking career, were extraordinarily dangerous.

Apparently, I would come off as nearly sober as I convinced my friends that I could drive home, often with a passenger or two. I would make wildly inappropriate phone calls in the middle of the night, or text people I had no business talking to. In the morning, I would wake up incredibly hungover with no idea how I got wherever I was. If I hadn't lost my phone the night before, I would avoid checking it as long as possible—basically until I absolutely had to.

Denial to myself and to others came naturally to me. I quickly learned ways to figure out details of the night before in order to hide that I had actually been blackout drunk. Later, this would become increasingly difficult and eventually impossible, but in the beginning—drunk me was quite clever. I would write myself text messages or take pictures, with the motive of being able to pretend that I remembered the night before. In the morning, when I eventually checked my phone, I would look for these clues before anything else.

I realize that this behavior sounds crazy, and that I must have known that this was not normal—but I didn't think so back then. I did whatever I had to do to seem normal. Deep down, I knew something was wrong or different about me—and that became a new reason to drink: *to keep up my denial.*

As time went on, three times a week became four, and five became six. By the time I was twenty-three, I was drinking heavily every night of the week. My decisions got worse, and my ability to cover them up gradually slipped from my grasp. The amount of alcohol I was consuming nightly went from two or three beers and a couple of shots to ten or twelve beers and as many shots. The most maddening thing to me back then was the breakdown of my composure while drinking.

As mentioned earlier, I started out being able to drink more than all my girlfriends. I was also able to drink most guys under the table and remain standing—to even seem sober to those who knew me best while I was blackout drunk. This power did not last very long.

I started to blackout earlier and earlier, and from fewer drinks—even though I was staying up later and drinking more. At twenty-three, as I mentioned, I would blackout after three or four beers on a night where I had twenty drinks. My behavior when drunk became more and more erratic, and I drove home from the bar nearly every single night. It's a miracle that I never hurt myself or anyone else, and I have no idea how I was able to get away with it. I am deeply grateful for the "luck" I seemed to have, cheating death as many times as I did, but others are not so lucky.

A friend I went to high school with was killed in a drunk-driving accident. She was in the passenger seat when her boyfriend, who was driving drunk, lost control of the vehicle and slammed into a tree. She was killed immediately upon impact, and I later found out that she had been pregnant. I remember how much she yearned to be a mother, so this compounded the tragedy.

What I realize now is that *I* could have easily killed someone I loved, far too many times. But during my active addiction, I was in denial about everything I was doing wrong. When reality *did* hit me, and it did every so often, I'd drink it away just like everything else.

I started out using alcohol to numb my social anxiety and low self-esteem and to be able to have a good time. Less than two years later, I was using alcohol to numb every aspect of my life. I got to the point where I psychologically and physiologically could not function without alcohol. I couldn't remember a life before it, and I couldn't imagine a life without it.

Who cared about the consequences; I was hooked.

It took nearly losing everyone and everything that I loved (more than once) for me to finally admit that the consequences of drinking far outweighed any "benefits" it still gave me. And, in the end, the only benefit I got from continuing to drink alcohol was avoiding the withdrawal—and that was not enough.

My younger brother Jonathan had this to say about my drinking:

"I remember you drank a little bit when I was younger, but when I really noticed was when you came back from Asheville and came back to live at the house, and at first it was just coming home with a six pack every night. It went from there; you started drinking more and more. That's when I really started realizing how much of an issue it had become.

As you know, I was high school, and I often had friends over and occasionally we'd drink, and I realized that there was there was something different. Say after maybe just three or four drinks, I saw your demeanor change, your personality change. It was kind of painful because I started wondering, 'Where's my sister gone?'

I really started realizing how bad it was when I would recognize juvenile traits, maybe that you struggled with in your youth, kind of just went nuclear after several drinks, and to me, it became clear that there was a problem. Often, there would be a lot of yelling, screaming, and not necessarily anger—but you were easily excitable.

The main issue I saw was sometimes you were kind of disassociated to the conversation was going on around you. So often, you'd react to things that didn't necessarily actually occur. You became paranoid, like you would get upset thinking that maybe people were talking about you when they weren't. Alternatively, sometimes people weren't talking about you, when in that mind frame, you may have wanted them to be. These were instances where it became pretty clear there was a problem.

What's particularly kind of sad about the situation was that, at first, as I mentioned, I would ask myself, 'Where did my sister go?' Then once enough time went by, and enough of these kinds of experiences piled up, I started to associate that type of behavior with your character. And that's was scary because I knew that that's not you—that's not Andrea. It seemed like I was watching you become a different person."

SCOTT

The consequences of alcohol addiction will last for years after the addiction has set in. The harshest for not only the individual addict, but for friends and family of the addict, is death. To the addict, that might not seem like a bad idea at the time. However, by the time he or she has become addicted to alcohol, they are no longer speaking for themselves. It is almost like the alcohol is speaking for them. You could almost picture the old cartoon, where the character has a devil on one shoulder and an angel on the other shoulder. The devil signifies the alcohol speaking for the person, and the angel signifies the person's actual conscious thought. A large majority of the time, the devil on the shoulder wins the argument.

In Chapter Three, I provided the full account of my dad's life as an addict. He suffered from a host of medical problems stemming from his alcohol abuse, including end-stage liver disease, liver cirrhosis, liver failure, kidney failure, hepatic encephalopathy (a good sign would be if a person is acting drunk but hasn't had anything to drink), esophageal varices (varicose veins in your esophagus), and death. Those were just the medical consequences.

My father also suffered familial and financial ramifications due to his alcohol dependency. I mentioned earlier that my dad and I didn't talk for several years because of a money issue that stemmed directly from his alcoholism. In his mind, he needed his next drink and to go hang out at the bar with friends, rather than taking financial responsibility and honoring his relationship with me by paying the bill for his phone.

Financially, Dad was ruined. Although he wasn't really good with money to begin with, his addiction made it worse. He made sure he had money to buy alcohol, but he didn't pay attention to his bills. Moreover, he was fired from a job that he was more than qualified for. I mentioned he was working as an IT analyst at a hospital in Michigan. His qualifications included a bachelor's degree from Indiana University for Medical Technology (his previous career) and countless certifications in Information Technology. He was a smart man! Unfortunately, he would be fired shortly after getting the IT analyst job due to his alcohol addiction.

Not only did he suffer a financial setback from being fired, the bills piled up and continued to pile up long after he had stopped working. The following is a list of bills that depicted a very ill man who was in and out of the hospital for various reasons. The biggest reason for his frequent hospital visits was his alcohol problem. Although these are just a few, I have a feeling that there were probably more medical bills that he received. These are just medical bills that he owed; this does not include the countless credit card bills, collections agencies, or his 2000 Pontiac Montana that he bought in 2009 for $7,000. It may not sound so bad until I tell you his interest rate was 21 percent!

Date	Organiza-tion	Amount	Descrip-tion	Notes
12/7/2006	Emergency Physicians	$750.00	ER Visit	Bill (over four months past due)
4/17/2008	Attorney at Law	$600.00	OWI defense attorney	Bill
4/22/2008	Superior Court	$660.50	OWI Conviction	Class A Misdemeanor. Fine $1500, suspend all but $300 + court costs. One year jail, suspended on one year reporting probation. 30 days driver's license suspension with credit from 3/28/08, followed by 180 days probationary license. Obtain addictions evaluation.

Date	Organization	Amount	Description	Notes
6/17/2009	General Hospital	$2,074.55	N/A	Collections
1/29/2010	MD	$67.22	Doctor Visit	Bill
4/10/2010	Addiction Recovery Center	$815.00	Relapse Prevention Program	Services suspended for unacceptably delinquent payments
5/4/2010	General Physician Services	$105.00	Doctor Visit	Bill (one-two months past due)
5/7/2010	General Physician Services	$32.83	Radiologic Exam, knee	Bill (one-two months past due)
5/12/2010	Medical Foundation	$51.20	Labs— Hemoglobin, CBC, Metabolic Panel	Bill
6/18/2010	Credit Corp	$646.66	N/A	Collection Notice for Del Pilar Medical & Urgent Care CTR PC

Date	Organization	Amount	Description	Notes
7/20/2010	Radiology	$155.86	X-Ray of Knee	Bill
10/1/2010	Finance Solutions	$1,525.51	N/A	Collections for Goshen General Hospital
11/16/2010	Medical Group	$101.43	"Medical"	Bill (over four months past due)
5/4/2011	Radiology Associates	$329.80	CT scan of Abdomen and Pelvis	Bill (Payment expected within 30 days)
5/4/2011	Hospital	$32.25	Hospital Care	Bill
5/5/2011	Hospital	$1,036.47	N/A	First Notice
7/2/2011	Hospital	$30.67	ER Visit (after insurance)	Bill
12/7/2011	Gastroenterology	$840.00	Hospital Consult for Esophageal Bleeding	Bill (Final Notice sent March 2012)

Date	Organization	Amount	Description	Notes
12/7/2011	Attorney at Law	$2,102.68	N/A	Collections for St. John's Health System
12/8/2011	Gastroenterology	$156.00	Hospital Visit Level 1	Bill (Final Notice sent March 2012)
12/8/2011	Radiology Network	$48.00	Chest X-Ray	Final Notice
12/10/2011	Gastroenterology	$210.00	Hospital Visit Level 2	Bill (Final Notice sent March 2012)
12/12/2011	Gastroenterology	$78	Hospital Visit Level 1	Bill (Final Notice sent March 2012)
12/13/2011	Hospital	$21,026.84	N/A	Final Notice
12/18/2011	Hospital	$5,846.77	ER, Hospital, Inpatient— Two days, Labs, Diagnostics, Pharmacy	Bill—Total due upon receipt

Date	Organization	Amount	Description	Notes
1/3/2012	Attorney at Law	$374.40	N/A	Collections for St. John's Health System
1/17/2012	Attorney at Law	$163.20	N/A	Collections for St. John's Health System
2/17/2012	Attorney at Law	$5,941.33	N/A	Collections for St. John's Health System
3/5/2012	Hospital	$49,782.08	N/A	Bill
3/19/2012	St. John's Health System	$374.40	N/A	Final Notice
3/23/2012	Hospital	$19,074.19	ER by ambulance, X-Ray, labs, etc.	Bill
3/23/2012	Fire Department	$350.07	Emergency Response, 2.5 miles	Bill (30 days past due)

Date	Organization	Amount	Description	Notes
3/30/2012	X-Ray Company	$203.00	N/A	Payment Assistance Letter
4/3/2012	Hospital	$563.94	Pharm, Lab, X-Ray	Bill
4/6/2012	Medical Specialists	$980.00	ER/Critically Ill/ Injured/ Hospital Visit	Final Past Due Notice
5/8/2012	Air Medical	$22,554.00	Medical Helicopter from Anderson to Indianapolis—31 miles	Final Notice
5/12/2012	Gastroenterology	$185.00	Hospital Visit LE	Bill
5/13/2012	Gastroenterology	$185.00	Hospital Visit LE	Bill
	Total:	$140,053.85		

On top of all of these medical expenses, he also had a list of medications he had to take. Again, these are just some of the

medications that I found in his belongings after his death. I'm not
sure how many more medications he was on.

Medication	Use	Dosage
Tramadol	Relieves moderate to moderately severe pain	50mg
Lactulose	Reduces the amount of ammonia in the blood of patients with liver disease	10g/15ml—60ml, 3x a day
Venlafaxine	Selective serotonin and norepinephrine reuptake inhibitors (SSNRIs) used to treat major depressive disorder, anxiety, and panic disorder	15mg/day
Gabapentin	Anticonvulsant or antiepileptic drug used to prevent and control seizures	300mg/2 at bedtime
Lisinopril HCTZ	ACE inhibitor used to lower blood pressure and relieve symptoms of fluid retention	20—12.5/1 per day
Amlodipine Besylate	Calcium channel blocker that widens blood vessels and improves blood flow; used to treat chest pain and other coronary artery disease conditions; treats high blood pressure	5mg/1 per day

Medication	Use	Dosage
Metformin	Controls high blood sugar in patients with Type 2 Diabetes	Twice per day (8:00 a.m. and 5 p.m.)

Melissa "Missy" Axsom

My dad is not unique in terms of the chaos and ruin he created while in his addiction. And like all addicts, he did not set out to become an alcoholic. As we hear all too often, addiction can begin as soon as a person receives a prescription medication for something as minor as a dental procedure. That's not to say that everyone who receives a prescription will become addicted to the medication, but this can be the case for some people.

Melissa "Missy" Axsom's addiction started with her wisdom teeth removal at the age of sixteen in the late 1990s. This would be the beginning of twenty years of pill addiction. After her dental surgery, she was prescribed Vicodin and liked the way the medication made her feel. One day, she walked into her twelve-year-old sister Jennifer's room and asked her if she wanted to watch the movie *The Burbs* with her. But there was more to the proposition.

"You have to take one of these while you watch the movie." Missy held a white pill in her palm. "It will make you feel awesome!" she told her sister.

Jennifer, too young to understand, took the pill her older sister gave her. Shortly after, Jennifer fell asleep, only to wake up a little while later and throw up. Jennifer told her mom.

Jennifer told me, "She just thought it was the most magnificent feeling in the world. My sister and I were very, very close, and she wanted to share that with me."

A short time after her wisdom teeth were removed, Missy contracted mono (mononucleosis). The doctor's discontinued her Vicodin medication and prescribed her Darvocet (an opiate that is no longer in production). Within a matter of a few days, the thirty Darvocet pills that she had been prescribed were gone.

Just like the majority of people in the late '90s, Missy's mother did not know much about the medications her daughter was prescribed. She only knew that the medication was prescribed to alleviate pain. There was not much information on the dangers of prescription medications, nor were there warning labels.

When the third refill was made, Missy's mother received some information about some potential risks to taking too much Darvocet. Therefore, Missy had to go through her mother to receive the medications. Even with this plan in place, Missy stole pills from her mother's room. After the third refill, Missy's mother decided that she would not give Missy any more medication.

"At first, it was a secret from my mom," Jennifer remembered, "and she would talk to me and my other sister about it, like: *I just like the way the pills make me feel, Mom doesn't know anything.*" Like a typical teenager would think. Missy felt invincible. Jennifer said, "I wasn't afraid for her until she quit school her junior year." (Missy would finish high school through night classes and received her diploma in 2000.) Her life spiraled downward from there. Even though she played softball and had good friends, after just three prescriptions, she started hanging out with people she would have never hung around. Many of these kids were using drugs and skipping school.

"My mother never thought to worry about household medicines being a problem," Jennifer continued. "We had cough syrup with codeine in it, and it was never a problem being left in our bathroom. So when Missy received the Vicodin or Darvocet, my mom didn't think anything of it."

From the time she had her wisdom teeth removed to when she began seeking out pills and over-the-counter medications to satiate her addiction may have only been a few weeks. Long after any medical need, the pills soothed her tension of familial problems that were occurring at the time. Missy's family lived in a community where split families and divorce were not the norm. Missy's parents divorced when she was about seven years old, and as a teenager, Jennifer imagines that she, like Jennifer, felt the weight of this difference acutely.

In 2003, Missy had her first experience with heroin. Prices for pills on the streets were very high, so the cheaper choice on the streets was heroin. According to www.therecoveryvillage.com, a bag of heroin can run as cheap as $5. That's cheaper than a pack of cigarettes and much cheaper than prescription medications on the streets. According to www.streetrx.com, one person bought (1) hydrocodone, 10mg/325mg pill for $10.

In 2004, Missy gave birth to her daughter, Olivia, referred to by her family as "Liv." It is unknown if Missy was on heroin at the time of Liv's birth; however, according to www.marchofdimes.org, babies born to mothers who use street drugs can have any of the following complications: premature birth, low birth weight, reduced head circumference, heart defects, birth defects, infections (Hepatitis C, HIV, Zika, etc.), Neonatal Abstinence Syndrome, also known as NAS (a baby that suffers NAS can also suffer withdrawals after birth), learning and behavioral problems, slower-than-normal growth, or Sudden Infant Death Syndrome (SIDS). Luckily, the family is happy to report that Liv did not suffer these consequences as a baby and is a vibrant young lady who is doing very well with school and social life.

Within a week of Liv's birth, Missy started to drop Liv off at her parents' house and began using heroin again. For the next several years, Missy would do anything she needed to for her next high. When Liv was in third grade, she completed a writing assignment that told a story of a mother "shooting up" in the living room. As a parent myself, this story breaks my heart. I want third grade kids to tell stories that are fueled by their imaginations and not portray the harsh reality of a drug addiction. The following is an excerpt from Liv's third grade writing assignment:

I know you're high and your daughter's down there suffering it. Every day even more silence. One tear fell down her cheek, then many more followed as Christine's mother packs.

"Honey, I'm leaving. Love you. Good bye. Better leave before the cops make me, huh?" "Yeah, I guess." Karla rushed down, "Wanna talk?" "No." She left quietly.

So I'm Christine and this is part of my life. My mom started using drugs at the age of 18 (heroin). Then had me at the age of 23. My mom used to do that in front of me and take me places with that until 3rd grade, when my g-ma took custody of me.

My mother then started dating somebody, who made her and my life worse then nightmares. I can't say everything but my mother still uses drugs and I know we could help her but she chooses drugs over a lot, maybe me. All I know is I can keep a smile on my face.

So to anyone who reads this, drugs are not funny or something to try. They ruin your life and the people around you.

+100,000 people die each year from overdose or drug related things, smoking, drinking. People might do it to "fit in." But in reality the people doing stupid things as drugs are the ones who are going to live in a bad life with regrets.

In 2017, Missy was jailed for petty theft. In most cases, a family would be devastated at the loss of their loved one to incarceration for a year. In the Axsoms' case, the family saw her sentence as a blessing. Missy would have a chance to get clean and live sober.

In June 2018, Missy was released from jail and the real test began. Sobriety didn't last. The family thought Missy was clean for about a week after she left jail, until she started to use heroin again.

By this point, Missy's family had fought so hard for Missy throughout her addiction. Her mother spent thousands of dollars to try to help her, even taking on a second job while Missy was in jail, to be able to support her daughter trying to change for the better. The unfortunate reality is that family may receive the blame for their loved one's passing, but in the case of an addict, that's furthest from truth. No matter what a family tries to do for their loved one, the person battling addiction has to want sobriety bad enough that they make the change for themselves. The blame cannot go on anybody else.

On July 27, 2018, Jennifer received a phone call from her sister, Sarah, informing her that Missy was dead.

She hung up the phone and began to scream.

Jennifer and her husband drove to Jennifer's mother's house. There were three police SUVs parked out front. "She's gone," her mom whispered.

Jennifer walked into the house and saw a police officer standing in front of Missy's bedroom door. Two other police officers stood in the living room. All three officers were crying.

The coroner arrived. He explained the "overdose protocol" to the family. He told them they would put her in the body bag, then onto a stretcher. Then they would wheel her out to the backyard and leave her arm out of the bag so they could touch her.

Jennifer's dad asked to see her as she was in her bedroom before they went through their protocol. The coroner allowed it. Soon after, her dad exited the bedroom, walked through the back door, came to the front driveway, and put his head on the hood of the car. He shared later that he shouldn't have gone into that room.

"Her arms were crossed over her chest. She was face down, but I could see her face was sunken in. Her knees were pushed out to both sides like she fell over while kneeling on the floor. She had sunk into the floor," he told Jennifer.

"She's on the stretcher now. Do you want to meet us in the backyard?" the coroner asked.

Jennifer thought, "I want to touch her one last time."

The family met in the backyard. Missy was on the stretcher in the backyard, covered by a black bag. Jennifer could see the tone of Missy's skin. It was soft.

As she alternated from looking at the bag to looking at the sky, Jennifer repeated, "I love you! I love you!"

The most painful moment for the family was when Liv touched her mother for the last time. She grabbed her hand gently, then hugged her mom over the bag. Jennifer looked around at all who witnessed this, and in the background, the three police officers watched on while holding each other's hands in a line.

"I know seeing Missy and our family's pain affected some of them because they showed up at her funeral," she later told me.

The next morning, Jennifer and Sarah woke up at their parents' house. Liv was not in her room. They checked Missy's room and saw Olivia laying on her mother's bed, sobbing. Jennifer, Sarah, and their mom joined Olivia on Missy's bed and cried with her. They lit a candle in Missy's memory and placed it in her bedroom.

In the aftermath of Missy's death, the family and community came together in powerful ways. Determined to do whatever they could to prevent other families from suffering the same fate, the family took action to raise awareness for opioid addiction. A writer from the local newspaper interviewed the family as they spoke out about addiction. At Missy's funeral, hundreds of people showed up; some showed up for the family and some showed up with their kids on drugs to walk them through and show them the death consequence of addiction.

One of the songs played at her funeral was "Sign of the Times" by Harry Styles.

When the priest approached the podium, his message was, "Just because you overdose, does not mean you don't go to heaven."

"After my sister's funeral, I felt Missy was at peace," Jennifer said. "Missy loved the rain, and when we walked out of the funeral home, it began to pour."

anna collins

In addition to medical prescriptions or cultural norms, mental health issues can also be a catalyst into addiction. In this story, anna collins (she always wrote her name with lower case letters) had suicidal tendencies years before she experimented with drugs or alcohol.

anna was in fifth grade when she had her first suicidal thought. The thought turned into a plan. She mixed fingernail polish, bathroom cleaner, and rubbing alcohol into a concoction that she was going to drink but decided to reveal to her mother, Belinda, the thoughts of killing herself that were occurring in her mind.

"I remember she was unhappy, and she didn't know why she felt that way. We sat down and began talking to see what she was unhappy about and if she knew what might be causing her to feel this way. I thought it was a mood and that it would pass. I thought this because I remembered that when I was fourteen or fifteen I felt the same way and it soon passed," Belinda remembered.

anna started at a new school for sixth grade. She took a pencil sharpener apart and used the blade to make scratches on her arm. Belinda was notified by the school nurse and social worker. She immediately took anna to see a counselor, who would try to find a medication that would help her. They began weekly therapy sessions. As anna got older, the tendencies continued, and she made use of a kitchen knife, an Exacto knife, or a box cutter to cut herself.

She made her first suicide attempt in March of 2000, at fourteen years old, by swallowing a package of Sudafed. As soon as she took the pills, she called her mother. Belinda was about fifteen minutes away at the time. In a panic, she called an ambulance and met the paramedics at her house.

In 2005, around the age of nineteen, anna moved to Texas with her dad, where she met a group of people that introduced her to cocaine. anna and her father had a difficult relationship. She felt misunderstood by her dad and step-mother. Whenever her dad would talk to her about her drinking or depression, he would only say things like, "Just stop drinking" or "Just stop feeling that way." He would do the same thing so many other family members do when their loved ones are dealing with addiction or suicide attempts. He couldn't understand; therefore, he thought more about what it was doing to him and his wife, rather than what addiction and suicidal thoughts were doing to anna. anna would eventually lose her relationship with her dad due to the disconnect over her addiction and suicide attempts.

Where most people might see this as unacceptable, it is actually very tough for a person to understand what the person dealing with addiction or suicidal thoughts is going through. anna fought the urge to use cocaine and alcohol on a daily basis and also fought the urge to kill herself daily.

In 2007, Belinda moved to Houston, Texas, and shortly thereafter, anna moved in with her mother briefly before moving into her own apartment. She continued to drink excessive amounts of alcohol and to use cocaine. While living in her own apartment, she was able to function on alcohol and cocaine, while maintaining a job in a supermarket for about three years. Her performance at work suffered, and before her boss could fire her, she resigned from her position. She took a new job but continued to use cocaine and abuse alcohol. If she couldn't afford cocaine, she would drink vodka straight from the bottle. In 2011, anna got to the point where her drinking and cocaine use was out of control.

In June 2011, anna moved back in with her mom when it was obvious that she was struggling with addiction and made another suicide attempt. This time, anna decided it was time for help and underwent 90 days of treatment at a rehabilitation facility in California. Upon returning from rehab in September 2011, her family had high hopes that she would stay in recovery. Unfortunately, she started hanging out with a group of people from rehab and relapsed with that group of people by using "speed balls," which is a mixture of cocaine and heroin. During her relapse, she had another unsuccessful attempt at committing suicide. Belinda remembered this time period as "the six horrible weeks" due to the amount of drugs and alcohol anna was using. She recovered for a week in a psychiatric hospital in Houston.

After leaving the psychiatric hospital, anna went to a mental health/addiction recovery facility in Knoxville, Tennessee, where she was treated as a "dual diagnosis." The staff at the facility treated her for addiction and her suicide attempts. While undergoing treatment, the staff suspected that anna suffered some trauma earlier in her life, but the family could not pinpoint what actually happened to her. After returning from rehab in December 2011, anna attended meetings regularly, helped others in sobriety, and became very close to her home group, as she stayed committed to her newly found sobriety. She even worked the midnight shift at a local rehabilitation facility and eventually moved on to selling insurance. Eventually, her social anxiety would take over and she would barely leave the house.

Even when she was doing extremely well in sobriety, every day anna would tell her mom how she thought about using and had several suicide attempts. When anna talked to her mom about her addiction and fascination with suicide, she would compare it to a person trying to figure out what they would eat for lunch that day.

"You know how when you wake up in the morning, you might wonder what you are going to eat for breakfast or lunch that day. In my mind, it's similar. Instead of saying, I wonder if I should eat a ham sandwich or a pizza for lunch today, my mind says, I wonder what drug I'm going to use today, or I wonder what a good way to kill myself today would be. I just can't stop these thoughts."

In 2013, 2014, and 2015, anna made three more suicide attempts. On one occasion, she swallowed a bottle of Tylenol. On another occasion, anna swallowed all of her anti-depression medication (Zoloft, Welbutrin, Lithium, Depakote, Klonopin, and Lamictal were medications she used throughout the years).

The incident in 2014 left her in intensive care for a week. Once more, in 2015, she started having suicidal thoughts and agreed to be hospitalized again.

August 24, 2016

anna checked into a hotel room, after telling her mother that she was staying with her boyfriend. She told her boyfriend that she was with her mother. Without the knowledge of her mother or boyfriend, anna attempted to overdose on cocaine in the hotel room. She was unsuccessful and taken to the hospital to be evaluated for a possible overdose. The physicians found small amounts of cocaine in her system.

August 29, 2016

anna was taken to the hospital again by her boyfriend, Jarrod, and it was agreed that she would be admitted to a local psychiatric hospital that night. She and her boyfriend stopped by her house to grab some clothes before going to the psychiatric hospital. When they got home, anna went into the bathroom for a few minutes by herself. Soon, she walked out of the bathroom and into the kitchen where Jarrod was waiting.

"You should probably call 911," she told Jarrod.

Those would be the last words she ever spoke. She collapsed onto the floor and went into cardiac arrest. Something she drank in the bathroom damaged her esophagus and made her heart stop.

In the hospital, they put her into a medically induced coma, where they attempted a new protocol that would cool the body to a very low temperature, for her brain to try to repair itself. To no avail. Her brain suffered too much damage and the protocol did not work. They tried to bring her out of her coma, but due to her brain frequently seizing, she was put back into a medically induced coma.

Her esophagus and stomach were so badly damaged that she was losing blood fast. The feeding tube couldn't function.

September 1, 2016

This was the day Belinda's worst fears would come true. As a result of the extensive brain damage, Belinda decided to take anna off life support.

Three hours later, anna passed away, and Belinda had to start finding answers to the question she asked herself for years, "How could I possibly live without my daughter?"

Present Day (2018)

This question would propel Belinda into radical searching and grief. Out of this, Belinda created "anna's team," who raises awareness for suicide and walks at events created by the American Foundation for Suicide Prevention in Houston.

Belinda is also establishing a foundation in anna's memory that will allow her to do more meaningful work to help other survivors of suicide and loss from addiction.

This story is familiar for many families. Members of anna's family could not understand her mindset as she struggled with addiction. "Just stop doing it" is a phrase many people have used, including me. The reality is that "just stop doing it" is like taking a simple step forward. However, in the mind of an addict, this is not a simple step. To the addict, "just stop doing it" means an action harder than climbing Mt. Everest. Until the addict or alcoholic takes the necessary steps forward and is ready for help, phrases such as this seem impossible.

Mason S. Wold

When a person is battling addiction, they may act in ways nobody would ever expect. When a person becomes addicted, they no longer speak or act in the manner a normal person would. As we've mentioned previously, the drugs start to do the talking and acting for them. Such is the case for Mason Wold. In Mason's case, a catastrophic event started his downward spiral into addiction.

Growing up, Mason was very close with his brother, Matt, and sister, Mindy. Matt recalled, "We did everything together. We were very close."

Mason was a junior in high school in Maryland around 2005. On a typical summer evening, Mason was hanging out with some friends when they got a crazy idea. A curved road near his house had a drop off, and as some teenagers may think, Mason and his friends thought it would be cool to ramp off the drop off in his car. Just as they headed for the drop off, a Chevy Suburban rounded the curve. Mason lost control of his car and hit the Suburban head on. The wreckage was horrific. Mason broke the steering wheel in half with his face.

Mason was in a coma for two weeks after the accident. His family thought they were going to lose him. Miraculously, Mason made a recovery, despite the severe head trauma he endured. After waking up from the coma, Mason did not know who he was or where he was. For four months, Mason underwent excruciating, intensive physical rehabilitation. He also suffered a broken hip, two broken legs, and brain damage.

After the accident, Mason dropped out of high school and never had the drive to sustain a good job or a career. He began to abuse the prescription medications that were prescribed to him. Mason would use any means necessary to find pills after he could no longer get a prescription. In 2015, while staying at Matt's house, he forgot to sign out of Facebook on Matt's laptop. Matt wanted to pull a joke on Mason and started to look into his Facebook account. His discovery was unsettling. Matt learned that Mason would use any pill to get high. The following is an exchange between Mason and another individual on Facebook:

Person 1: "I don't have any oxy (oxycodone or oxycontin), but I do have vicodin and klonopin."

Mason: "That's fine. I'll come pick them up now."

Upon this discovery, Matt admitted that he may have been in denial because he thought Mason was just being a young guy trying to have some fun. He didn't think it was a real problem.

Mason was caught for various small crimes, such as theft and possession of narcotics. He was incarcerated in a local jail six times. Matt paid between $500 and $1,000 on the first three occasions to bail him out of jail.

Each time Matt bailed him out, he allowed Mason to stay with him under the condition of not using any drugs. Matt thought that this strategy would help keep his little brother clean. "You can stay here to get back on your feet, but no drugs."

Mason continued to get in trouble and was sent to jail multiple other times. Even though Matt stopped bailing Mason out, he continued to visit him in jail and put money on his commissary (money to buy items while in jail, like snack items, hygiene, etc.).

Matt also gave Mason money several times when he needed it and allowed him to stay at the house several times. Looking back, Matt feels he may have been blind as to what Mason was using the money for.

In 2016, Matt found out that Mason was using heroin. While on a family vacation to North Carolina, Matt was informed by a neighbor that Mason broke into Matt's house and stole jewelry, Matt and his wife's wedding rings, and various electronics. After stealing the items, Mason used Matt's wife's vehicle without permission as well. Mason took the items to a local pawn shop and sold everything for approximately $775 (the value of all the items was close to $5,000). When Matt confronted him, Mason tried to apologize.

"I'm sorry! I feel horrible for taking advantage of you."

"Mason, I'm done. After everything I've done for you, and you do this to me?! I can't talk to you anymore until you get your life together," Matt told his brother.

Matt was able to recover about half of the items Mason sold, including their wedding rings. Matt had to pay the pawn shop the same amount they paid Mason to buy it. Deep down, Matt knew that Mason was apologetic for taking advantage of his older brother. Through the drug-fueled mistake, Mason knew that Matt loved collecting watches, so Mason did not take any of Matt's watches.

Mason tried to show his older brother the ways he was getting his life back together, such as getting clean, staying away from his friends who were using heroin as well, and getting a job. Each time Mason would try to tell his brother the good things he was doing, Matt would find out that Mason was spotted at a local drug house, known for selling heroin.

Matt felt he did everything for his little brother that he could. Along with the thousands of dollars he gave to or spent on Mason, he also offered to pay for his rehab. Mason always told Matt that he could do it on his own. Unfortunately, nothing Matt offered enticed Mason to get clean. Matt realized that he could only help Mason if he wanted the help. There was nothing Matt could do if Mason did not want the help.

"The addict has to want the change. They have to want to be done with it themselves, not because they feel like they are letting somebody else down."

In July 2016, Matt parted ways with his little brother to focus on his wife and three children. Matt's hope was this would be the wake-up call Mason needed to turn his life around.

"I can't continue to waste time, money, effort, and heartbreak for somebody that doesn't want to change their life."

Mason continued to talk with their mother, who would fill Matt on everything going on with Mason. Their mother was understanding of why Matt could not talk to his little brother. While they were not talking, Mason would get placed in jail two more times.

"Each time he landed in jail, I would tell my mom that I knew I would one day get a dreaded phone call that Mason is dead. Unless he does something drastic to change his life."

May 9, 2017

The phone rang.

"Matt," a close family member said. "Mason's dead."

"STOP LYING!" Matt yelled.

"I wish I was lying. He's gone. The cops are here."

"If you're not lying, put one of the cops on the phone!"

"Sir, this is Officer McNamara. Your brother Mason has passed away. It appears he overdosed on a bad batch of heroin that was laced with fentanyl. It killed him instantly."

Matt was just getting to his gym with his oldest son, Junior, when he received the call. His wife, Jen, was already in the gym. In a fog, Matt went inside to tell Jen what happened, then left.

"My head was spinning. I didn't know what to do."

Matt and his son headed to his sister Mindy's house. He called Mindy on the way.

"Mindy, it's Matt. I just talked to the police . . . and Mason is dead."

With Mindy on speaker phone in the vehicle, Matt, Mindy, and Junior cried together. Matt dropped Junior off at Mindy's house, and Matt and Mindy went to their brother's house, where his body lay. The neighborhood was known for drug trafficking. On the way, Matt called his mom and dad, who lived in Georgia, and gave them the bad news.

"That was the worst conversation I have ever had with my parents. I don't wish that on my worst enemy. To this day, I can remember the sound that came out of my dad's mouth when I told them. It was a sound that I can't compare to anything. It was like a moan of complete anguish and sadness; every negative feeling that you could make in one sound came out. It was horrifying. It—it haunts me to this day."

When Matt and Mindy were at the house, they watched paramedics carry Mason out in a body bag through the front door.

As the oldest sibling, Matt took charge of funeral planning and taking care of the family, so the reality of the loss of his brother didn't strike hard until several days later. Matt explained that he had several moments of tears during those days. After several days, Matt had the realization that Mason would never call him again to ask for $20. Mason would never come to their house again to watch a Notre Dame Football game.

In the wake of Mason's death, the Wold family focused on their children. Matt has three children (ages twelve, nine, and eight) and Mindy has three children (ages thirteen, ten, and four). Matt and Mindy decided that the best course of action for them was to be very open and honest about why Uncle Mason died.

"If his death keeps our six kids from ever touching drugs, then something positive came out of this tragedy. Addiction hurts everybody around the addict. My children are devastated to this day. My fourteen-year-old son, Junior, wrote a paper in high school about how drugs will change the person and the family."

The following is Junior's ninth-grade paper:

This I Believe

I believe that drugs can change a person for the worse and also affect everyone around them. On May 11th, 2017, my uncle Mason lost his battle with addiction and passed away from an overdose from Heroin. In the 3 years before his death, I noticed the changes in his personality and in the year since his death, I noticed the changes in my family.

Growing up, my uncle was a silly, fun, and care-free kind of person. He was the uncle I loved to be around and loved to talk to. He would always take my brother and I outside to play football. He would also take my brother, sister, and I to the park down the road from our house, and even though he played like he had two left feet, he still had fun challenging me to basketball, and lost to me every time. During Notre Dame football season, he would visit us to spend time with us and watch the game every Saturday.

About three years ago, I started to notice the changes in his personality, mood, and physical changes. He wasn't the same person that my family knew and loved. He became a person that was unpredictable. He would be happy and laughing one day and then be mean and quiet the next time I saw him. He was not the fun uncle that I enjoyed being around anymore. He rarely came over to watch football games, take us outside to play, and other family gatherings that he always came to. But I didn't think much about it at first because I was young and naïve. It took me a while before I noticed how secretive and defensive my father was when he brought up my uncle in a conversation. It wasn't until we took a vacation to North Carolina and he broke into our house and stole our jewelry and electronics that my father informed me about my uncle's drug addiction. It was like my eyes opened for the first time. After we found out that he stole from us, my father cut him off from our lives and I never saw him after that.

After that, it was like I never had an uncle in the first place, I forgot about him and never really thought about him. I was angry and hurt by his choices and the way he betrayed my trust. It wasn't until I heard my father talking about him over the phone one day that I thought about him for the first time in over a year. After my dad got off the phone, he was crying, it was the first time I ever saw my father cry. He told me that my uncle had overdosed on Heroin a few hours earlier. I had a mix of emotions, I was sad, confused, and scared. I didn't know what to think and it wasn't until I sat down with my father that I truly realized what was happening. I broke down and couldn't stop crying. It was like a bathtub that was overflowing with water and I could not turn off the faucet.

A week later, we had a celebration of his life and everyone reminisced on who he was prior to his battle with Heroin and what he meant to my family. It brought members of my family together who had not seen each other for years. I could hardly recognize some of my father's cousins who I was so close to when I was young, but lost contact with them over the years. It was a fun and sad at the same time but also a memorable experience that will remain in my heart for the rest of my life.

As shown from my personal experience, I believe that drugs can change someone's personality for the worse and cause them to act like a different person. Drug addiction can alter a person and change their relationships with those close to them as well. Through my uncle's death, it has brought my family closer and makes us appreciate the time spent with each other.

As a family member of an alcoholic who died from his addiction, I can tell you first-hand that you cannot make your loved one recover. Although you can plant seeds in an attempt to help them, you cannot make them see the dangers of their actions. Your loved one has to see these dangers and want recovery for themselves. Just like in Michael's case, her family knew what she was trying to hide. No matter what they tried to do, no matter how many times her dad checked on her, it was not until she was lying on her floor looking up that SHE made the decision to go to rehab and live sober.

Survey any way you have enabled or perpetuated your loved one's actions and cease immediately. You can lead the horse to water, but you cannot make them drink it.

LET'S GET REAL

1. Are you in denial of how much you drink or use?

2. Do you find yourself lying to everyone- even your best friend- to cover up your drinking and/or using?

3. Are you worried that if you were to quit drinking that you would be judged by other people in your life?

4. You will invest in your health on the front end or the back end. Do you want the investment to be fairly cheap and painless, or do you want medical bills to exceed $140,000 and force your loved one to take you off life support?

5. Do you have resentment, guilt, shame, or fear of judgment toward the loved one you lost to addiction? Rather than a junkie, can you view them as a teacher of ways in which not to live?

TREAD

CHAPTER 6
Michael - Part 2

MICHAEL

Friday, December 11, 2015:

I WAKE UP SHAKING. Cold sweats. My dad tells me check-in time is at 8:00 a.m. I can't stop shaking as I feel my body is completely depleted, but I am ready. I am so ready. Ann (my stepmom) makes me granola with plain Greek yogurt, and I eat it all (who knows what the food will be like in rehab) then I immediately throw it all up in the sink.

Last night, Ann presented me with a bag that contained dominos and a tan dachshund to remind me of Sampson and Smokie. I hugged the dog and know already this toy will be my lifeline. I ran out of Evan Williams last night, so Dad and Ann gave me an expensive bottle of whiskey to nurse on through the night. When I looked at that bottle, a wave of anger came over me.

Anger I let it get this far, anger that this became my current reality. I took one last sip from the bottle and shoved it away. I wanted nothing to do with it anymore. A massive wave of sadness and frustration overtook me and tears filled my eyes. As I grabbed tissues out of the bathroom to wipe my eyes, a slight feeling of determination hit me. I knew it was my time to fight.

Dad yelled upstairs to the bedroom, "Are you ready, Michael?"

"Ready, Dad."

Ann gave me a hug, tears in her eyes, and walked us to the car. It was freezing outside.

On the drive up through the mountains, I couldn't stop shaking. Couldn't catch my breath. We got to the town a little early, so we went to a park so I could go to the bathroom and walk around outside before heading to the treatment center check-in.

"I don't feel good. Dad-" I could barely stand. I was nauseous, and I could barely feel my hands anymore.

"Well, Michael. You were supposed to keep drinking!"

"I am done."

The detox was setting in on me. My dad looked scared. Almost panicked. We got back in the car, and I couldn't stop shaking. My hands wouldn't open. My body was shriveling up in the car, I was dizzy, and I couldn't focus on anything.

"There isn't a bar open this early, or I would take you there and we would take a shot together!" That made me chuckle.

"Let's see if they will check me in early." My shakes were getting worse. My heart was not slowing down, and my mouth was so dry. "I'm not doing well, Dad."

We drove fast through the little town to Serenity. I was delirious, but I took in as much of the scenery as I could. It was peaceful. There was a lot of snow. I took in the Christmas decorations. There were white lights on all of the trees, wreaths on the telephone poles, and all of the stores had lights around them. We were in the mountains, and that was comforting.

I saw the sign, "SERENITY." It was big, pine-colored, and carved out of wood. We pulled into the parking lot and for no reason I could explain, I felt at home. A rush of love and relief came over me. I was ready to not be sick everyday and a slave to whiskey. I was ready to stop throwing my life away and to keep my word. I was ready to take back control of my life. I was ready to not feel so lost.

My dad carried my bags. With every minute it felt like I was becoming physically weaker. Somewhere along the drive up to

Serenity, I lost the ability to stand up straight. I couldn't form words. My teeth chattered if I stopped talking. A lady by the name of Pam greeted us at the door. She was tall with glasses. She had on a nice sweater and dress pants. Then a nurse in black scrubs took my suitcase, jacket, workbag, and stuffed weenie dog. Pam gave my dad a clipboard with all of my admission paperwork. I couldn't hold the pen, so I just honestly signed the documents with a squiggly line and Dad did the rest of the writing.

It was just after 8:30 a.m. My shaking was getting worse.

"She's fading!" My dad called out to a nurse. The same nurse who grabbed my bags came immediately back with a wheelchair. Dad had to go. Although I was delirious, I will never forget this moment.

"I love you, Michael Harrington." My dad's eyes flooded with tears. "You got this." He hugged me so tight. We sobbed together until his shirt was wet.

"I love you so much. Thank you, Dad."

"I'll be seeing you soon." I felt a wave of intense love and hope and belief fill me up. I also felt slightly scared. I didn't want to let myself down. I never wanted to feel like this again.

Dad walked down the hall and out the door.

The same nurse who grabbed my bags came back and put me in a wheelchair. She wheeled me to the clinic where another nurse greeted me. She was short and had shoulder-length blonde hair and was also wearing black scrubs. She introduced herself as Dawn. She seemed so nice. I was too weak to stand, and I could barely talk.

"Stay with us, Michael."

"I can't open my hands. I can't stop shaking. Please let this stop."

Dawn gave me Pedialyte and Librium. She took my blood pressure, and I passed out briefly then quickly came to. I scared Dawn. Her eyes got big, and she asked for another nurse to come over to help. She gave me more Pedialyte and another Librium. Within about ten minutes, my shaking was subsiding. I could stay awake. Within an hour, I felt as though I was becoming stable. I was able to open and close my hands.

Before moving me into the detox wing, another nurse came in to take my picture for my lanyard.

"You'll wear it the whole time you're here," Dawn said.

When I looked at the picture I wanted to throw up. I was so swollen and red. It looked like I just had my wisdom teeth taken out or that I was a chipmunk packing nuts in my cheeks. My hair was pulled back in a bun. I looked forty years old. I couldn't get over how red I was. It was clear that bloating and swelling were the side effects from my drinking. My eyes were bloodshot. Next to my picture on the lanyard was a number and a red string.

"That's your code for dialing out when you want to make calls. The red string on yours is because you are a high-risk patient for seizures, so we have to be able to identify this if you pass out."

Awesome, just awesome, I thought. *I'm not only in rehab, I'm the worst of the people in rehab.*

"Great," I said.

Dawn wheeled my chair into the detox wing. Everything was so clean. It smelled like a hospital, and for some reason it was comforting because, to me, that meant healing and health.

"So, Michael, your dad tells us that you love Christmas."

I immediately started crying. "It's my favorite time of the year."

"Well, when you are feeling better, I will show you the best Christmas tree on campus. It happens to be in the Women's Lodge where you'll stay after detox."

"Really?! Thank you. Thank you so much."

"Your dad made sure we knew!" My eyes filled with tears. My dad is so awesome. A feeling of determination came over me. I don't ever want to put my family through any more pain. I am not going back.

It was dark in the detox wing as patients were still sleeping. We were separated from the men on campus (thank God), so I just had to worry about looking like crap in front of other women. The irony of this was not lost on me even then- caring about how I LOOKED when I had just been wheeled into rehab.

The nurse moved my wheelchair to my bed, and my suitcase along with my workbag and stuffed weenie dog were at the end of the bed.

"Go ahead and try to get some sleep, Michael. We will be back in a couple hours to check on you." I grabbed my stuffed weenie dog and hugged him tight. I laid down.

I felt relief. I felt safe. I felt like I was home.

But I couldn't sleep. I lay there in bed and thoughts were racing through my head: *I am actually here. This feeling that I am feeling is awful. All I want to do is get better. Am I really going to make it? How did I end up here?*

I finally fell asleep. A bright light woke me, as it was dark in the detox wing unless any lights were turned on. A nurse I hadn't seen before took my vitals (blood pressure, checked my pupils, asked me to open and close my hands, put pressure on my arms, and asked me to fight against her). She palpated my stomach area, and I winced when she pressed a spot below my ribcage on the right side.

"That's your liver," she said. "It will be sore for a while- as you heal."

My poor liver. I had no idea how bad it really hurt. I hadn't even noticed my body for so long because of my constant state of being drunk or high. Now, my body was waking up. I was worried about the damage I caused. Were other things going to surface as I continued to heal? The nurse said she would be back later.

I saw a couple girls getting up and walking around. I just laid back down, as I was too tired to engage. At noon, a nurse woke me up for lunch.

"Do you have a preference on the food?"

"I am not picky."

I sat up in bed and saw a girl folding clothes into a rolling suitcase.

"Are you leaving?!"

"No, they are just letting me join the Women's Lodge. My name is Lindsay."

"I'm Michael."

"This is my second time here, unfortunately. But this is a great place. I hope to see you over there sooner than later."

"Thank you."

She walked out. Lindsay had been the only one in the clinic with me. I was now alone in this massive space. There were seven beds lined up ready for more addicts to fill them. The ceilings were high, so my voice echoed when I talked. I sat on my bed, now feeling more alone than ever. I grabbed my stuffed weenie and hugged it so tight that tears filled my eyes. I couldn't remember the last time I felt so many emotions. As I sat there, I began to feel stronger, so I got up and walked, holding the wall to steady myself in the hallway. I found a TV room, which looked awesome, and then I managed to get to the bathroom. I had nothing in me so I just peed. It hurt. I could feel my kidneys screaming. They were screaming from dehydration. When I came out, I washed my hands and looked in the mirror. I was full of shame and sadness. I stood there and tears filled my eyes. This is me. I am in rehab. I dried my eyes and walked back to my bed. Shortly thereafter, the nurse came with my lunch: a turkey sandwich, salad with tomatoes and croutons, a banana, and a brownie. It was so delicious. I couldn't believe how nice the food was.

"Let me know when you want me to show you around, Michael. I believe you will be in this wing for at least a few days before being cleared to be healthy enough to go to the cabins and be on normal patient schedule."

The nurse handed me a piece of paper with the daily patient schedule. It was full! I immediately noticed the workout classes on the schedule as well as all of the different "breakout group sessions." I also noticed the times: we started our days at 6:30 a.m. and ended at 9:00 p.m. I looked for the free time. None. Just during lunch and small fifteen-minute breaks in between activities. I thought to myself: *I feel like I'm back in grade school.* The nurse held me up and walked me around the detox wing. She showed me how the TV worked, where the board games were, and gave me a book to read about alcohol: *Under the Influence: A Guide to the Myths and Realities of Alcoholism.*

"Serenity teaches you the Twelve Step Program, Michael. You will learn more about it when you leave detox and are able to begin the work."

"Oh, AA. I tried that in my 37-day sober stint." My mind immediately went back to the rooms of AA in Telluride and I started to remember bit and pieces of the program. I honestly really did like it. I liked the structure of the step work that is involved in AA. I felt scared and relieved to see something familiar.

I looked at the book and opened it, but I couldn't follow the words. The letters swam and jiggled in front of my eyes. I tossed it on my bed and went to the TV room. There was a case with old DVD's. Nothing new. I chose *Just Go With It* with Adam Sandler and Jennifer Aniston.

I watched the movie twice in a row. Dinner came, which was chicken noodle soup. The night nurse, Leslie, introduced herself to me. She gave me Klonopin which, she told me, is an anti-seizure medication. I fell asleep. I was woken up at 5:00 a.m. to take my blood and vitals. I couldn't go back to sleep, so I watched *Just Go With It*— again.

Day 2: Saturday December 12

At 5:00 a.m. the nurse woke me up. This was the first day in I don't even know how long that I woke up sober: with nothing in my system. I think this was a miracle. I felt woozy and the nurse helped me up to walk. It was hard to find my balance but I managed. I continued to sip on Pedialyte. Another girl checked into detox. I wasn't alone anymore. She was tall and fit, with pale skin and black hair. She looked scared and was not particularly nice to the nurse. She had a kind of regal quality. Her name was Caitlin, and she told me that she was a massive white wine drinker. She said she would drink about four or five bottles a day. I smiled internally because it was a relief to hear that someone else was just like me. I couldn't go back to sleep, and I couldn't bring myself to read, so I watched *Just Go With It* AGAIN.

At about 7:30 a.m., a girl walked in and asked for me. She was short, had tattoos, dark chin-length hair, and was in black baggy sweatpants. Her name was Sara, and she told me that she would be my sponsor. I knew AA had sponsors. She said she was going to be my mentor-sponsor during my time at Serenity.

"The nurse said I'd be in detox all day," I told her.

"I'll check on you later then," she said.

Around 2:30 p.m., the doctor arrived. He was tall and lanky and wore glasses. He had on a nice collared shirt and khaki slacks with his white doctor coat. He seemed warm, like a doctor on TV.

"Michael, I want to tell you that if you hadn't have come into Serenity when you did- and if you kept the behaviors and the drinking up, I am quite sure you would have been dead within less than two months."

My throat sucked in on itself. My heart pounded. I worried I was going to have another seizure. *Two months?* I couldn't wrap my head around it. It was making me nauseous. *How did I let it get this far? Two months?* Blood rushed to my head, and I just sat there and put my hand on the doctor's leg in disbelief.

"Maybe even sooner," the doctor said. "At the rate you were going with your dehydration and lack of nutrient intake, your body was not going to keep up. It already wasn't keeping up, which is why you had your seizures, which you ignored."

I shook my head. "Yep. I definitely ignored it. You're right on that one." I felt so embarrassed. Here I am, an adult, someone who is supposed to be able to take care of herself, and I couldn't. I was being scolded. It was awful. I was full of shame. I didn't know what to say to the doctor. I sat on my bed with my head hung low.

"We are very happy you are here. You are a lucky girl."

"I know," I said.

"Do you have any questions for me?"

"When will the pain in my liver stop? Every time I stand up straight it hurts so bad."

"I would imagine by the time you leave in about a month, the pain will subside. Remember, you haven't been very nice to it, so it is healing as well, and tenderness is to be expected. Just let someone know if the pain becomes unbearable."

"I will. Thank you." I thought to myself, *maybe this is why so many people don't get sober and they stay out drinking—because of all of these feelings, the whole detox thing, the shaking, seizures, liver pain, tremors- it's awful.* I never wanted to go through this moment again. NEVER AGAIN was now mantra.

Day 3: Sunday December 13: I MEET JAIME!

I did it! I survived my first full day yesterday without any substances. 12.12.15 is now a holiday in my world. Yea! I honestly didn't believe I would live a day without drinking or doing drugs. And yet I had done it. Incredible; simply incredible.

I took my first shower since arriving. My sponsor Sara popped in and said tomorrow would be my first full day out of detox with the rest of the ladies in the rehab.

At 11:00 a.m., another girl checked into detox. Her name was Jaime. She came into the room with a big boot on her foot and a walker. She looked close to my age. I told her all about the facility. She was exactly my age- twenty-nine! She told me she had to wear the boot for another week because she had ankle surgery. Jaime came straight from the hospital because she was in a 32-day coma from drinking.

"You were in a coma?" I asked.

"Oh yeah. I went in to the coma because I lied to the doctor about how much I was drinking. He knew I was drinking a lot and told me to wean off before the surgery. I didn't do that. When I got out of surgery, I went into extreme DTs and after about 72 hours I had completely lost my mind! I was seeing terrifying things like snakes and skeletons and rodents. Finally, my lung collapsed, which made my brain start to swell. Fortunately, my mom had come to California to help me with my ankle surgery. She was sleeping next to me in the hospital room when my lung collapsed and called 911. Doctors came in and put me in a coma to save my life, and I stayed in it for seventeen days. When I came out of the coma, I remained in the hospital for another fourteen days. After that, I was sent to an old person home to re-learn how to walk and talk for another ten days and now, I am here."

I just looked at Jaime and was beside myself. Jaime was a miracle. We laughed throughout the entire afternoon and she watched *Just Go With It* with me. I told her I had already watched this movie five times. I knew that Jaime and I were going to be friends.

Day 4: Monday, December 14

I woke up, and Sara came and took Jaime and I to breakfast with everyone outside of the detox wing in the dining hall. There, I met the other female patients. I looked around at all of them. They were all very different: a couple of older women, some women who were around my age, and younger ones. All of them were in baggy sweats and sweatshirts like myself. They all had such sad and mad looks on their faces. Most of them walked around the dining hall with their head down and their body language just screamed "don't talk to me." I could tell immediately that I was going to be the happiest, most outgoing of them all.

I went through the buffet line and picked out my breakfast: grapefruit, eggs, oatmeal, and fresh berries. Sara had a seat for me at a large round table, so I sat down and listened to the conversations at the table next to me. Everyone sounded so negative.

"I really don't want to go back and do session with Carol," one said.

"Some of the things they make us do are so stupid."

"The assignments are lame."

"I just want to sleep. Diane is such control freak."

I was floored. I was so happy to be there- so grateful. Did they realize how expensive it was to be there? Rehab costs just over $17,000. The staff, the food, Sara, Jaime- all of it had been so nice. But I hadn't really started yet. I had no idea what the process would be like after detox (and that had not been a cake walk). These women were already in the work. I chewed my oatmeal and the oats stuck to my tongue. I continued listening to the griping and complaining at the next table. I felt scared. Was the program stupid? A waste of time? Pointless? I'd convinced myself this place could save my life. I became terrified it wouldn't work.

I chewed my blueberries and kept my mouth shut. I looked at Jaime. She had a look of shock on her face, but she just smiled at me and continued to eat her grapefruit. I will focus on Jaime, I told myself. She is just like me- positive. Not like those women.

After breakfast, Sara walked me to the Women's Lodge.

"I want to show you something," she said. She grabbed my hand and walked me through the front door.

The Christmas tree! It was big and full of lights and ornaments. I began to cry. I hugged Sara. It was so beautiful. I walked up to touch the branches. It was artificial- I could see the pole through the plastic pine needles, but it may as well have been my family's tree like we had when we were growing up. It hit me only then that I was going to be here, locked up, for Christmas. Another event I would miss.

I just wanted to be home and snap my fingers and have all of this magically go away. I was crying again, and Sara just stood with me. As I was crying, I was also lit up on the inside looking at the tree. I touched some of the ornaments. I walked all around it and was able to smile. NEVER AGAIN.

A couple women in the lodge just stared at me. There were about ten of them and they all seemed to roll their eyes.

"Just keep your Christmas cheer to yourself," one called over from the couch.

This is a nightmare, I thought to myself. I was trapped in rehab with a bunch of Scrooges in an anti-Christmas snow globe. I didn't need enemies right now, so I just smiled at them and said "Okay."

Sara introduced me to Carol. She was one of our techs and also the Zumba/Dance instructor! Carol was also sober. She was once a patient at Serenity! I found that fact deeply comforting.

She said that in the lodge was where all group sessions were held, where we met with our designated counselors, had AA meetings, activities, and did our homework. She then showed me the snacks and the COFFEE!

That afternoon, I attended my first group therapy session. We had group therapy every day. After some prodding, I shared what brought me to Serenity. About how I started drinking all day every day, about Evan Williams, my drug dealing affair, and missing my sister's wedding. In turn, I got to hear how everyone else got there. Meth, pill popping, the rest were here for drinking, like me. When they spoke, it was like they were telling my same story, but different.

We were all the same. For the first time, I didn't feel riddled with shame because all of these ladies did the same things I did. It was comforting.

After group, I was able to make phone calls. I called Dad and Mom, and I was so relieved to hear their voices. "I know I am in the right place," I told them.

A nurse called me off the phone. The nurses explained that I would come in every day, three times a day, to get my meds. They told me that as I made progress my medications would change to fit my needs, and that hopefully by the time I went home, I would be taking absolutely nothing. They also told me I would be out of detox on Wednesday and in a cabin with Jaime! GOOD DAY.

Day 5: Tuesday, December 15

My first full day in the Lodge! I was introduced to my counselor, Haley. Haley was amazing. She made me feel so comfortable and safe. Haley was in recovery, too. She used to drink and do copious amounts of drugs. I knew- I could just feel- that she understood my insanity. The crazy awful things that are paired with addiction. I didn't hold back in this first session, and it was glorious. She just *got* me. It's a feeling that catapulted me into diving deep and not holding back.

Haley explained the twelve-step program to me. She gave me my first Big Book (Alcoholics Anonymous). She explained why Serenity is a twelve-step rehab and why they felt it was was a foundation to set people up for a sober life after treatment. That was when I got motivated. I love structure. I love knowing why I am doing what I am doing. I knew from her tone that this was not going to be a walk in the park. I told Haley that I was ready to do the work. I told her that I was done and that I was not going back. She gave me my first assignment: Read the first ninety pages of the Big Book.

I can honestly say that if I had worked only with a "normal" therapist- one who hadn't been an addict and wasn't in recovery- I would not be as successful in my healing. I'd been around plenty of "normal people," and they never understood. They tried, but unless they had been in an addict's shoes, I doubted they would ever fully understand.

I also got the news from Dad that my sisters and mom were flying in to see me on Saturday. (There are strict rules for visitation at Serenity, and visitors are only allowed on Saturday evenings to attend dinner).

I told Jaime, and we stayed up and watched *Just Go With It* and *Sea Biscuit* and talked for hours. Jaime understood me. She didn't judge me and I didn't judge her. Jaime became my first sober friend.

Day 6: Wednesday, December 16

MOVING DAY! Or so I thought. The nurse told me that my potassium and magnesium levels were dangerously low and until I got those up, I couldn't move in with Jaime. They said this is common with alcoholics. They told me that because I was not eating really anything before coming into rehab, my body needed time to heal and soak up the nutrients I was finally giving it. I was frustrated but I understood. They said most likely on Friday I'd be able to move. Bananas and electrolytes became my new best friends.

Day 7: Thursday, December 17

This was THE BEST night's sleep I had so far at Serenity. It was the best night's sleep I had had in over two years. I was finally feeling totally clear headed. My body was starting to come alive and function. My liver was still extremely tender to the touch, and I still felt it throbbing throughout the day. I resumed a full day at the Lodge and met with Diane, the Spiritual Advisor, and yet again- she was one of us. Sober from a massive drug addiction and alcohol. Diane used to be homeless and slept on the streets and now here she was, on the other side, helping addicts like me. I opened up to her about my spiritual beliefs. I told Diane that I was not religious but that I absolutely believed in something bigger than me. I told her about my moment on the floor in my house where I saw my Grandma and

Aunt Mary Michael above me. I told her how they were transparent and floating, but they were absolutely talking to me. I told Diane I knew I couldn't get sober on my own. That I desired to build my faith and to be able to let things go and trust.

Diane hugged me. "Okay," she said. "We will work on this together."

In our down time and at lunch, I started to get to know the girls more. We all would share insane stories from our pasts. We could all laugh about the crazy things we did that normal people would not find funny: making ourselves look stupid, stealing, cheating, waking up next to random guys, exchanging sex for drugs, missing important life events, puking and pooping our brains out from detoxing . . . oh yeah . . . good stuff. I finally felt that I had nothing to be ashamed of.

Day 8: Friday, December 18

I was cleared to go to the Cabin with Jaime! Wahoo! My family was coming the next day. I grabbed my suitcase, work bag, and stuffed animal and walked the pathway up to the cabins with Jaime. We were in cabin #20. I walked in and saw what looked like a stand-alone standard hotel room. Two queen beds, a bathroom, a table, and a dresser. It was so awesome to get out of the detox wing. I finally felt like I was "a part of." Moving into the cabin is when I realized that I still had a long way to go. I still had three weeks left, and I was already feeling maxed out on my emotions. I was feeling scared knowing that I could no longer run from my feelings. How was I going to keep processing and feel okay in my body? I already was feeling extremely uncomfortable. I just wanted to flip a switch and feel okay and happy in my body. I took a couple deep breaths outside of the cabin. I let the cold air flood my lungs as I looked around at the snow. I thought back to what the doctor said about me probably dying if I didn't come here. That gave me motivation. Let's go, Michael. NEVER AGAIN.

Day 9: Saturday, December 19

Family day! I slept so well. I felt like Jaime and I were soul sisters. We laughed all the time. Talked about super inappropriate things that only addicts and alcoholics would find funny. Jaime's family was coming that day, too! We spent the morning decorating our cabin with paper snowflakes that we cut out of printer paper and anything we could find that exuded Christmas, as our supplies were limited. The afternoon was spent doing homework. Our assignments included journaling how harmful drugs and alcohol were to us and the people around us and what our values were (Values?! I'd never, ever considered mine. Sleeping with drug dealers was not a value. Missing family events- also not a value. Drinking before work, after work, losing jobs, quitting jobs, disappointing people- those were not my values). There were daily reflections also- writing assignments. The assignment that really hit home was doing Step One of the Twelve Steps: Admitting that I was powerless over alcohol and that my life had become unmanageable. Actually writing down how UNMANAGEABLE my life had become in all areas: personal, financial, work. Ugh. It made me sick, and yet it also drove me. NEVER AGAIN. *One day at a time,* I told myself. *I will never go back.* The real work was beginning, and all I wanted was for 4:30 to get there so I could see my family.

I showered, put on jeans and a nice shirt instead of staying in the sweats I wore every day. A girl in rehab was a makeup artist so she did my makeup. After she did my makeup, I looked in the mirror and I felt pretty. Then I looked down at my lanyard. The redness had faded and my eyes were no longer bloodshot, but I was still swollen. *Never again*, I said over and over.

4:30 p.m.: Family Visitation

There they were: Mom, CT, Twinney, Dad, and Ann. I hugged Mom, Twinney, and CT forever. They brought presents. Best Rehab gift—Christmas Movies: *Elf* and *A Christmas Story*. I cried. I gave them a tour of my cabin, the Lodge, and showed them my binder of things I had been working on with processing. I felt relieved to see them, SOBER. They were so relieved that I was there, that I was ready. It takes what it takes. The time flew and it was time for them to leave. CT took her scarf off and put it around my neck to wear. It smelled like her. Casey gave me her necklace. We all cried, and I hugged them all so tight. They piled into Dad's car and left. When they left, a wave of determination flooded me. There was no going back. I knew that I was ready a week ago but seeing them solidified it for me. *I am not dying. I am living. I am going forward.*

Days 10 -14: Sunday, December 20- 24

I dove deep into work in the group sessions and with my counselor. Every day I was getting stronger and more alert. I was working hard on Step Two, which was coming to believe that a power greater than me could restore me to sanity. I had to write out what "Came to Believe" meant to me. It meant a lot of things. It meant an attitude change. It meant looking at how I needed to change my ways of thinking and have more humility in my life and not be so prideful. It meant looking at how my life became insane. It meant writing out how I wanted my foundation for life to be now with beliefs that mattered to me: practicing gratitude, having faith, trust, and love instead of fear, ego, and not trusting.

This was no small feat. One afternoon before we all broke out into small groups, the counselors talked to all seventeen of us together. We sat down and listened to what they had to say about the harsh reality of our disease. I was alarmed when they said that the relapse rate was between forty and sixty percent. I looked around the room. That meant that out of the seventeen of us, not even half would stay sober. When I heard this, a switch flipped. *I will be one of the eight who make it. I will fight.* I surrendered to do whatever they told me.

What also gave me fuel was watching the majority of the women not take this process seriously. It made me angry. Every time some of them slacked off, rolled their eyes, complained about other women or their counselors or techs, I wanted to punch them. I could see that a lot of them didn't get it. A lot of them faked doing the work. I pitied them and I judged them. What a waste of money for them to be here, and quite frankly, a lot of them were angry that they were there. Just hearing some of the girls talking about going back out and drinking or using, it made me sick. I ALMOST DIED. A lot of them almost died. I didn't understand why they didn't want it. But I had to let that go. My counselor told me to focus on myself. Let their apathy become my fuel. A lot of the women thought that they could beat their addictions without doing the work. Sorry to say they were sadly mistaken. When the other girls were laughing and not doing their homework, I just doubled down and worked harder, drank more coffee, and continued my grind.

Every day I was gaining more clarity around the reality of the destruction that I had caused. It made me uneasy to think of what a manipulator I was. I started opening up about everything I did to Max- the lies, cheating, and manipulation. I dove deep into coming to grips with how unhealthy I actually was. I was an emotional rollercoaster, let me tell you. I had been suppressing hardcore for years, and now that I was sober, I was FEELING ALL OF THE FEELINGS. It was weird. The main emotions I was feeling were anger, sadness, frustration, and shame. About a week into my therapy work, I realized that I did not love myself. Just even thinking about loving myself made me so uncomfortable. It made me squirm. It made me sad. I had no self-respect. I knew this was going to be the hardest part of my journey- learning to truly love myself, forgive myself, and accept myself.

I'd have these waves of awareness, like I was being smacked. I could hardly keep up with them, and then it would be time for another "Daily Reflection" that we were required to fill out each evening.

- What was the most significant event/insight that affects my life and sobriety today?
- What behaviors did I exhibit that I was proud of?
- What behaviors do I need to work on?

- Is there something I kept to myself that would have been better to share with someone else?

- What feelings have I felt today? What was going on for me at that time?

- Do I have any secrets that I am holding onto? What are they?

- What did I think you learned from or needed to work on as a result of these experiences?

I hated these daily reflections in the beginning because they made me think and get honest with myself. Something I was not used to doing. I was not used to sharing how I truly felt because I didn't want anyone to know. I didn't want to be judged. What was amazing is that as the days progressed, I didn't feel judged at Serenity. I finally felt like I could be me.

Day 15: Christmas Day

MERRY CHRISTMAS! Everyone was trying to embrace my Christmas spirit. I was a total Elf and I will just say that they tolerated it! Haha! It had been two weeks at Serenity and I had already learned so much. That day, though, I was filled with a lot of mixed emotions. I had a lot of anger and sadness in me still. Anger that I was there in rehab doing all of this work and that I couldn't just figure it out on my own. I was sad because I wasn't with family, sad that my disease landed me here. Why did I have to be an alcoholic?

I shared all of this with Diane and she said, "Michael, rehab is the best present you could ever give yourself. Please understand how big this is."

I had to really think about it. I was just so focused on what I was missing and not was I was gaining. Diane really helped to change that part of my mindset. It took a hot minute and whenever I started to get sad, I just thought about how many more Christmases I would have NOW that I made the choice to give myself the gift of sobriety.

Day 16: Last Day in my Twenties

Thank goodness! My mindset had really started to change. I was in so much gratitude to be in rehab, leaving my twenties, and starting my thirties off on the right path. Did I get nostalgic for a minute not having the typical drunken "Dirty Thirty" birthday party? Of course I did. Of course I was sad. I had envisioned being with Twinney going out with all of our friends, having a couple drinks, and doing just a couple lines of blow to stay awake to remember the night. I thought I would be partying the night away in a cute outfit with Twinney surrounded by so many friends. But then I had to come back to planet earth and tell myself I would've been puking in the bathroom- I would've blacked out and not remembered it.

Day 17: 30th Birthday!

Twinney was the first phone call I made. I am happy. I am alive. It honestly felt like a re-birth being in rehab for my 30th birthday. Good lord, get me out of my twenties. Yes, they served a purpose absolutely. But bring on my thirties. I found a lot to be grateful for that day. I was grateful for my sobriety. Grateful to start a new decade out healthy. I was grateful for my life and my willingness to continue to persevere every day. I was reading out of the NA (Narcotics Anonymous) book, and I came across a quote that really hit home with me.

> "Even in a remote corner of paradise, the disease can find us—
> and so can recovery. She kept coming back, and found freedom
> through fearless inventory work."—Pg 315, NA

Days 18-20: December 28—December 30

These were some hardest days at Serenity, as more work was required of me to grow. I had to read "effects" letters from my family in front of my entire group. Each one of my family members got to write me a letter explaining the effects my alcoholism had on them. Here is some insight from the letters (Mom, CT, Dad, Ann, Twinney, and Aunt Molly):

- Our worries about Michael have resulted in losing sleep, breaking down in tears, changing travel arrangements, spending countless hours worrying and talking with her sisters and other family members, feeling hurt and manipulated, and feeling emotionally drained and helpless. (**Ann**)

- She had been coming out to my house suffering from anxiety and hangovers, not being able to sleep. She affected my work; I would postpone business meetings so I could watch over her. I know she has a disease and needs to overcome it. (**Dad**)

- Your chemical addiction to alcohol affects the whole family. It was your emotional well-being and physical health that frightened and worried me the most. I saw you falling through the cracks, and it scared me as I know it scared you. I as your mother, did not know how to fix this downward spiral. The pain you were experiencing is something that your family was experiencing too. (**Mom**)

- Michael, you are a very special woman. Your spirit is enormous. This difficult time in your life grieves me because you are not whole at this time. I love you, and when you are not well, then your family is not well. The family is one; when you have pain, we feel pain too. (**Aunt Molly**)

- You have missed out on sharing some of the happiest moments in my life with me. I didn't get to feel your hands on my belly when I was pregnant with Bri or have you laughing with me making sure I looked picture perfect on my wedding day. Though my heart has been broken by the absence of your presence at life events, it is starting to heal knowing that you will be here now for the rest to come. **(CT)**

- I feel as though I don't know you anymore. The biggest effect your alcohol abuse has on me are all of your lies. It breaks my heart feeling like I don't even know the one person who is closest to me. I don't know you anymore. Up until Rehab, I would pray I got a text from you in the morning praying you would be alive. The worry about your life and health caused me to be angry and upset with you because I just didn't understand why you didn't want to fight. **(Twinney)**

These letters broke me. Until this moment, I didn't see this in the depths of my addiction. I didn't see how selfish I was being. How could I? I had lived my life driven solely by the need to get high or drunk.

Day 21: New Years Eve!

I was so happy to put 2015 behind me.

Leaving behind: Fear, alcohol, drugs, isolation, low self-esteem, negativity, a group of really close friends who no longer serve me on this new path.

Bringing In: SOBRIETY, love, acceptance, surrender, sober friendships, embracing my higher power, learning to let go, surrender in order to rise.

NEW YEARS DAY: January 1, 2016

I am right where I need to be. I have surrendered to the process. Surrendered my old life so I can live and not just exist.

Day 23: January 2nd
Marcy Visits

I was well through Step Three now: Made a decision to turn our will and our lives over to the care of God as we understood him. What I loved about this homework and talking about this in group and with Haley was the simple fact of being able to say, "AS WE UNDERSTOOD HIM." It didn't have to be God. It could be whatever made me comfortable. I would say God or Higher Power. What I knew after processing this step was that I had willingness. I was willing to believe. I was willing to see that self-will, self-centeredness, and selfishness were not conducive to living sober and that those things fueled my alcoholism. Yucky. No more!

I was so excited that my best friend Marcy was coming to visit. Marcy came all the way from Telluride. Marcy had tried everything she could to help me. She is the one I affected the most outside of my family. It's hard for me to fully understand why she was still there, still by my side- through all of the lies, disappointments, and embarrassing moments. Marcy is the definition of unconditional love.

She came for Saturday night dinner! Dad and Ann were there, too- they hadn't missed one. Marcy said I looked the best I had looked in a long time. She cried. I cried. She brought me presents from Christmas and my birthday. I was enveloped in love.

Days 24 and 25: January 3 and 4

This last week I experienced a lot of breakthroughs with my emotions as I dove into Step Four which stated: Made a searching and fearless moral inventory of ourselves. This step tore my character apart. I was totally gutted like an elk in hunting season. I exuded selfishness, dishonesty, jealousy, fear, ego, judgment, being inconsiderate, self-seeking, and was so prideful. Yep- I was a true alcoholic by the nature of my actions. Having to write this down and give examples was awful and humiliating. I was so angry with myself. This is not how normal people live. Good lord, I felt like a terrible human being. I cried a lot through this. This work really shined the spotlight on me and my awful behavior. Everything I did in my life was to better me. It was to get me where I wanted to be, even if it was at the expense of others. My biggest defect: Judgment. WHEW! I judge a lot. Haley said I had to look inward, and she asked me, "Do you think you judge a lot, Michael, because it is a reflection of what you wish you had in your life that you don't? Do you also judge because people are exuding behaviors you do that you wish you didn't?" Zing!

When I wasn't angry processing these thoughts, I had moments where I was in gratitude that I had a family that still loved me despite my rude and selfish ways. Talk about a wake-up call.

Good news: I had a choice now. I had the choice to bring awareness to my actions and choose better. I was determined to not ever exude those traits again. What I desired now: sobriety, patience, love, tolerance, care, humility, understanding, and grace. You thought I was driven before . . . oh, no, no- this really made my entire body fueled with desire to never go back. Never.

I had a sense of ownership going through me as I was gutted. I was ready to not be embarrassed of where I came from, but rather be in acceptance, learn from it, face it, own it, and make the appropriate corrections.

Day 26: January 5

It Gets Real

It was my day to facilitate an AA meeting for all the ladies in the Lodge. This was a big deal. I planned my topic all day. I was going to read a story I found in the Big Book, "The Keys to The Kingdom." This story really touched me. All of the women gathered in the Lodge in the communal area in a circle. We had a lady who brought candy, and everyone grabbed some before I started the meeting. When I started the meeting and started reading, one of the girls, Elizabeth, was laughing on the couch. She was eating Skittles and not paying attention. She began snickering and throwing the candy at another girl who had just come over from detox. I stood up, slammed my book on the ground, looked Elizabeth in the eyes, and said:

"ARE YOU KIDDING ME? SERIOUSLY, ELIZABETH, ARE YOU KIDDING ME?" Elizabeth just smirked. The other girls looked excited, like watching a storm roll in across the sky. I stormed outside and started bawling. Jaime came after me.

I yelled, "Does she have no respect? Who does she think she is? She is going to relapse. What an ungrateful human being." I cried with anger. I felt sorry for myself. Here I was, fighting for my life, doing the work, preparing myself for life after rehab, and I had to put up with ungrateful immature women like Elizabeth. This was summer camp to them. I, on the other hand, understood the severity. I never wanted to feel the feelings I had been feeling those past three weeks ever again. I thought about what Diane told me. Focus on my own recovery. Jaime just stood next to me, silent, supporting. "NEVER AGAIN!" I screamed at the sky. *I will not lose everything again.*

I gathered myself. I walked back in and finished leading the meeting like the warrior I know I am.

Days 27-29: January 6–8

Step Five: Admitted to God, to ourselves, and to another human being the exact nature of our wrongs. My brain hurt. I sat with Diane, my spiritual advisor for three hours, literally three hours, and told her EVERYTHING. Literally, every little thing I did in my drinking and drugging. I held nothing back. If I was going to start over, then I was not going to leave anything suppressed inside. Words do not do justice to how cleansing and refreshing it was to get it all out of my system. Diane is a saint for listening and the most beautiful part about this experience is that she did just that- she sat and listened without a shred of judgment.

That afternoon, I met with Haley about what would happen when I left Serenity. What was my plan for sobriety? I had been in a bubble and Haley had to pop it. I needed a game plan, she told me. How specifically would I stay sober? How would I implement the tools I'd learned here? My gut said OH HECK YEAH I am staying sober, but I would be lying if I told you that I didn't have a little doubt in me. What I did know for sure was that I was going to an AA meeting the day I got out and that I wouldn't miss a day. My plan was:

- Attend ninety meetings in ninety days,

- Get a sponsor- go through the Twelve steps and start back at One.

- Do the work and focus on one day at a time.

Day 30: January 9
Graduation

I was full of emotions: happy, sad, scared, grateful, and hesitant. I wrote a good-bye letter to alcohol that I got to read in front of everyone! Women and Men.

Goodbye Alcohol,

You were ruining my life. You have ruined it in more than one way- financially, emotionally, spiritually, and professionally. You have caused me so many problems: lying, manipulation, false sense of reality, not being true to myself, and putting me on the back burner. Goodbye to who I relied on for happiness, my best friend (or so I thought), and the one thing I valued. Goodbye Alcohol. You fueled my disease and now you will only be a distant memory.

Now, onward and upward. The journey begins. One day at a time. Goodbye to the fog. Hello clarity. Hello surrender and acceptance. Welcome back values, love, truth, honesty, and above all: WELCOME SOBRIETY! Evan Williams—I am hitting the ground running and I am not looking back.

No regrets.
Signed your ex, Michael

I spent the afternoon with Jaime, reflecting on our time at Serenity. Like the epiphany in one of the movies we watched over and over, I actually felt like I was re-born. I would now get to discover who Michael is. What I did know for sure is that she is an alcoholic, and she is sober.

Day 31: January 10
Homeward Bound

The box canyon mountains of Telluride were calling, and I was on my way. I said goodbye to the sisterhood. I took a good look around the room. Some would die, some would relapse, and only a couple would keep the gift of sobriety. I swore in my deepest heart that I would be one who would hold onto the gift. We stood in a circle and said The Serenity Prayer one last time together:

> *God, grant me the serenity, to accept the things I cannot change.*
> *Courage to change the things I can, and the wisdom to know the*
> *difference.*

I had a plan to go to an AA meeting that night in Denver, and then Dad and I would drive to Telluride the next day.

I felt delicate as I left. I felt emotionally skinned alive. As we pulled out of the driveway, I smiled. Serenity helped save me. Serenity gave me permission to not feel shame about who I was. Serenity allowed me to completely surrender in order to rise.

"Now there is a sense of belonging, of being wanted and needed and loved. In return for a bottle and a hangover, we have been given the keys of the kingdom." (A.A. pg. 276)

Now, the real work begins.

LET'S GET REAL

1. Have you been to rehab and did that give you the boost you needed for your sobriety? Did anything internally or externally get in the way of your success in treatment?

2. If you haven't been to rehab, imagine for a minute that you had the opportunity to go to rehab. Would you take it, or would you be too scared of the work involved?

3. What is your biggest fear about getting sober?

4. I want to ask you to take a moment and pause. Michael was so caught up on not being with family for Christmas, New Years, and her 30th birthday. Once she was able to understand that taking care of herself NOW would allow to her have MANY MORE Christmases, birthday celebrations, and New Years, she was grateful. Are you not getting sober because you are way too focused on right now instead of how much better your life could be for you and others?

CHAPTER 7

Andrea - Part 2

ANDREA:

September 2013

TWO WEEKS AFTER I made the phone call to my mother telling her that I needed to come home, I crashed landed at her house, back in Georgia.

The way I had been living during my year in Asheville was not sustainable. It was, by a wide margin, the worst year of my life. For the past few months, I'd vowed not to drink before or during work. Every morning, I woke with my hands shaking. I constantly struggled to catch my breath, and I lived in a constant state of panic. The symptoms would only subside once I got off work and was three or four beers in, or after three back-to-back shots.

I wanted to stop. I wanted to, but I couldn't. When I was still living in North Carolina, everyone I hung out with seemed to be drinking as much as I was. I was hardly ever alone, but I felt incredibly isolated. Eventually, it became clear to me that I wasn't going to get sober in Asheville. I needed to come home, and I knew that I needed to quit drinking.

I built up a story that if I came home, I would be able to quit drinking. I did not know the extent of my addiction. I did not have a plan. I did not ask for help. But I tried.

And I tried.

And I tried.

For six months, I *tried* to quit drinking every single day. Most days, I failed—but I had decreased my intake enough to stop getting full-blown delirium tremens. My daily withdrawal symptoms weren't as unbearable as they had been. My hands still shook, but not as visibly. I still had extreme anxiety—but not to the point of panic. I didn't feel like I was constantly drowning, but my breath still came in short and shallow.

I do not view these things as signs that I was making any headway towards real recovery, but I was at least starting to understand that my daily life was easier and less painful when I drank less alcohol.

So, I began to look at alcohol as the cause of my pain instead of the cure to it. That is not the whole truth, but the mindset kept me from crossing back over the line into life-threatening drinking again.

That is, until it didn't.

January—March 2014

I had a couple of weeks or so of straight sobriety when I decided to see a doctor for depression and anxiety. I can't remember if she asked about alcohol, but I imagine that if I wasn't drinking at the time, I would have said so. I am not sure about this, but it's possible I omitted how much of a problem I had with alcohol.

After talking to the doctor and taking an assessment that looked like a standardized test, I was diagnosed with Bipolar 2 and put on Prozac (an antidepressant) and Lamictal (a mood stabilizer). I was told not to drink on these medications, and I had every intention not to. But eventually, I did.

My behavior became more erratic with and without alcohol in my system. I was losing touch with reality at times, and my emotions were wild. I continued trying to drink less alcohol through this time period, having a max of six beers a night, but it seemed to be getting more difficult to hold myself to these self-imposed limits.

At my six-week checkup, I told my doctor how I had been feeling.

I'm almost certain I left out my drinking this time. I can't remember if she asked me about my alcohol consumption, but I do not remember lying about it. It is possible that I would have minimized how big of a problem I had. She switched my mood-stabilizer to Abilify, and after the two or three weeks waiting for it to start working, drinking all the while, chaos ensued. I lost the ability to make my own decisions seemingly overnight.

St. Patrick's Day 2013—One "Last" Hurrah

Since my move back to Georgia, I had had minimal contact with my Asheville friends because most of them were heavy drinkers, and I was trying to *stop* drinking heavily. A day or two before St. Patrick's Day, one of my girlfriends asked if I'd like to come up for the weekend—so that we could "go out on the town" like we used to do.

I remember rationalizing this trip to myself: I missed the city and the bar scene of Asheville. I missed my friends who were mostly made up of drinking buddies. And worst of all—I missed not caring at all.

When I woke up on March 18, 2013—I wished that I hadn't woken up at all. In the space of only two days, crashed my car, got cut off in one bar, kicked out of another, and in one grand display like a firework boat on July 4th, burned every bridge I had left in North Carolina. For the first time in my life, I was completely without rationalizations. Finally, it was impossible to ignore that my alcoholism was the cause of all the pain I had inflicted on myself and on others.

As soon as I got home, I announced to everyone in my life that I was done drinking alcohol for good, and I meant it this time. My family supported me, as always.

I immediately made an appointment with my doctor and my therapist upon getting back. I was completely honest about my alcoholism this time. My doctor switched my medication to something milder, something less likely to cause erratic moods. I began working with my therapist specifically on the issues and causes surrounding my addiction to alcoholism. I was done trying. I quit drinking, and I vowed to never drink again.

March 2013—April 2014

For over thirteen months, I stayed effortlessly sober. I really had had enough, I said to myself. My primary reason for abstaining completely from alcohol was the same as before, to avoid experiencing and causing pain. However, I found myself coming up with a lot more reasons the longer I stayed sober.

After some initial adjustment, my body began to feel better than it had in years. Even though I was only twenty-four, I felt and looked years younger than I had when I was twenty-one. My mind became exceptionally clear. I had worried initially that my mind would never recover from the years of alcoholism, but after a couple of months had passed, I felt an acute ability to focus, and my cognitive and analytical skills thrilled me.

My emotions became increasingly more manageable after two or three months of sobriety. I was still on two medications for Bipolar Disorder. The medications I was on no longer made me feel crazy without alcohol in my system.

I believed I was doing everything I could to both stay sober and to grow as a person. I went to weekly therapy for addiction recovery. I was being treated for the mental disorder I was diagnosed with. I was consciously learning new things, as well as doing everything I could to improve myself as a person.

This included:

- Constantly reading personal growth books
- Attending school and becoming a Certified Nutritional Therapy Consultant
- Working out daily, for the first time ever
- Consistently working to improve my relationship with myself and others

- Learning financial responsibility
- Trying out new hobbies and activities
- Writing for pleasure again after a very long hiatus

I believe my first real journey into sober living was easy for two reasons. The first, I've already covered—I really was done with my drunken life. The second reason was subconscious, only realized in hindsight.

During my first thirteen months of sobriety, nothing bad happened in my life. I was no longer creating my own hardships, and fate was kind to me that year. I did not face any adversity great enough to challenge my "fragile recovery." I call it fragile because my sobriety was untested.

I did not know that something crucial was missing from my recovery. In therapy, I was uncovering and dealing with all the painful things that I used to cover up with drinking. In my daily life, I was becoming a better person in many beautiful ways. The one thing I wasn't doing was learning how to cope when life hits you with tragedy. That was my undoing.

April 22, 2014

I was two weeks shy of turning twenty-five and fourteen months sober from alcohol.

Sometime around mid-afternoon, my mom called me. This was unusual, as she'd normally text me if she needed to reach me when I was at work. I don't remember exactly what she said to me, but I do remember that the tone of her voice was unnervingly serious.

She calmly yet vaguely told me that I needed to come to her and my stepdad's home as soon as I got off work. I asked her what was wrong. She wouldn't answer anything except that she, my stepdad, and my many siblings were all okay. Those are the people I asked my mother about, my/our immediate family members.

I didn't ask my mom about my dad.

In 2014, my parents had been divorced for eighteen years. Both of my parents remarried years prior to this, and my dad had remarried twice. I don't remember the last time I saw my parents in the same room.

However, I felt immediately that it was likely a death in the family, even though she did not tell me this. I suspected that it was my Uncle Ken (her brother and only sibling), who had been battling cancer for years.

It was 6:00 in the evening when I got to her house. She and my younger brother Jonathan were standing outside in the driveway when I pulled up.

My mom spoke first.

"Honey. It's your dad. Something happened."

She stepped forward and opened her arms to hug me. I embraced her out of habit, but my mind was racing.

"What happened? Is he hurt? Where is he?"

The words tumbled out of my mouth. My mom was sobbing into my shoulder; I don't think she wanted to say the words.

My younger brother Jonathan was only seventeen at the time, but he already towered over us at almost six feet tall. He was solemn, and at that moment, he looked years older.

He said, "Dad died last night."

"How?" I asked.

My mother said, "We don't know all the details yet, but we know he was found dead from a gunshot wound to the chest," she took a deep breath, "and he was holding the gun."

*   *   *

More information came in the hours, days, months, and years since he passed. My father had committed suicide at sixty years old after struggling with alcoholism for his entire adult life. His blood alcohol content at the time of death was 0.16. He left behind five adult children and his wife of six years.

I believe he was profoundly tired of his life. He cared deeply about what others thought of him, and so on the outside—his life always looked perfect. He lived in a nice home, he and his wife drove nice cars, even his social media was carefully curated to show a picture of a happy husband and father.

His alcoholism was known to our entire family, and he sometimes went a couple of years between relapses—but he always went back to drinking. It was the way he coped with life.

I was about to learn that it was mine, too.

There were two weeks between my dad's death and his memorial service. Though I did not drink during those two weeks, I still barely remember anything. I believe I was in shock. I know I wasn't processing what had happened. I certainly wasn't grieving yet. His death didn't seem real. He'd died while on vacation in Alabama, and I didn't go and see his body before it was cremated. It was like my dad had simply vanished.

May 22, 2014—Memorial Service for Adrian Carr

Due to the choices of certain family members, my father's five adult children (including me) had no say in his memorial service, nor were we invited to speak. The whole thing felt phony, like a cardboard set in a play. I did not know most of the people there, but it was very clear from the ceremony that my dad's friends and acquaintances had known a very different version of my dad than I had.

He was heralded as a warrior for Christ, with sword-wielding imagery and all. It was jarring. My dad was raised by his Cherokee grandmother, and he'd always leaned more towards American Indian mysticism than Christianity, at least from how I knew him.

No one mentioned that it was a suicide. No one said anything about depression or alcoholism. I understood at the time that many people would never consider bringing up these ugly truths at a memorial service, but I wish that I had said something. I felt like his struggle and eventual defeat were not honored.

I was very angry after the service. I don't remember whose idea it was to "celebrate Dad's death" with a small (but raging) house party, but that's what happened. That night, I was at my sister's home with all my siblings and our significant others. Everyone began drinking, and for the first time in thirteen months, I desperately wanted to drink, too.

I want to say that I wanted to drink because my dad had just committed suicide, but that is only partially true. I just wanted to drink, and my dad's death was a beautiful, deadly excuse that no one could blame me for.

I told myself: *This is just for tonight. You put it down before, and you're not going to pick it up again. Just for tonight.*

I started with a single brown glass bottle of Angry Orchard hard cider. Seven minutes later, I was grabbing my keys to head to the liquor store up the street. Fifteen minutes later, I was back at the party with a bottle of 1800 Silver tequila. I lined up a shot glass on the kitchen counter and downed at least five shots.

Thankfully, my tolerance had fallen to such a low level that I was vomiting in the guest bathroom within an hour. I passed out on the couch before I could drink anything else.

MAY 2014—DECEMBER 2014

For the next eight months, I wasn't quite back to Asheville-level drinking, but I was worse off than I had been in a long time. Everything hurt so much more this time, but in a different way. The last time that I had been stuck in the relapse and recovery cycle, I had not 100 percent admitted that I was an alcoholic. But right before I got sober the first time, I had admitted it. It was a fact about myself that I could not un-learn.

Though I was sober many more days than I drank during that time, my behavior when I blacked out was worse than ever. I was back to living in constant terror, and I woke up to withdrawals every time I drank. Everything was just like before.

During this time period I was, on average, sober about 90 percent of the time, but ten percent of the time I was back in the dark world of an alcoholic.

I couldn't understand why I couldn't just quit again, like I had before. At the same time, I wasn't using any of the tools I had gained during my first go-around in sobriety. Instead, I blamed myself and called myself a failure after every relapse.

JANUARY 2015

I had always been aware of Alcoholics Anonymous; most everyone is. I had even been to an open meeting one time when I was fourteen and my dad asked my sisters and I if we'd come with him. I only remember that it was in a church basement in the next town over from mine, near where my dad lived at the time. I remember everything was white, and that there was coffee.

When I decided to go to an AA meeting, I did so with an open mind. I was desperate and willing to try anything. I was afraid I was going to die.

I can't remember my first meeting in detail, but it was in the basement of a Baptist church, and I remember the feeling I had when I left with my first white chip. I felt hopeful that I did not have to do sobriety alone. My mind, on the other hand, wasn't so gung-ho about many of the things I had heard. I didn't like the idea of being powerless, and I wasn't sure that I agreed with alcoholism (or any addiction) being a disease. It especially bothered me that the people in the rooms with decades of sobriety often said that they "needed AA" in order to stay sober. I didn't want to go to meetings for the rest of my life. I wanted a cure.

My gut told me something was not right about the energy in the room—but I was desperate for a solution. I ignored my instincts and "kept coming back" almost daily, for seven months.

JANUARY—JULY 2015

I have struggled with how much I want to share about both my experience in Alcoholics Anonymous and my subsequent negative viewpoint of it which I still stand by today. My goal here is to tell my story in a way that helps others, so I am only going to share my personal experience. This part of my story is for those out there like me who "worked it," but it didn't work. You are not alone. If you want more information about the flaws in AA, there are many resources out there that break down and analyze why Twelve Step Recovery works for some people and doesn't work for others.

That said, I never relapsed so frequently in my life than I did during the seven months that I attended AA meetings. It was not the people that broke me down; it was the program fanaticism and the dogma. It was my two different sponsors and their useless (sometimes harmful) advice, though I do believe that both women were doing their best.

I gave away my personal power with the first step, as everyone who goes through AA does. This aspect of their program works for some people. It was devastating to me. The story about alcoholism being an incurable disease leveled me.

Before AA, I struggled greatly to control my drinking, but I had never given up on myself being able to recover. After AA, I felt more powerless than I ever had over alcohol, over my life, over my future, literally everything. After AA, I believed that I had a disease that was literally incurable and that, to stay sober, I would have to attend meetings and resist the urge to drink for the rest of my life. Again, it works for some, but not for me.

I stopped going in July of 2015, and it took me months to break free from the mindset I had cultivated based on AA's teachings. Remarkably, though, as soon as I stopped attending—I felt more hope than I had in a year. My relapses kept coming, but they were fewer and with more time in between each one.

One thing I agreed with from AA was that willpower was not going to keep me sober. I had to look for something deeper. It gradually came to me that fighting my desire to drink was a war that I wasn't going to win—that I was fighting the wrong fight. I didn't want to fight against something; I wanted to stop wanting to drink at all. I desired freedom. It was that mindset that would save me.

At least it *would*, after one last rock bottom.

Halloween 2015

A friend was having a costume party, and I volunteered to be the designated driver for myself and a couple of friends. In a way, I was trying to somehow "ensure" that I would not end up drinking at the party.

It's likely clear by my including this story that the night did not work out as planned. My memory of the party goes completely blank shortly after arriving, but I was told that the following things happened:

- I downed more hunch punch than a nineteen-year-old on prom night.

- I was obnoxious, irrational, and confrontational without a discernible reason.

- I fell at least two different flights of stairs.

- I kissed a female friend who was in a monogamous relationship.

- I supremely pissed off everyone who was there.

- And finally, I passed out in my friend's teenaged sister's bed—clothed, thankfully.

The next morning, I woke up confused, yet horrified—just like every other time I pulled something like this while blackout drunk. Only this time was both the worst and the best of all those awful nights.

It was the worst night of them all because of what I said earlier—I knew better than to trust my willpower alone. I also knew that I didn't want to drink anymore. I knew, and I took that first drink anyway.

It was the best night of my life because it was the last one and because it made me, at a level I had never experienced, want to quit drinking, for good this time. Not one day at a time, forever—for the rest of my life. The only thing I took one day at a time *this time* was getting through the three days of withdrawal that followed.

November 1, 2015—Present

Just like the first time I quit drinking, I never wanted to hurt myself or anyone else by drinking again. The difference between the first time and this time was the complete mindset shift I had regarding my addiction to alcohol. I knew with absolute certainty that **I was NOT powerless**—not over alcohol—and not over my life and my future. I had become aware that it was entirely within my power to never pick up a drink again.

I began to wholeheartedly trust in the Universe that created me. I believe that no one on Earth is handed more than they are capable of handling and that everything happens for a reason. I went back to therapy and was honest about my alcoholism this time. I dove headfirst into personal development. I began looking for purpose and meaning in my life, and I found it.

I am extremely grateful for my journey, even the worst parts, because it has positioned me to help others who still stand where I once stood. It is my purpose going forward to help others struggling with addiction—and I will not be stopped—not by alcohol, not by anything.

LET'S GET REAL

1. If you have tried to quit drinking in the past, what made you start drinking again?

2. How can you create an environment of support for when you quit again?

3. Are you aware of what triggers you to drink? Brainstorm ways to handle each trigger before you encounter them.

4. If you have tried recovery programs before, what about them did not work for you? Are you open and willing to find another option in order to get and stay sober?

CHAPTER 8
Scott - Part 2

South Bend Tribune—Wednesday, May 23, 2012
Brian Scott Leeper, Sr. (Obituary)

ANDERSON—Brian Scott Leeper, Sr., 52, of Anderson, IN, formerly of Mishawaka, IN, passed away at 7:08 p.m. Saturday, May 19, 2012, in St. Vincent's Hospital in Indianapolis, IN.

Scott was born on June 20, 1959, in Dayton, Ohio, to Curtis, L. and Joan (Jarnagin) Leeper.

Surviving Scott are his father, Curtis L. Leeper of Anderson, IN; two children, Jennifer (Edward) Montgomery of Mishawaka, Scott (Ashley) Leeper, Jr. of Stella, N.C.; four grandchildren, and a grandson, who is due to arrive in August; and his sister, who lives in Michigan.

His mother, Joan Leeper, preceded Scott in death.

Scott was a veteran of the U.S. Army.

Scott graduated from Indiana University/Purdue University with a Bachelor in Science in Medical Technology. He was a Phlebotomist with the South Bend Medical Foundation. Scott then pursued a career in the Information Technology field as a successful Information Technology Specialist. He was an instructor for Productivity Point/Signal Learning Center and

Maple Tronics. Scott went above and beyond his ability as an instructor and received several certificates of accomplishments along with earning many Certificate of Excellence Awards as a Microsoft Certified Trainer.

Scott loved fishing on Wabedo Lake in Minnesota. He enjoyed golfing and hunting, especially "putting deer in trees"! Scott was an avid Chicago Bears fan and Chicago Cubs fan. He also loved Notre Dame and I.U. basketball. Scott had a witty sense of humor and a gravitational personality. He was a loving family man who adored his grandkids. Scott had a love for animals, especially man's best friend. He will be dearly missed by all who were a part of his life.

Family and friends may call on Thursday from 5 until 7 pm at the Bubb Funeral Chapel, 3910 N. Main Street, Mishawaka, where funeral services will also take place on Thursday at 7 pm, with Rev. Ervin Mize officiating the services.

Contributions may be made to the American Liver Foundation, Heartland Division, in Scott's memory.

After tragic events, a person's life can change almost instantaneously. Depending on life obstacles, existence or lack of a support structure, family life, work environment, and various other details, the person suffering a loss can have a successful bereavement period or hit their own rock bottom. For the next couple of years following my dad's death, I made a series of uncharacteristic decisions and dealt with my own mid-life crisis.

May 24, 2012

The day of my dad's funeral was a blur. I was numb. I felt sad but couldn't cry. I felt anger but wasn't mad. I was exhausted.

4:00 p.m.

The funeral home seemed inviting, but dark. I didn't want to walk in. This place signified the finality of my dad's passing, and I didn't want to believe this was actually happening. As I walked to the double doors of the brick building, a middle-aged man with a black suit opened the door with a sympathetic smile on his face.

I walked to my left, down the hall to the open doors. As I entered through the doors, I turned to the right, where I saw the flag case that held my dad's ashes, surrounded by displays of flowers donated by various people and organizations. What was once a heavy-set man who stood at 5'8" tall and weighed close to 325 pounds was now in a small, triangular, wood flag case urn that displayed the American flag. Underneath the flag display on the front of the urn was a picture of my dad with a big smile on his face on Lake Wabedo holding a walleye that he'd just caught, with the words:

Brian Scott Leeper
June 20, 1959
May 19, 2012

I just sat and stared at my dad's urn. I couldn't move. I couldn't cry. I couldn't do much at all. In the room with me was my wife (who was six months pregnant), my sister, Jenny, and her family, and my grandfather, who seemed more disgusted at the fact that dad died than anything. Knowing my grandfather, he was doing all he could to hide his emotions.

5:00 p.m.

I'm a pretty social person, but for the first time in my life, I didn't want to talk to anybody. The line of people coming for the viewing and the funeral lined the hallways and went through the front double doors. As people passed by the doors that led to our room, they observed a table that displayed a stack of computer certifications that would make most computer gurus drop their jaw. I even had a few of them tell me that dad was a computer genius. I thought that my hand was going to fall off from shaking so many people's hands and hugging so many others. Through it all, I tried to muster a smile, but I wasn't fooling anybody. There wasn't anything to smile about.

I don't remember much of the funeral. I was in a fog and would be for quite a while afterward.

August 18, 2012

Three months had passed since my dad died. I was stationed at Camp Lejeune, where I was a criminal investigator.

I was at the Naval Hospital around 3:00 p.m. when my wife went into labor. All my pain seemed to subside as I launched into supportive husband mode, trying to keep my wife comfortable. I caressed her hand as she received the epidural, held her leg as she pushed since it was extremely swollen, and tried anything to keep her calm during this process. We'd already picked out a name for our son—Jaxson. I just liked the name, but Ashley will tell you we named him after Jaxson Teller from the *Sons of Anarchy* television show. I kept picturing the moment I would meet my son. The reality of being a dad and holding my baby boy in my arms made me smile and cry simultaneously. Through the expectation, I was on high alert. My last hospital visit was tragic, and I made it my personal responsibility to ensure that Ashley was comfortable and safe throughout the entire process. During labor, Jaxson got stuck on Ashley's pelvis, so we even tried a game of tug-o-war to help her push even more, but the pain was excruciating for her, so the birthing team decided to conduct an emergency C-Section. I was not ready for what would come next.

The last time I'd been near an operating room, or even a hospital, was the day Dad passed away. I kept my dad in the back of my mind but was fine with being in a hospital. Two orderlies wheeled Ashley into the operating room and handed me a pair of blue scrubs.

"Wait in the hallway," one of them told me. By now, my anxiety was screaming at me. I looked through the little circle window of the door leading into the OR. I could see Ashley's head sticking out from underneath a blue curtain that separated her head from the rest of her body. She wasn't moving her head at all. I could see doctors and nurses moving back and forth from behind the curtain. I couldn't see what was happening on the other side of the curtain, but I assumed that they were making the incision in her belly to deliver my son. I stopped looking through the window and paced back and forth as tears ran down my face.

The only thing I kept picturing in my mind was the team of doctors that came out of my dad's operating room, telling me they couldn't save him.

"God, please let my wife and son live!" I thought to myself. Throughout the agonizing minutes, I only imagined the last day in the hospital with my father, three months prior.

The doctors brought me into the operating room, where my wife was prepped, and the doctors were ready to deliver my son. Within minutes, I heard my son cry for the first time, and I was called over to cut Jaxson's umbilical cord. My son was born! As soon as I turned to walk back to my wife, I caught a glimpse of the other side of the curtain. Ashley's stomach was opened up like the hood of a car! I probably turned white, and the doctors were probably wondering if I was going to be THAT husband and pass out. I walked back over to Ashley. "He's beautiful!" I told her as I kissed her cheek. Wife and baby were both totally safe!

Although my wife and son were perfect after delivery, our relationship quickly suffered. Not only was I dealing with the death of my father, but now I had to learn how to be a dad. Over the course of the next several months, we fought constantly. I felt like I was married to a roommate, rather than my wife. While she seemed to be dealing with some post-partum depression, I was unknowingly dealing with depression, anxiety, and PTSD from my dad's death. Our intimacy suffered. Sex was almost non-existent because I was also dealing with erectile problems. I couldn't achieve an erection, and when I did, orgasm was almost impossible. The fact that I was not aware of the condition I was walking around with made everything around me worse. I didn't realize that I was suffering from PTSD. I didn't understand that the ED was a result of the post-traumatic stress. I didn't know how to cope.

According to a study in *Depression and Anxiety* by Lukoye Atwoli, PhD, MMed, MBChB, of Moi University School of Medicine in Eldoret, Kenya, and the University of Cape Town in South Africa, and colleagues, 2,813 individuals (30.2 percent of the respondents) chose the unexpected death of a loved one, out of a list 27 traumatic events, as the event that triggered PTSD. The study also indicated that the loss of a parent doubled the odds of PTSD. If a respondent believed that they could have prevented the death, the odds were almost tripled.

The ADAA (Anxiety and Depression Association of America) states that PTSD is diagnosed after a person experiences symptoms for at least one month after a traumatic experience. The ADAA lists symptoms as the following:

- Flashbacks and/or nightmares

- Emotional numbness; avoidance of places, people, and activities that are reminders of the traumatic event

- Difficulty sleeping and concentrating; feeling jumpy; being easily angered

- Negative thoughts, such as "I'm a bad person" or "I can't trust anybody"

- Distorted blame of self or others about the traumatic event

- Feelings of detachment or estrangement from loved ones

Sexual dysfunction can also be a sign of PTSD. An article by Zachary Zavislak and Laura Tedesco in *Men's Health* magazine, dated April 21, 2015 said the following:

By some estimates, nearly one in five U.S. soldiers returning home from Iraq or Afghanistan suffer from PTSD.

And the majority of these veterans-those age 40 or below, who are in the prime of their sexual lives—face an 81% higher risk of sexual problems than those without a PTSD diagnosis,

*according to a 2013 study published in the Journal of Sexual
Medicine.*

*Further research released last year in the same journal suggests
a stronger link: Servicemen with probable PTSD were 29 times as
likely as those without PTSD to report ED (Erectile Dysfunction).
Among men with genital injuries, for comparison, the risk of ED
went up only ninefold.*

"Cope with what? I'm fine. Nothing is wrong," I would tell people,
if they asked if I was okay.

Each day I went to work as a criminal investigator, where I worked
cases such as theft, child neglect/abuse, domestic violence, various
types of assaults, and the occasional classified case, my attitude toward
the work I used to enjoy quickly turned sour. Whenever I would have
to respond to a minor call, such as a couple fighting loud enough for
neighbors to hear, I was disgusted. "At least you're not having to pull
the plug on your loved one!" I thought with seething anger.

If there was anything I didn't agree with or anything I didn't like, I
complained. I began to distance myself from friends and colleagues. I
began to have problems physically. I had bulging discs, degenerative
disc disease, arthritis, and other problems in my neck. Soon, I started
to have sleep problems. I couldn't go to sleep or couldn't stay asleep,
which would lead to falling asleep at the wheel, or almost falling
asleep while conducting interrogations!

Within weeks, I was on ten to fifteen medications at the same
time (listed in a previous chapter). The medications just piled onto
the psychological problems I was already having. I became a zombie
of sorts. I was numb, not really feeling much at all, physically or
mentally.

Even though I didn't feel that anything was wrong, at Ashley's
request, I started to see a counselor. Before long, I was seeing a
psychologist and psychiatrist twice a week each. I was in a shrink's
office four times a week! After each counseling session, if I didn't
have to return to work, I immediately went home and cracked open
a beer. Some days, I would drink a twelve-pack, and other days, just

one or two. It depended on how angry I was after a stranger tried to "psychologize" me.

Looking back now, I realize that I was turning to the bottle to deal with my problems, just like my dad did. The consequences in the coming months would be almost unbearable.

May 19, 2013

It was a year from the date that my dad died. I still don't remember a lot from that day, but I do remember drinking, a lot, while I reminisced digging into my dad's foot locker. I tenderly looked through all of his papers and knick-knacks that I kept—his obituary, a baseball, my Little League baseball hat that he still had (I played on the Hardees team).

May 20, 2013 (1:28 a.m.)

I must have passed out drunk. I woke up with my face in the carpet in the living room of our house in the little town of Stella, North Carolina. The lights were still on. I looked up. I was all alone. Ashley must have gone to bed. I didn't see her or Jaxson. I looked around and saw everything I kept in my dad's foot locker spread all around me in disarray. I knew I had to get up in a few hours for work, so I put everything back in the foot locker and went to bed.

"I have a problem," was the last thought that I had before going to sleep.

By this point, my relationship with my wife was nearly a memory. I did not want to be married to the person I had been with since my senior year in high school (thirteen years at that point). Regardless of everything we went through, I told myself I was done. I didn't realize until much later how I was projecting my grief and anger onto my wife. I simply thought that she was taking me for granted. At the same time, she was dealing with post-partum depression and learning how to be a mom. I didn't pay any mind to that aspect, though. I just felt that she wasn't putting forth effort into our relationship in areas such as communication and intimacy. As things got worse, I told myself that I would not allow my son to be raised in a house where his parents constantly fought and hated each other. I grew up in a similar environment and didn't want that for my son.

Within my son's first year of life, my wife and I signed legal separation papers, and I was secretly having an affair with somebody who worked in my building. She liked some of the same things I liked, such as classic cars and guns, so it felt comforting. I hid this affair from everybody I worked with, but it quickly became public knowledge. People at work started gossiping, and my Marine Corps career was in jeopardy, but I was not concerned about that. I felt that I had earned my behavior because I had lost my dad.

"I shouldn't get in trouble right now because I'm dealing with my dad's death," I thought to myself. "What's it matter, anyway? I'm legally separated." In the Marine Corps' eyes, this did not matter. I was still married, legally separated or not.

August 18, 2013

My son turned a year old. I should have been excited about this. My mom and grandmother even came down for his birthday. It was the most awkward birthday party I had ever attended. Thankfully, Jaxson just enjoyed his *Lorax* cake, and we found orange icing and cake everywhere, including chunks of cake in his diaper!

September 14, 2013

Ashley told me that she needed to protect herself and find support. She packed up and moved back to Indiana with Jaxson. I was still adamant that we were getting a divorce and was indifferent to the idea of living states away from my son. I think this was due to the combination of depression, medications, and projections of my own pain onto Ashley. I even drove the moving truck back to Indiana for her as she drove her car back.

After returning to North Carolina from Indiana, things continued to unravel. The career-killing relationship that I started made such a ruckus around my office that I was forced to turn in my badge and investigator credentials and had to work the front gate. A command investigation ensued.

During the command investigation into adultery, the forbidden relationship ended, and I found myself completely alone. The people I'd considered friends or colleagues were nowhere to be found. Maybe they were trying to help, but I was so depressed and riddled with anxiety that I probably pushed them away unwittingly.

December 8, 2013

One winter North Carolina day, I was driving my F-150 to one of my four counseling sessions for the week. A thought crept into my mind.

"What if Ashley and I can make this work?"

With that thought, I called her. To no surprise, she was very guarded, but she was still receptive to the idea. Soon, we started over. We started a courtship like we just started dating. She was living in Indiana and I was still in North Carolina, so we had a long-distance relationship to start with. It was a blessing and kept us from trying to jump right back into a marriage.

We talked over internet video calls so that we could see each other and I could see Jaxson. To her dismay, I was also smoking and using chewing tobacco (dipping) at the same time while we were on our video calls. I thought, "What the heck, we're all going to die one day anyway. My dad died in his fifties, and so did my grandfather on my mom's side."

Between December and May, Ashley and I continued to talk. She drove down multiple times with our son so we could be together. This was our honeymoon phase. The real work was coming.

June 20, 2014

After a long command investigation into adultery, administrative separation (adsep) proceedings began. Adsep proceedings are different from military courtroom proceedings. No actual charges were being filed, but they were making a case to kick me out of the Marine Corps because of misconduct (adultery). My case was short work for the members of the command determining my fate. All five command members voted for Other Than Honorable (OTH) Discharge, with only one recommending a suspension.

After thirteen years of service, six countries visited, and two combat tours in Iraq (2003 and 2006-2007), I felt I was being thrown away like a piece of garbage. If there was any part of me that was trying to be positive, this verdict destroyed that. The victim mentality just became stronger. My negativity became louder. The world sucked and I was a victim. My dad died, I almost lost my family, and now I'd also lost the only thing I ever knew as an adult, the Marine Corps and being a criminal investigator.

At the time, I had a Top Secret clearance. If I'd had an Honorable Discharge, I would have been able to work at any federal agency or any police department of my choosing. With an Other Than Honorable discharge, no federal agency or police department would want to hire me.

June 22, 2014

I moved back to Indiana. I was conflicted emotionally. On one hand, I was losing my career and had no idea what or who I would become. I had no identity.

"Who am I?" I thought constantly.

On the other hand, I was being reunited with my wife and son. We were going to make it work this time. I didn't know what gave me faith that this could work. Between the fourteen years that we were together and the simple "what if" thought that entered my mind spontaneously, I wanted to give it another shot. I'm not even sure if I had faith it would work, but I knew it was going to take work from both of us.

I didn't know what career I wanted to pursue. Over and over, even though I was the epitome of negativity (the irony was not lost on me), came the thought: I wanted to help people in some capacity. I just didn't know what that looked like yet.

July 2014

I was hired as a headhunter for a staffing company in my hometown. I was happy to find a job that would be helping other people find employment. I was hired to find people who had skilled trades, such as welding, maintenance, etc. The problem was that I didn't have any experience with any of this. The skilled trades department was booming at the time I took it over. I quickly learned that this was not the profession for me. At the ten-month mark, I was fired. I still wanted to help people, but I had to go back to the drawing board.

April 2015

After a couple weeks of job searching, I was hired by a non-profit organization to manage several thrift stores in the northern Indiana area. Although I was not a fan of working in retail, I jumped at the chance to take this position because these stores funded a rehabilitation center in South Bend. My mission to help people seemed to start to take off. While managing the stores, I gave motivational speeches for the men in the rehabilitation center. The facility hosted men from all walks of life—from hardened criminals from the streets, to men who cooked in restaurants, to men who worked in offices. A perfect example of how addiction does not discriminate.

During my speeches, I wanted to be as blunt as possible about what was happening to these men in their addiction, from alcohol, to pills, to cocaine, meth, heroine, etc. I told the men the story of my dad; then one day, I asked the men present to visualize being in my dad's position and their loved ones in my position. Something happened in the room—like a current shot through the chairs. Some of the men openly cried. Some opened their jaws in shock and awe.

The following was also a scenario I posed to the men in that room and many rooms since:

"Let me ask you something. If I walked past you on the sidewalk in your neighborhood and punched you in the face, got you on the ground, and kept kicking you in the stomach, would you stay in the fetal position and take it, or would you stand up and fight back?

The tension in the room started to build. I could see some of the men start to puff their chests up, in preparation to fight. "I'd fight back!" a few of them exclaimed.

"Good! Then why aren't you standing up and fighting back when life is kicking you while you're down? Why are you staying in the fetal position and taking it?"

I could see a light switch on in the men's faces. I felt a collective sigh. A collective realization. There seemed to be an awakening. The men told me they understood finally that they were not fighting back. They were merely taking the beatings life was giving them. Most of them came up to me after each speech and thanked me.

"You spoke to me on a level that nobody has ever spoken to me on," one man said with a tear in his eye. I went home that night feeling more fulfilled than I ever have in my life.

Within a few months of my employment, the rehab facility in South Bend closed. The men and the equipment were moved to another location in Indiana. From that point forward, until the next January, I never gave another speech. I only ran the stores, and once again, I was on the hunt for other ways to be fulfilled and to help people. I resigned from the organization in January.

January 2016

I decided to chase money, rather than fulfillment. I was hired by a local garage door company to be the Commercial Service

Scheduling Coordinator. I saw dollar signs when they told me that I would be starting with a salary $15,000 higher than my previous job. Fulfillment was no longer important. With this salary, I could easily provide for my wife and son. I was in charge of scheduling commercial service and field service calls all day. At first, I thought this was the place for me and sidelined my need for fulfillment. When I was interviewed, I was asked about how I deal with stress and that if I came into work every day knowing I was going to lose, then I would be just fine. I laughed and told them that I had to clean up poop inside a dressing room at my last job and had been to combat twice.

The interviewer continued to talk about how I would be scheduling service calls for the day, taking service calls from customers, taking service calls from salesmen, taking service calls from management, and finding a way to take care of all customer needs with five crews, spanning a territory of 6,400 square miles.

"You just need to be able to try to put twenty pounds of crap into a five-pound bag on a daily basis," the interviewer said. Piece of cake . . . I thought.

The job was tough, but the tougher part was dealing with people who didn't know how to hold each other accountable or how to take orders without complaining. This was a tough pill to swallow for somebody who spent thirteen years in the Marine Corps. Take orders, follow them, give orders, inspect what you expect. That's just how things were done in the military.

The one thing that kept my sanity was the gym. The day I started at this company, I started going to a new gym down the street. This was just a little hole-in-the-wall gym right next to the train tracks. The building was brown, and the equipment was older, but the plates were iron. I didn't need anything extravagant. I'd lifted on and off since I was a kid but walking into this gym seemed intimidating. I all but forgot how to weight train. I walked over to one of the bench presses and put a 45-pound plate on both sides. The bar weighed 45 pounds also, so it totaled 135 pounds. I'd lifted this before, so it shouldn't have been a problem. I checked around the room to see if anybody was paying attention to what I was doing. Nobody was looking, time to try this out. I lay on the bench and pushed up. "You gotta be kidding me!" I thought, as I felt like an old Buick was weighing down on my chest.

By the end of that first workout, I fell back in love with fitness! One of the walls had numerous pictures of bodybuilders, and I became enamored with the idea of competing. That night I went home and told Ashley my thoughts.

"I know myself. I know if I don't set a drastic goal, I will fall out of the gym again within three months," I explained. "I think I am going to compete."

"Like . . . bodybuilding?" she asked, looking at me like I had a second forehead growing.

"Yeah! Bodybuilding! I think it would be a good goal to set!" I said triumphantly.

"Ok . . ." she said, her voice inflection telling me that she thought it was just another hare-brained idea of mine.

The next day, I was talking to one of the members, Dell, about abdominal exercises. "Do you want to compete?" he asked.

Looking around like I had a recording device attached to me, I replied, "Yes! I just talked to my wife about it last night!"

With that, we got started to compete in a show in South Bend in just five short months. At the time, I was around 190 pounds and about 25-percent body fat. But I worked tirelessly and competed in the show in South Bend in June. I placed second in that show and later placed fifth in a show in September of that same year.

My training and competitions were the highlights of that year, as the job was less than fulfilling and I was simply chasing a paycheck. By January 2017, this clearly was not the path I was supposed to be on, because, once again, I was fired.

But something fruitful had come out of this—a vision for a way to fan my love for fitness and help people. For the next several weeks, I worked around the clock to obtain my personal trainer certification.

March 2017

By March, I was certified and started working at a local gym as a trainer. I fell in love with teaching people various aspects of leading a healthy life and watching them use these tactics to better themselves. My heart was full when I helped a person get under 300 pounds for the first time in years. I laughed when a client would jokingly cuss at me, give me the finger, or tell me they hated me. That just told me I was doing something right. I knew they would be back the next day for more.

I was only getting paid for my sessions that I booked, so I knew I had to hustle. I worked in the gym for twelve to fifteen hours a day to gain clientele and train those who signed up with me. It was tiring, but I enjoyed it. In the first two months, I made the gym $20,000 in personal training packages. I was on fire. I saw greater visions emerging—leaving the gym at some point and starting my own training business.

As time went on, I started to realize something. The people who signed up with me were motivated. Something in their personal lives motivated them to make a change. This realization helped me sign people up, but I found quickly that motivation has a shelf life, a very short shelf life. When motivation is depleted, the person no longer shows up for themselves. If they weren't devoted to this new regimen as a long-term lifestyle, they quit. People quit on themselves at various stages of their training. I had some people sign up for 96 sessions but quit after using fourteen sessions. Others would complete 64 sessions but just quit coming to the gym after they used all their sessions. This gave me a revolving door of clients. I knew it was already time for me to take the next step in my health professional career. I wanted more tools to help transform someone's life. I wanted something that would help people make lasting life changes. I wanted to make a bigger impact in the lives of others. I entered a training program to become a health and life coach. In the forefront of my thinking was that if I could keep one person from going down the path my dad did, I would be fulfilled. As I started looking into becoming a coach, I branched out on my own as a personal trainer.

I started my coaching practice in May 2018 and would receive my certification from the Health Coach Institute in July 2018.

LET'S GET REAL

1. Imagine your name or your loved one's name in the obituary where my dad's name is. Step into that for a moment. Use your senses to feel into this. It's a horrible feeling, isn't it?

2. Are you reeling from a loved one's untimely death from addiction? Are you stuck in a pit of misery as a result? What are you doing to change that?

3. What are some resources you can use to assist you in growing from this tragedy?

4. If you have grown from it, how are you reaching another friend or family member dealing with an addiction?

SWIM

CHAPTER 9

The Many Paths To Recovery

THERE IS NO excuse to not recover.

The tragedy is that we see people only try one path, or two. When they only try one or two or even three paths and it doesn't click, they get defeated and end up going back to their addictions. Your addiction doesn't give up that easily. It will fight with everything it's got to keep you in the morass. It will feed you every reason why you don't have a problem, or why you're beyond hope. It will feed you LIES in the form of very good EXCUSES. WE saw in ourselves and we see people every day come up with a million excuses to not recover or why they can't recover:

- You have to be rich—rehab is expensive!
- You have to be a celebrity.
- You have to quit your job.
- You need to believe in God.
- You have to have a loving family.
- You have to have a lot of time.
- You have to know where to start.
- It's too hard to overcome an addiction.

- My addiction isn't that bad- I'm probably not even an addict.
- AA, NA, Al-Anon, Refuge, Rehab, Sanctuary, Ibogaine- none of them work.

We're here to tell you is that if you truly desire to get help for your addiction, you can. Here are just some ways people currently use to live sober:

- Rehab
- Sober Living Residences
- AA
- Refuge Recovery
- Recovery Coaches
- Meditation
- Retreats
- Online Support Groups
- Social Media
- SMART
- Community Support
- Persistence in a self-made daily practice
- Counseling

At the time of writing this book, there are likely even more ways people are recovering from addiction- and even better- long-term, life-long sobriety.

What is important to understand is that not everyone is going to recover the same way. The only essential ingredient is a commitment to find a workable path for you and not to give up. What we also want everyone who is reading this book is that recovery and sobriety take work. You can't just expect to show up to a meeting or pop a magic pill and be cured from your addiction. The business of recovery is an inside mission. It's a process. Sometimes it's laborious; sometimes you won't feel like it. The only person who can do the work is you. There is no KABOOM effect. But you're now in a high stakes game- your actual life is on the line. (If you have any doubts about this, go back and read the stories in the first half of the book.) What we also want to re-iterate is that RECOVERY IS WORTH IT.

Will some people have it easier than others when it comes to getting sober? Possibly. Not one person is the same. Just because someone may have any easier go at it doesn't mean that they will maintain it. Nor does it mean that if recovery is hard for you that you can't have a lifelong, powerful, amazing recovery. What it boils down to: how badly do you want it? Are you willing?

MICHAEL:

What works for me is AA. I love it. I love the structure and the community. I am a social person, and the community that is involved in AA for me is beautiful. I can walk into any AA meeting around the world and immediately feel connected before I even say hi to anyone. I love having a sponsor and working the steps. My sponsor is an amazing mentor and has been there for me in my darkest moments in sobriety as well as my largest triumphs. The most amazing thing about AA is that this is all service. No one is getting paid to help me or another alcoholic. It comes from a deep desire from the people in the rooms of AA to help other people live a beautiful life. I have never met such selfless people until I walked into the rooms of AA.

Am I a spiritual person? Yes. However, I will say that is not the reason I love AA. I love AA because for me, it is an awesome blueprint for a way of living. The Twelve Steps hold me accountable to always growing and not staying complacent. AA challenges me to make sure that I am actually living in sobriety but even more- living to my greatest potential instead of merely existing (white-knuckling life) without alcohol and drugs.

A lot of people out there think that you have to believe in God for AA to work for you.

Well, I want to give any atheists a little hope via my awesome friend.

Alex is from Canada. He is an atheist. He's a loving, rational, practical, retired musician who has been sober for a very long time.

M: Alex, since you do not have a spiritual practice and do not believe in God, how do you handle all of the God talk in AA?

A: My notion of a higher power is the notion of good. What a concept, right? Just the power of good. I believe that if I have a daily practice acting in a kind, loving, and patient manner, then the chances are, I'll receive similar in return. 'Do unto others as you would have them do unto you.' This seems to be a spiritual law and it shows up, one way or another, in most spiritual disciplines you look at. Good enough for me. As opposed to so much of "God" talk, which, to me, just seems way too egocentric. 'Oh, look, God just found me a parking place.' I mean, seriously. I'm not saying there isn't a place in the world for comforting fantasy but that way of looking at the world simply doesn't work for me, nor did it ever. 'Be kind. Do good. Keep my head out of the future.' That works for me, and I think it's better for everyone if I make those things my daily practice. I know there are thousands of atheists in the program like me, and I suppose in a way I feel an obligation to let them know that I also feel the way they do, too, and it's no barrier to progress in AA. My wife and I have one friend in the program, now sober six years, who told me flat out she wouldn't have stayed if I hadn't spoken up about not believing in God.

M: How do you view the Twelve Steps then if you do not have a spiritual practice or believe in God (there are a lot of God words in those steps!)?

A: Well, I do believe in having a spiritual practice. And as I said, I believe in a universal good. I just don't have a religiously oriented, 'God is up in heaven' spiritual practice. I just translate for myself in meetings. When people say God, I just say "good." I view the twelve steps as not only a spiritual but a completely practical way to live your life, especially the last four steps, nine through twelve. In the concern they show for others, those are very 'spiritual' steps. Those in particular are the steps I can refer to and practice on a daily basis to improve life and the lives of others around me.

M: How do you view meetings?

A: I think they're absolutely essential. I've never known anyone who stayed home, read the big book, and stayed sober. You can pray to baby Jesus till your knees bleed but if you don't go to meetings, my experience is that you won't stay sober. That's at least what thousands of meetings have shown me. Alcoholism is essentially a disease of isolation. I don't care if you yukked it up in every bar from Tokyo to Toronto, if you're a real alcoholic, then chances are some deep, essential part of you feels disenfranchised from the mainstream of life. So what's the answer? For me, it's the community of Alcoholics Anonymous. Meetings are where I see real bonds formed, trusting friendships built, laughter that's genuine. Meetings are where an alcoholic's life can be brought into focus in a meaningful way.

M: Awesome. Now let me ask you, when Step Three of the Twelve Steps says you 'made a decision to turn our will and our lives over to the care of God <u>as we understood him</u>,' what do you do in this case?

A: I turn it over to my belief in good, the power of good.

M: What about when everyone says "The Serenity Prayer"?

A: Honestly?! Yeah, yeah, it's heresy I know, but I say the meditative mantra I was given when I trained in Transcendental Meditation. The AA book says 'sought through prayer and meditation,' right? Well, I've been meditating for, let's just say, a VERY long time. TM works for me, complements the program, and enriches my life in ways every bit as essential as AA.

M: Do you believe people can get sober without AA?

A: (Laughs) Well, yeah, George Bush got sober in church, didn't he? He got sober in church and if stories are to be believed, he was pretty out there when he was drinking. But, honestly, he seems to be the exception. For most people, AA and the Twelve Steps just seem to be the most practical, effective way of changing alcoholic behavior and helping people find a way to a better life.

M: Why do you think people go back out and don't stay sober?

A: Any one of a thousand reasons, really. I know for sure the number-one reason many people who desperately need AA come but don't stay is the mention of the word "God." They hear that and they run for the exits. They've already had enough of religion in their lives and if they see AA as a religious program, boom, they're gone and most never come back. To me, the most important words in the Twelve Steps- and some of the very few words underlined in the book are 'God as we understood him.' Without that caveat- put in between, at the insistence of an atheist- I don't see how AA would have survived. Certainly not with the worldwide outreach and scope that it has. But until the newcomers grasp the concept that it doesn't have to be a 'Catholic God' or a 'Baptist God' or whatever, then it can be difficult for them to feel at home in AA, and they just don't stay.

M: And, in your experience, what other reasons do people have for not staying or going out?

A: Loads. People often just don't want to do the work, and the Twelve Steps only work if you actually work them. Or, some people, if they've been in AA for a while, think, 'Hey, I think I'm cured! I can drink again!' Well, that doesn't usually turn out too well. Or one alcoholic may develop a very big, it's the end-of-the-world, resentment at another alcoholic. Who knows? If a creative alcoholic is seriously looking for a reason to go back out there, in the time it takes to say the Serenity Prayer, they'll find one. What I know is that people who stay sober go to meetings and usually, a lot of them. If you look around any meeting, the people with the most time are usually the ones who go to the most meetings. That, and doing the other things that seem to work: talking to another alcoholic, talking to your sponsor, getting involved in service work, doing coffee, chairing a meeting, manning the phones. I've heard a lot of old timers say that back in the day when people still smoked, cleaning out the ashtrays was one thing that suddenly made them feel connected to the program. Crazy, right? But things like that seem to work. Bottom line is, getting out of 'me' and into 'we' seems to be the essential thing here. Just doing something as simple as reaching out your hand to a newcomer can make a huge difference to their sobriety and yours. It always struck me that on page 86, 'Upon awakening . . . we ask God to direct our thinking, especially asking that it be divorced from self-pity, dishonest, or self-seeking motives.' It doesn't say anything about alcohol! Getting out of 'me' and into 'we,' yeah, that seems to be the right answer for pretty much any situation an alcoholic might encounter.

So there you have it. Alex is living proof that anyone can not believe in God or religion and still succeed in AA. He is a non-believer who truly believes in the AA program and process and makes the program work for him on a daily basis.

RECOVERY COACHING

Another way to dive into recovery is to work with a recovery coach. Coaching is about creating forward movement with the client. Coaching is about habit change. Coaches dig deep into finding the root cause for why the client has always acted in a certain way and empowers them to make the necessary changes to live a fulfilled life.

Riley's Story:

Riley is a hard-working middle-class woman who works in finance. She is very well-known in her community and very well-respected. She wasn't comfortable going into the rooms of AA and sharing her addiction with a bunch of strangers. She wanted to have privacy in her recovery journey.

M: What made you decide to hire a coach to maintain your sobriety?

R: I wanted the privacy. I didn't want to put my problems out to my community. In my profession, I work with a lot of people in the community handling their finances— anywhere from investing, creating retirement plans, and doing taxes. People at the rehab I went to talked about coaches and the benefit of having one as another option for continued maintenance for my sobriety. I was resistant to the idea at first. I had tried therapy, and I hated it because I felt worse every time I left a session. I looked online and happened to stumble across a coach that was in recovery. Something inside me thought this could work.

M: When you started working with your coach, what were your initial thoughts?

R: I honestly didn't know what to expect other than I loved the client testimonials I had read about her. I had looked her up on Facebook and Instagram and saw from her posts that she knew what she was talking about. I also really appreciated how open she was about her path and her struggle and also her triumphs and sincere love of life in sobriety.

When we had our first call, I thought that she was awesome! I was also a little nervous but ready to do the work. I had little over a month of sobriety under my belt from being in rehab, and I knew I needed someone in my corner to help keep me sober and accountable. She totally understood me because she had been an alcoholic herself. We created a game plan to move forward in my life and create sustainable healthy habits that I do every day.

M: Can you elaborate on what you mean by sustainable healthy habits?

R: Of course! We started off by establishing a morning and evening routine to create consistency in my life, and I love it. My morning routine consists of starting off with listing things I am grateful for and really feeling those feelings. My coach emphasized when it comes to any change, you have to really *feel the feelings* and not just go through the motions. Then I make sure to eat a healthy breakfast to nourish my body. Lastly, I review the alarms that my coach had me set in my phone that go off several times a day that say things like "be present," "pause," "gratitude check," and "feel the feelings." These alarms are crucial because they allow me to put my focus back on what matters, which is gratitude, pausing so I can really gauge where I am at in my day and to be present. That is something that I never was doing when I was drinking. I was never present, and lastly, to feel the feelings is major. I never felt my feelings, and my coach has helped to give me permission to feel my emotions instead of suppressing them.

At night, I do a checklist of how I acted throughout the day: Was I selfish? Judgmental? Impatient? Unkind? I call myself out to see my progress and to see areas that I still struggle with. Then, I write down my "Wins," which can be anything positive such as "I got up when my alarm went off! I held the door open for a stranger. I was patient with a client." My coach emphasizes how important it is to have self-awareness of everything I do because everything I do is a choice. When I do self-checks throughout the day such as pausing, I am able to see where my thoughts are going. I am able to get curious about them instead of beating myself up for having sentimental thoughts. I realize it's part of the journey. Coaching really has me focus on what I am thinking about, and if its about drinking, then I pause, get into gratitude, really think about *how much better my life is now*, and then the temptation seems to lift. Instead of suppressing my feelings, I now acknowledge them and process them.

My routines help me stay present and fully aware of my actions and the thoughts that I am thinking. I liked the person I was becoming but I felt tremendous guilt about my past. My coach focuses on positivity and gratitude and no negative self-talk. She told me I can no longer feel shame and guilt for my past. That it does no good. So I focus on being grateful for what has happened because it is allowing me to be much better now. It has been eye-opening to have someone help me see how important it is to be aware of my thoughts and to recognize if they are helping me or hurting me. It was clearly hurting me to stay stuck in shame and guilt. What is helping me now is to be grateful for what happened and to look at how my past can help me now.

M: That's awesome. How long have you been working with your coach?

R: I have been with my coach for just over six months, and I don't see myself leaving her anytime soon. I have really begun to see the benefits of having someone in my corner to talk to about all of my feelings and to not ever feel judged. My coach continues to help me grow in acceptance of this new way of living sober. We have started to scale back now, only meeting every couple of weeks over FaceTime instead of every week, which is nice because in those sessions I get really honest about where I am with life. She holds me accountable through text and email several times a week, which is what I believe has been a major factor in my success.

M: Why is accountability a major key to your success?

R: Well, it's why I love my coach. She expects me to check in with her and be honest. She gives me exercises and things to do that really challenge me and force me out of my comfort zone. My coach asks me to get in action by being involved in the community and do volunteer work where I can find it. She asks me to acknowledge people for their hard work. Even if it's the stranger that is bagging my groceries, my intention every day is to get out of my small self. She doesn't let me slip backwards, and if I start to, we address it and find out why I start to self-sabotage.

M: What about community? I know for a lot of people getting sober, they really desire to be around other people going through the process.

R: I have an awesome support group from several friends. The friends I hang out with do not drink around me, and they are there for me because I asked them to be there. Also, my husband is extremely supportive as well as my co-workers. My coach told me to be upfront and honest about my journey. To have no secrets because I have been so secretive in my past. It honestly feels so good to be able to confide in people that are close to me and that support me.

M: Do you ever see yourself not having a coach to help you with your recovery?

R: I honestly don't think so. I think having someone that is always there for you is key. Yes, I think we may scale back our sessions as I continue to get more and more time under my belt, but honestly, I love having that person that gives me tough love with love. A person that challenges me and sees my blind spots so I can get through and keep progressing. A couple things come to mind that have happened for me since working with a coach that I never thought would happen for me. First, I am able to pause before speaking or acting. Pausing has been huge for me when I want to act or react in a way that might not be the best. Second, I have come to really love myself and my past. My coach has really shown me how to be in gratitude and no longer shame and guilt. I honestly didn't think I would ever have that perspective on my past.

M: What is the biggest change you have seen in yourself since working with your coach?

R: My self-confidence and loving myself. Seriously. I didn't think I could ever feel as confident and comfortable in my skin as I do now. I am confident in being able to express my emotions, and I no longer feel guilty for having emotion. Also, I look at everything that is going on within me or around me with curiosity and not judgment. I can't believe what a difference it has made for me to change my perspective on being curious instead of judging. Being curious allows me to really look at *why* I am feeling the feelings I have, such as frustration, impatience, sadness, shame, and guilt. I get to get curious instead of beating myself up about it. It is through coaching that I have been able to love more and judge way less. Also, I honestly didn't think I could ever love myself the way I am starting to now. Like I actually *really love myself*. It's crazy! Every day, the negativity lessens and I just don't even care to be around it. I make self-care a non-negotiable for me now. I make sure to block out time in my week for it because my coach made me realize if I do not take care of myself, I can't take care of others in the capacity they need me to. I used to have a short fuse and lose my temper with co-workers and even my husband, and now I pause. This pausing and self-awareness has led me to getting a promotion, a $6,000-a-year raise and being seen as a leader in my company. My positive outlook on life is truly incredible. I feel proud of myself because I'm the person I wanted to be.

Recovery 2.0:

Through more than twenty years of recovery from addiction, noted yoga teacher Recovery 2.0 founder Tommy Rosen learned a lot about what works and what doesn't work in recovery. From his explorations on the yoga mat and in Twelve-Step rooms, Tommy found a path to sustainable recovery that includes mind-body practices, a profound look at diet, and a holistic and inclusive perspective on the Twelve Steps. All of this has allowed Tommy to realize that recovery happens in stages. He has discovered that by utilizing the best practices of the Twelve Steps in combination with yoga and meditation, he could achieve lasting freedom from addiction. In Recovery 2.0, Tommy shares his own past struggles with addiction and the powerful insights that helped him to identify and break free from the obstacles that stand in the way of recovery. Tommy shows you how to build off the key tenets of the Twelve-Step program combined with an innovative approach where deeper levels of detoxification and transformation allow you to uproot addiction and thrive. Recovery 2.0 offers:

- A new way of looking at addiction as a vibratory frequency that has roots in family history and one's "Addiction Story," which helps to destigmatize addiction and remove associated guilt and shame.

- Fresh perspectives on how to get the most out of the Twelve-Step teachings and community, while avoiding pitfalls.

- Daily practices in breathing, meditation, and yoga that will give you access to the extraordinary power within you.

- Inspiration to help you discover your personal mission and be of service to others.

Recovery 2.0 focuses on not just surviving addiction but thriving in recovery and living a life second to none.

How Evan Found Success with Recovery 2.0

M: Can you give me a little back story on your alcoholism?

E: Yeah, of course. I would say it's nothing special. I started drinking in high school, and then all the way through college I just partied my face off. I sometimes wonder how I graduated. Anyways, after college I was able to control it for a while because I was now in the "real world" and had to be responsible. I did the typical thing- got married, had a couple of kids- and then work just became more and more stressful. Life became stressful being a dad and a husband

and always feeling like I had to perform. What started out as just having a couple of beers at home after work with the family escalated to hanging out with co-workers after work for a couple, then coming home buzzed, and then to deal with the family I hid a bottle of vodka upstairs in the closet and would escape to take pulls off of it. Before you knew it, I was a mess again. My wife became so angry and resentful because I wasn't present, and she knew something was up but I didn't want to talk about it. I didn't know how. One fine day, my wife found an empty vodka bottle upstairs in the closet and I was found out. It was a meet-your-maker moment.

M: Wow! What happened?

E: I broke down. My wife broke down. She gave me an ultimatum. She said to "get help or get out." So I panicked. I had heard of AA just through people talking at work about their lives, and I knew about it in college as well again, just from people talking it because someone they knew was going. It took me about a week to get the courage to go, and when I finally went, I got there right on time, took a seat in the back, and just listened. It wasn't as bad as I thought it would be, so I went back again a couple days later and people came up to me and introduced themselves to me, and to be perfectly honest, it was comforting and so then I just kept going back. I was maintaining my sobriety, but I slowly realized I didn't really love going to the rooms. I wanted to explore other ways to stay sober, and I had heard a guy in the rooms talking about Recovery 2.0.

After a meeting I pulled him aside, and I asked him all about it. That night, I went home and got on my computer and visited the website and Facebook group and just fell in love.

M: Evan, tell me why you absolutely love Recovery 2.0.

E: What's not to love?! For me, it's the community and the founder, Tommy Rosen. The community is awesome. I connect with people all over the world through the Recovery 2.0 Facebook Group! If you don't have Facebook, then you connect through their website (recovery2point0. com) or their YouTube Channel (Recovery 2.0). It's incredible. Tommy Rosen has built a worldwide recovery community. I never feel alone, and that is the best part about it. I love that I can jump on the Facebook group at anytime and just connect and have a conversation. On top of that, there are events you can go to that Recovery 2.0 put on. At these events, you can get coached, do yoga, deepen your meditation practice; it really just has anything that anyone in recovery could possibly want, in my opinion.

M: What is one thing you find that is crucial to having in your recovery that Recovery 2.0 offers?

E: Constant community engagement. I crave community. Like I said, I could reach out at any hour of the day on the Recovery 2.0 Facebook Page and someone will respond. That is what I find to be so beneficial about social media. It is the ability to connect. I can remember several times in my early recovery when I wasn't feeling great—I almost drank again, and I just made a post to the Facebook group, and I had people almost immediately reaching out to me and supporting me. Also, I love how Recovery 2.0 posts about different conferences and workshops that are going on all over the world! Recovery 2.0 offers many outlets for people to get educated on Recovery. I mean, c'mon, I used to be the most unpleasant, not-present dad or husband and now I am. I actually remember and enjoy time with my family and being able to be excited about life. I work out five times a week, I meditate, I left my stressful job and now work for a company that I have already received several promotions at. All of these things that have happened in my life I celebrate with my Recovery 2.0 community. Also, Recovery 2.0 has given me the skills to be able to go through hard times in my life, such as my father's death, and I didn't drink. It's wild! I wouldn't have it any other way. It's truly incredible the way I live my life now, and I owe it to Recovery 2.0 and everyone involved.

REFUGE RECOVERY

From RefugeRecovery.org: "Refuge Recovery is a non-profit organization grounded in the belief that Buddhist principles and practices create a strong foundation for a path to freedom from addiction. This is an approach to recovery that understands: All individuals have the power and potential to free themselves from the suffering that is caused by addiction." Refuge Recovery has in-person meetings all over the world, as well as online meetings.

The Four Truths of Refuge Recovery:

1. Addiction creates suffering.

2. The cause of addiction is repetitive craving.

3. Recovery is possible.

4. The path to recovery is available.

Their Eightfold path to Recovery is an abstinence-based path and philosophy. The Eight parts of the path do not have to be done in any order, but are all meant to be developed, experienced, and sustained. They include: Understanding, Intention, Communication/ Community, Action, Livelihood/Service, Effort, Mindfulness/ Meditations, and Concentration/Meditations.

A quote from Refuge Recovery states that, "No one can recover for you. We take refuge in the fact that we have the power to do so." More information can be found at RefugeRecovery.org.

Interview on Refuge Recovery with Tiffany Swedeen, R.N.

A: Tiffany, would you share a little about yourself and your addiction?

T: I'm Tiffany—a registered nurse, certified life and recovery coach, and a single mom in recovery from addiction to opiates and alcohol. Opiates always "worked the best" for me, but I was addicted to any substances that could help me escape or avoid my thoughts and feelings. I'm also in recovery from religious trauma, self-loathing, depression, and anxiety—the sources of pain that led to my use of substances. I've been in active recovery for four years. I don't use a sober date—for one thing, I don't feel like my relapses meant I was starting over on day one. I've not been abstinent from all mind-altering substances since I ventured into the world of recovery, but I've been building and improving upon it since early 2014 when I first sat across the room from a chemical dependency counselor and said, "I'm in serious trouble. Please help me." I accomplished what most people consider sobriety/abstinence in fall of 2016.

A: How did your addiction start?

T: My opiate addiction started with my own prescription. Officially, I was prescribed Vicodin to treat migraines that I'd struggled with for a couple years. But I was also trying to treat emotional suffering. I was a single mom with a teenage daughter at home. My relationship with my long-term boyfriend was failing—it was chaotic and co-dependent. I had extreme job burnout, working as a caregiver, constant overtime, and taking care of my own ill father. Vicodin helped me cope, but soon, my Vicodin prescription was no longer strong enough to numb out or avoid painful feelings and situations.

Eventually, my addiction progressed to the point that I did something I thought I would never do. I started to steal leftover narcotics from the hospital where I worked. I'd become tolerant, meaning I needed more to make the drug work. If I ran out of opiates and couldn't get more, I drank heavily until I no longer noticed or cared about the opiate withdrawal symptoms.

A: Were you addicted to alcohol as well?

T: Alcohol was my backup drug of choice. When I finally became sober, that was the hardest thing honestly—to not drink. Drugs essentially became almost impossible to get (I never did buy them on the street, so I had very little resources), but alcohol is always accessible and acceptable. There's been times in my recovery when life is hard, and my mind starts to revert to my addictive thinking patterns— and it's alcohol that I think of first because it's so easy to obtain. Luckily, the probation program I am now in doesn't allow any alcohol consumption—they test for it a couple times a month through urine or hair, and in a way, this acts as a kind of safety net.

A: Can you tell me about how you started recovery?

T: My recovery started in 2014 when I reached out to a chemical dependency counselor because I realized I was in serious trouble. I'd been in active addiction for three years, but I didn't want to tell anybody. I was terrified to tell my manager at work and didn't understand that there were confidential resources available. I didn't tell anybody in my family. I didn't know of any friends who were sober or recovering to talk to. I felt so extremely ashamed myself and horrified at my actions. I stayed silent for a long time.

My plan was just to see a counselor privately, but I refused to go to group meetings because I was afraid that I would be recognized. My biggest fear was that I would be turned in to the Department of Health (DOH). That's a major consequence for health care providers that have addiction and substance use disorder if it impairs their ability to work. The DOH intervenes and might even take their license. But even worse is what happens when one doesn't reach out: the addiction grows. That's what happened to me. Addiction is progressive, and recovery requires effort and significant support. The once-a-week session I was attending was not enough for me to make progress.

My counselor suggested I attend an eight-week long Mindfulness Based Relapse Prevention course (MBRP). Mindfulness means staying in the present moment, learning to tolerate discomfort, accepting and understanding feelings and emotions without having to escape. I would learn to stop, breathe, and respond mindfully to external and internal stimuli without giving in to cravings and urges.

My time attending that course was the only time during active addiction that I was able to stay fully sober seven days at a time. I didn't use any opiates the entire eight weeks. I did drink some during those eight weeks, but I never drank within a few days of the class.

The reason it didn't stick is because I didn't stick with it. I was still so horrified and ashamed and secretive and self-loathing that, after the eight weeks, I didn't hook up with any of the community. I didn't go to the aftercare meetings. I was afraid somebody would recognize me or turn me in. The program alone didn't prevent my eventual relapse, and my addiction did still spiral out of control over the next couple of years, but the concept of mindfulness and the foundations of that program remained with me—even though I wasn't consistently practicing what I had learned.

A: What happened next?

T: My addiction consumed me. I was in and out of counseling and attended a handful of meetings when I was desperate. It all came to a screeching halt in May of 2016 when my employer accused me (correctly) of stealing pills and made me take a pee test on the spot. My urine was super dirty—I had so many drugs in my system; drugs I'd taken from work, family, and friends. The human resources director said, "Here's your choice. You go into the Department of Health probation (a rigid recovery and accountability program they call 'alternative to discipline') or be terminated and probably lose your nursing license as well."

They gave me a deadline; I had to get into treatment within a week. I ended up going to a local treatment center's intensive outpatient program closest to me that met my probation requirements.

Part of what I had to do—what I still have to do in probation—is attend three peer support group meetings a week. Peer support groups usually mean Twelve-Step groups; that's the first thing people think of, and even the smallest towns usually have a meeting. I was willing to do anything I had to do to recover and keep my nursing license at that point. I went because I had to, but it wasn't speaking to me. I felt shame at the meetings. I actually would leave every meeting wanting to drink or use much more than on days where I didn't attend a meeting. I didn't connect with a higher power, even if I was allowed to choose my own. Religious trauma is a big part of my story and being forced to hold hands and say The Lord's prayer at the end was traumatic. If I left early or didn't join in, I didn't make connections and get to know members. I also seriously struggled with the idea that these Twelve steps were a prescription that was supposed to work for every single person, and if they didn't—the person had failed, not the program. My background in nursing, critical thinking, and evidence-based practice tells me that humans are dynamic, unique individuals, deserving of an individualized care plan. Some people might only need five steps, and others might need fifteen steps. But there was no room to question or get creative.

The intensive outpatient program wasn't promising from the beginning. I felt like I was getting this lip service- 'if you just find a higher power, show up to this class, watch our thirty-year-old videos, and attend meetings, you'll get better'. They'd give some handouts on nutrition, supplements, and meditation, but there was no opportunity to practice together or go in depth. They were big on feeding us ice cream multiple times a week as well. This didn't speak to my heart at all. I realized I was writing check after check and even with insurance, it cost me tons of money. It wasn't fulfilling or effective treatment.

A: It sounds like you may have been just going through the motions. Can you tell me more?

T: My brain was finally sober; I was starting to see everything more clearly. I watched my peers in the program relapse, one after another. I was starting to wake up a little bit back to my old self, and my old self had never settled for status quo. I had always been an overachiever; I'd always been very resourceful. My inner self has always pushed me: "Let's do better, let's find better. This is your one life, you've got to find what works best for you."

I finished the three-month program; by that point it made sense financially to not start over. I thought, "I have to get out of here." I started seeking out an aftercare program and counselor that would make sense for me. I did a little research and got a word-of-mouth referral about a facility about thirty minutes away. I had read online that the owner/operator was also a nurse and had completed the same 'alternative to discipline' program I was in, but ten years ago. I decided to give it a shot.

When I went in for my first session with their counselor, and I noticed he had meditation cushions in his counseling room. He had books on Buddhism and pictures of him in Tibet. I didn't know anything about Buddhism yet, and I didn't know much about meditation, but I remembered the MBRP eight-week course. Around that time, I also heard Russell Brand talk about Transcendental Meditation during an interview as one of the main factors in his addiction recovery. I thought, "He's been on heroin. If meditation can treat his addiction, then it can certainly help mine."

It was a total fluke, finding a mindfulness trained counselor at this new program. I'd been looking for a place that had good reviews and outcomes and offered individualized care plans. It honestly was this amazing life "coincidence" and a major inflection point on my journey.

The counselor asked Have you heard of Refuge Recovery? I facilitate it every Saturday night here in this city.' This was still thirty minutes away from me. But the drive didn't matter at the time—I was willing to do whatever it took to get well.

A: Can you tell me about your first recovery meeting?

T: In the fall of 2016, I went to my first Refuge Recovery meeting alone, and I was nervous. But I didn't feel the same as my very first Twelve-Step meeting—I wasn't crying and trembling and wanting to run away. I'd been in treatment for a few months by this time, and I had a feel for the recovery culture and community. I was surprised by the experience, though. The room that I walked into was very quiet. Everybody had to take off their shoes at the door; I could see through the window that there were about ten people sitting on cushions on the floor.

I was nervous because I didn't know what I was getting into. And that can always be a little uncomfortable. But I was also excited because it looked like these people were putting their tools to practice right in front of me, and that's what I was so looking forward to. That's very different from my experience in Twelve-Step meetings where much of the individual work is done alone or one-one-one with a sponsor.

One of the first things the facilitator said was that in order to create community, we would start the meeting with everybody saying their name. He stated there was no need to label yourself by anything other than your first name; we drop any judgments or labels right from the beginning.

That felt so great. I'd always been uncomfortable speaking up at Twelve-Step meetings because I didn't know what to call myself. Should I say I was addict? An alcoholic? I never felt like I fit in those boxes exactly, and it felt like the meetings had rules I was supposed to know and follow whether they felt valuable or made sense to me. This was different.

I didn't want to leave that room. I didn't feel addicted in there. I just felt normal. I felt like "this is possible, I can do this."

The facilitator stated that addiction and cravings are directly related to our human need to avoid suffering. Humans seek pleasure and run from pain. Avoiding suffering is normal. Those of us that use drugs or alcohol to relieve suffering (whether one is aware of the reason or not) are not inherently different than other people.

A: How did the messaging make you feel?

T: I thought addiction was my problem. I thought substances were my problem. I thought I was a bad person who couldn't stop stealing pills. When I learned in this meeting that I was a human with a human condition, I felt so normalized and accepted. After that, I was able to start accepting myself, which empowered me to make significant changes and cope with my cravings in a healthier way.

Another thing that drew me in immediately was that Refuge Recovery teaches every person has the power to relieve themselves of the suffering addiction causes. Everyone has the power to recover from addiction—everyone is capable.

One of the chapters is entitled, "Recovery is Possible." That is also the Fourth Noble Truth, in Buddhist terms. There is a path (the Eightfold Path) to follow that leads us out of addiction. It's a journey, and it's going to be the rest of my life working on it, but it's within my reach and it's for my highest well-being.

I wanted to cultivate more of those things. I wanted more compassion and forgiveness in my life. I wanted to learn how to get over the cravings and stop obsessing about substances. Refuge gave me tools to deal with my cravings in the moment—meditation, resilience, self-love, *mindfulness*. Leaving the meeting, I felt much more encouraged than I had when I was told to "eat sugar, call your sponsor, and don't pick up."

A: Who would you recommend Refuge Recovery to?

T: Anybody could benefit from Refuge Recovery. It is for "addictions of all kinds" which could even mean someone who's addicted to negative thinking. The program is focused on self-help and self-actualization. Refuge values and promotes compassion, loving, kindness, generosity, mindfulness. Who doesn't want more of that in their life?

Everybody is empowered to find their path and learn from their own experience. So that means if somebody comes into Refuge Recovery, and part of their program is to have a higher power, that's absolutely supported. Lots of people go to both AA and Refuge because there's nothing about Refuge that makes them incompatible.

I recommend Refuge Recovery to those who feel that they don't fit in with Twelve-Step groups, but also to those who love their Twelve-Step group and are looking for some in-person, real-time, group-guided meditation to add to their recovery toolbox.

Even if you've tried meditation and didn't like it, or found it to be uncomfortable, I think Refuge is a great place to try again. They make it simple and accessible. Also, just like any other peer-support group meetings, if you've been to a Refuge meeting or two, and you didn't find that you loved it right away—remember, that each group is autonomous, and it is worth checking out more than one if possible.

Refuge Recovery is still a relatively young recovery program. So, it's not in every area yet, but it's growing rapidly, and there are online meetings twice a week as well at www. intherooms.com.

If this program sounds like something you feel would be beneficial for your community, but there's no meetings near you, I encourage you to research about how to start a meeting in your area yourself. There is plenty of assistance and information available to walk you through the process on Refuge Recovery's website.

A: Is there anything else you would like to add?

T: This is your one life, and your recovery matters. Everyone deserves an individualized, holistic, practical, deeply spiritual yet completely non-religious program. Don't settle for meetings that don't serve your sobriety and your soul. If you're not connecting with what's available, if you're not finding what you love, *build* what you love. You can make it happen—and you can be a service to others by making it available.

SMART Recovery

You can learn about SMART recovery at SmartRecovery.org. Straight from their website: SMART recovery is "an abstinence-based, not-for-profit organization with a sensible self-help program for people having problems with drinking and drugs. It includes many ideas and techniques to help you change your life from one that is self-destructive and unhappy to one that is constructive and satisfying. SMART Recovery is not a spin-off of Alcoholics Anonymous. No one will label you an 'alcoholic,' an 'addict,' or 'diseased,' nor 'powerless,' and if you do not believe in a religion or spirituality, that's fine, too. We teach common sense self-help procedures designed to empower you to abstain and to develop a more positive lifestyle. When you succeed at following our approach, you may graduate from the program, or you may stay around to help others."

In SMART Recovery, they do not focus on your past, except on what you can learn from it. They focus on the present, how you are living now, and on the current causes of self-destructive behaviors. Then they help you to figure out what behavior changes you can put into place in order to create a positive lifestyle change, particularly related to addiction and recovery.

SMART Recovery's Key Areas of Awareness and Change place emphasis on:

1. Enhancing motivation

2. Refusing to act on urges to use

3. Managing life's problems in a sensible and effective way without substances

4. Developing a positive, balanced, and healthy lifestyle

SMART Recovery uses evidenced-based cognitive behavioral and non-confrontational motivational enhancement techniques, such as REBT (Rational Emotive Behavior Therapy), which proposes the idea that your thinking creates your feelings and leads you to act. Their approach is to teach you how to change your beliefs and manage your emotions that lead you to drink or use.

SCOTT

Another road to recovery is the Intensive Out-Patient program, or IOP, which was the resource Geoff Mickleson used, who had an addiction to opiates and heroin.

S: When did your addiction problems start?

G: I started with drinking as a teenager and eventually moved into prescription pills. After pills, I started snorting heroin because it was cheaper.

S: Did you ever overdose?

G: In five years, I overdosed four times. I was involved with "drug court" during two of those overdoses.

S: What is drug court?

G: Drug court was an accountability tool for the people dealing with an addiction to drugs that did not have a major felony drug charge on their record. The city started this due to the overwhelming growth of addicts going to jail, rather than getting help for their problem.

S: What was the next step for you after drug court?

G: Intensive Out-Patient. IOP taught me a lot about myself and my addiction. It taught me that I was just as addicted to the chaos as I was the drugs, such as the parties, the late nights, easy women, things like that. The typical sex, drugs, and rock-and-roll mindset. The fast lifestyle.

S: Describe IOP.

G: While on drug court, I had to go through twelve weeks of classes, meetings, support, and accountability, while I conducted daily business with my job and life. Then six months of aftercare. I failed a drug test during my first round of aftercare and had to undergo a second round of IOP. If I failed again, I would have been placed in an in-patient facility for rehab.

S: What is aftercare?

G: Aftercare was going to meetings and getting drug tested randomly.

S: What did IOP teach you?

G: IOP taught me how to identify the triggers that made me want to use and call somebody when I had the urge to use. During IOP, I learned my urges would only last about thirty minutes.

S: What was your biggest takeaway from IOP?

G: I actually feel IOP would not have worked if I didn't make the decision to want to change to begin with. After the fourth overdose, something clicked. I knew something needed to change or I was going to die. This wasn't a phase. Nobody is going to save me but myself. IOP provided the tools and made me accountable. I would get drug tested before every class. They were instant-read tests, but they still sent the samples off to a lab to be tested further. IOP only works if you make it work. The majority of the other people in drug court were just waiting out their time to get through the process and go right back to drugs when they're done.

Geoff's success story from his addiction is not the only one, as you've heard many others in this book. Happily, for his family and friends, the effects have diminished drastically since he took responsibility for his actions. Family and friends of addicts, understand these success stories can be your loved one's story as well. Time is of the essence, but it only takes an initial thought, just like Geoff's. *Nobody is going to save me but myself.*

My father was in and out of AA for many years, which was no surprise to me. The Twelve-Step Program of AA works for many people. As you've read, my fellow author, Michael, credits her sobriety to that program. My other fellow author, Andrea, did not find the help she needed. Unfortunately, my father fell into the relapse category after attending AA, many times. Bottom line, these three examples are perfect examples of how different approaches to sobriety work for different people. If you or a loved one tried AA and it didn't work, that does not mean there is no hope. It simply means that a different approach is required.

After thinking about the conversation with my dad, where he confessed the inner thoughts that drove his life—about how he was fat, nasty, and how nobody loved him or wanted him—it is easy to see that he needed one-on-one support to dismantle these beliefs and hold him accountable to a new path. I believe, if he would have worked with a coach, his chances of staying sober would have been significantly higher. I may not have clear evidence pointing to this fact, but if a coach would have worked with him about his mindset, about self and personal development, he may have found value in himself, rather than the bottle.

My dad also attempted to work through an addiction recovery center in Goshen, Indiana, but his services were suspended due to not being able to pay the $76 required to attend. I don't blame the recovery center. Although this is just speculation, I imagine he probably used that money to buy more alcohol.

As you could see from the stories in this book, the addiction affects the village. Family and friends of addicts deal with the challenges of loving an addict through their challenges. Unfortunately, with the stigmas that have been placed on addiction, loved ones feel that they will be shamed and judged from the general public if they were to open up about this challenge. Loved ones also fear that the addict will go deeper into addiction, lie about their addiction, or become completely estranged from the family, if the family or friends bring it up. This puts the loved ones in a very harsh scenario of "I don't know what to do!" All too often, this paralyzes the loved ones into inaction.

"I'm afraid they'll get mad and stop talking to me."

"I'm afraid they will see death as a way out if I tell them this will kill them."

"What if they just lie about it?"

These are statements and questions I've heard and even said myself. But I'm here to tell you, inaction is worse. Many families are afraid that their loved one will go deeper into addiction if they confront the issue. Maybe they will. But ask yourself the opposite, "What if they were just waiting for somebody to just be present and care for them by speaking up?" I didn't take any action for my dad; as a result, he died three months before he would have met his grandson. My inaction led to taking him off life support and watching him die. Now, maybe that was what would have happened anyway. But if that was his sole fate, even with some type of intervention, maybe I could have had a couple more years with him.

My call to anyone in the position I was in with my dad is to look deep within yourself and find your boldness for your loved one who is dealing with addiction. They aren't mad at you. They aren't yelling at you. It's not your loved one who is creating these fits of violence toward you. It's the drugs or alcohol talking and taking action for them.

Where there are many resources for the addicts that are well-known, many people may feel uncertain about what help is available for the friend or family member. Happily, there is more support for families and friends every day. Here are some sources you can consider:

> Another source for loved ones is the Al-Anon Family Groups. Al-Anon is an international organization that utilizes the Twelve-Step program for families of addicts, in order for the family to better cope with the challenges of addiction. Al-Anon is set up in a similar way to AA. Al-Anon supports friends/family members and helps them to learn that they cannot control the addict's behavior and are not to blame for their loved one's drinking problem. The meetings are also designed to assist the family member or friend in understanding that the only person who can change one is oneself (the alcoholic must be willing to change themselves), and the program offers a variety of tools and strategies for the friend or family member to take steps toward their own health and empowerment. Al-Anon is a place where family members and friends can receive help and support from those dealing with similar circumstances. One thing that must be understood about Al-Anon is the aspect of anonymity. These groups are very serious about their anonymity, so only people who want to participate (versus conducting journalistic research) are allowed at the meetings. You can find an Al-Anon chapter near you by visiting www.al-anon.org.

Another group very similar to Al-Anon is Nar-Anon Family Groups. This is a group for family and friends of narcotics addicts. These groups, along with Al-Anon, are spread throughout the nation, so there may be a group in your area. You can find a Nar-Anon chapter near you by visiting www.nar-anon.org.

The approach I see less commonly is a coach who works with loved ones of addicts. A coach will be able to work with loved ones on the challenges of shame and guilt, as well as learning how to cope and interact with their loved one as they set boundaries. By working with a coach, the loved ones will have a program structured specifically for them and will be working one-on-one. Coaching is an effective tool in many arenas due to the unique nature of each challenge and the tools provided. Search your area for a recovery or family coach, or message one of us to find a Family Recovery Coach. The great need for and lack of coaching support for family and friends of addicts has inspired Scott's new program to launch in 2019.

The purpose of this or similar coaching programs is to build awareness around the mindset of the loved one of an addict or alcoholic. This program will assist the loved one in releasing the shame or guilt felt because of the feelings of failing the person who has the problem. As we deal with the pain and struggle of a loved one's addiction, this problem starts to take a toll on our own mindset. We start to be ashamed of our loved one, guilty for not knowing how to fix the problem, and feel a heightened fear of judgment from society. Coaching works to heal the false beliefs, the guilt, to release the shame and build a healthier self-identity. Coaching supports you in reclaiming your own identity, dreams, and goals- your life. Nurturing yourself, changing your mindset, and focusing on your healthy life vision will allow you to be the best support for an addict, without taking on their addiction. Building these mental muscles can allow the family to stay strong during the time of struggle. Furthermore, if the family unit can become stronger, the addict has a higher chance for successful recovery.

LET'S GET REAL

1. Think of Alex's story and being an atheist in AA who absolutely loves the program- does this give you hope to know that you don't have to be religious to go to AA?

2. Do you still believe that continuing to drink alcohol gives you any "benefits?" If so, please examine these closely. Are they truly beneficial? How do the cons outweigh the pros?

3. What is keeping you drinking?

4. Have you tried one of these roads to sobriety? Did it work? If so, are you still applying what you learned? If not, what other avenues are you willing to try? Have you suggested any of these to a loved one?

5. After reading these stories, do you have any remaining excuses not to pursue recovery?

6. Have you tried to help a loved one but ignored the fact that they have to help themselves?

CHAPTER 10

Part 3 - Living Sober: Michael, Scott, Andrea

MICHAEL:

S OBRIETY IS A gift. I knew after getting out of Serenity Treatment Center and re-entering the "real world" that I had to put my sobriety first. Something happened to me when I was at Serenity and I am not quite sure how to explain it. All I know is that a fire of conviction was lit within me and it propelled me forward into a life beyond my wildest dreams.

I was nervous. I knew I couldn't be quiet about my sobriety or I would resume old patterns and relationships. I was afraid of every new step. I feared being judged being back in Telluride where I'd humiliated and harmed myself. My entire family thought it was the worst decision possible to go back to Telluride. Deep down, I knew that it was going to be good. I'd gotten a taste of the recovery community before I went to Serenity, and to be honest, I was excited to get back to the rooms of AA. I loved what I had learned at Serenity about the twelve-step work. It was working for me, and I was driven to continue to work the program.

Just as he had brought me to Serenity thirty-one days before, my dad arrived in his black Acura station wagon to drive me back home. As I pulled into Telluride, so many emotions hit me: happy, sad, grateful, mad, embarrassed, determined, scared, you name it. It was sunny. A bluebird Colorado day. The sky was a deep blue with no clouds in sight. I looked at the beautiful box canyon peaks at the end of town. This was my beautiful, quiet little piece of heaven. I felt so much gratitude to be here. To live here. Another wave of determination flooded me. I was ready to live a new life.

One thing that was weighing heavy on my heart was addressing my relationship with Max. I knew he was a full-blown alcoholic, and I was so mad at him. He called me a total of three times while I was in rehab. He didn't even call me on my birthday. I had talked in detail with my counselor about this before I left, and my game plan was to evaluate the situation once I saw him, to go to as many meetings as possible, to find a sponsor, and to keep the lines of communication open with my family. I knew if I couldn't bear to stay at our house (which was technically mine because his name was not on the lease) that I could always stay at my dad's place. I deep down knew that Max and I would not stay together. I can honestly say that I really didn't even want to see him. But I wanted to honestly analyze the situation. I knew that no matter what, I was keeping the house and Max was going to be the one to leave. I just had to put myself in the situation to gain the courage to make the necessary adjustments.

When I pulled up to my house on Main Street in Telluride, I was disgusted. I opened my car door to get out, and dad got out of the car as well. There Max was, walking through the yard to greet me at the sidewalk where Dad parked. I got out of the car, and Dad opened the hatch and handed my big brown suitcase to Max. I hugged my dad so tight and said I would call him later after I went to my first AA meeting back home.

Max and I walked across the yard and up the stairs of our house, and I opened the door. I paused for moment. The last time I actually remembered walking up these stairs was when I fell through the door and collapsed to the floor and called my dad to get help. It was all too fresh. Still too real. I couldn't believe that I was already back home. I looked down the hallway through the front door, and I was disgusted. Everything here was as it had been except even more dirty. Dishes in the sink, dust everywhere. It smelled awful. Like old liquor and food. Max set my suitcase down in the bedroom. I stood and looked at him. The whites of his eyes were actually yellow (a sign of liver failure), he couldn't stand up straight, he was so skinny, and I just gave him quick peck on the lips to get it over with. I realized I really felt no connection to this person. But my dogs! I cried and hugged Sampson and Smokie so tight. These two little guys made me feel that everything was going to be alright.

That night, I went to the meeting. I only lived four blocks from the church! That made me happy. I opened the doors and walked down the stairs to the basement, and the first person I saw was Dave-O. There he was, with his ball cap, mustache, khaki pants, and black work vest. Dave-O was also the first person I saw the first time I tried to get sober in these rooms. He hugged me for what seemed forever.

"Welcome back. We missed you. Glad you are here."

"I'm so happy to be here, Dave-O."

Many more people came up to me and gave me hugs. I knew I had found my family. I shared about rehab with the members and how I believed this time would be different for my sobriety. NEVER AGAIN. I told them I was looking for a sponsor and that I was going to make ninety meetings in ninety days as my counselor recommended in rehab. This room was full of love. Full of hope. This is the side of Telluride that I wanted to be a part of.

The next night at the meeting, a lady by the name of Robin approached me after the meeting and said she would love to be my sponsor. I was so happy. Things were falling into place.

After about a week of being home, going to meetings every day, (Tuesdays and Fridays I went both in the morning and in the evening), I was feeling comfortable going and looking for a job. What I knew I needed was structure in my life. I needed to stay busy. I realized more than ever that I needed to address the situation with Max. All I cared about were my goals: stay sober, meet with my sponsor, never miss a meeting, call my family every day, and get a job.

Being back in Telluride, I was aware now of my previous behavior (the blackouts, the drugs, losing jobs, the infidelity). Back in my previous environment, I carried a huge weight of shame and guilt and embarrassment. Every time I walked by the liquor store or drove past my dealer's home, I felt sick. I just kept telling myself that I would rather feel this than go back. I will never go back. I kept telling myself "one day at a time" and "this too shall pass." I read pages 86 and 87 of the big book every day to keep me grounded and to decompress at night.

In rehab, I had talked with my counselor about getting a simple and stable job. Something that had daytime hours so I could get to my meetings. At this point in my life, I had no idea what I truly wanted to do. I just knew that I needed consistency so I could get in to a solid routine. I talked to Robin and she agreed. She said that the sooner I got to work, the better. I poured over the "help wanted" section of the local newspaper and saw several opportunities for concierges.

I finally got the nerve to go and apply for a concierge job. Questions ran through my head as I headed to the interview. Did these people do a background check? Would they even consider me? Well, they did, and I got the job. I called my sponsor, Robin, immediately. She was so happy. The first thing I told my employers when they asked about my schedule was this:

> "I need you to know that I am in recovery. I just got back from rehab, and my sobriety is everything to me. I need to be finished with work by 5:00 p.m. every night so I can make AA meetings."

Both of my bosses actually smiled at me and said that wouldn't be a problem. They appreciated my honesty and even said that they were proud of my recovery. Relief flooded my limbs. It was in that moment my confidence grew and shame slowly fell away.

This job was the gateway to a new Michael. A new way of life. Slowly but surely, with every AA meeting and every time I met with Robin, I was becoming more comfortable in my new world. I knew that I was not going to be a person who kept my sobriety a secret. I knew that in order to continue to be successful I had to RECOVER OUT LOUD.

MAX

As weeks went by, I became more convinced- Max had to go. One night, I came home from my AA meeting and he was passed out on the couch. I saw the empty Evan Williams bottle next to him. I was angry. Max was killing himself, and I was not going to have any part of this. I called his father and said that Max needed to go to rehab. Max was resistant at first, but then he knew he needed to go. The next week, he checked into Serenity.

FIRSTS

Once Max left, I was living on my own and not in a relationship for the first time in many years. Robin explained to me many times that I was going to confront a lot of "firsts." These stand out as the most significant:

My first boyfriend:

Tucker. At first, I felt so awkward. I didn't know how to act or flirt or be intimate without having whiskey or cocaine to take the edge off.

I met Tucker when I was hostess for a fine dining restaurant in Telluride. I picked up a couple shifts working at night to stay busy in my sobriety. Tucker was busser/food runner. I instantly felt a connection to him, and it was weird to feel real feelings. Tucker was easy to talk to, and during a slow time at work he had mentioned that he didn't drink. He wasn't an alcoholic; he just simply said it was something that wasn't benefitting his life anymore. I was instantly relieved. I made the move and asked if he wanted to hang out after work one night and he agreed. We walked back to my house and just talked. It was comforting knowing that we just didn't have to have sex the first time we hung out, which was totally out of the norm for me. I actually got to know him. Tucker was/is an amazing person.

Tucker loved me for me. He loved ALL of me: my insane energy, my constant laughter, my type A cleanliness . . . everything. And I loved him. To have these feelings for someone was incredible. The feelings were deep and flooded my entire body. They were genuine and real. Also, the sex was awesome. Seriously. Of course, it was somewhat strange because I was feeling all of the feelings and sensations of physical intimacy without numbing myself. I remembered everything. I was PRESENT. Honestly, I had no idea what it truly was like to be fully present during intimacy. There was no hiding. It was beautiful. I share this because I truly didn't know what real intimacy was like- I had never been physically intimate with someone without being drunk or high. Intimacy is such a sacred part of a relationship. I love it. I can't believe I spent so many years just going through the motions of sexual intimacy and not actually being present. Tucker helped me to feel beautiful. He helped me believe that I am beautiful. I am forever grateful for this relationship.

My first summer softball game:

I honestly didn't think I would ever play softball again. I was the person who passed out on the pitcher's mound, yelled and cussed at the batters as they came up to bat, and was also carried out of the park over the shoulder of my best friend's husband. I couldn't bear to think about what everyone would say when they saw me show up to play. Robin helped me to truly understand and process the simple fact that I have no control over what anyone else thinks and what matters is what I think of myself. Robin reminded me that the way to create self-esteem is to take estimable actions. I signed up with a new team to be the pitcher. As I walked into the park, a wave of anxiety flooded my body and I got dizzy. I paused. I saw Marcy. Marcy who had supported me every step of my journey. I continued towards our team bench. Everyone was happy to see me. I received hugs, engaged in small talk, and put my cleats on. I stared at the cooler of beer and just smiled. A couple gals asked if I wanted a beer, and I simply said, "Nah, I'm good." And that was that. Easy. Walking up to the pitcher's mound I got excited instead of embarrassed. A wave of determination flooded me. I was here to show myself and the people here that I was different. To my surprise, it was painless. I felt a feeling deep in my chest that everything was okay. I was going to be okay if people asked me how I was. Honestly, nobody said anything to me. I played well. I pitched and batted a phenomenal game. It was weird drinking just water and not going to the cooler for a beer. I had to take multiple moments and pause and get into gratitude. I was filled with so much happiness. The weather was perfectly sunny and warm. After the game was over, Marcy sat next to me as we watched the sunset. Her eyes filled with tears. So did mine. She was happy to have her friend back. I was happy to be back. I was grateful to be present. Grateful that my sobriety was allowing me to have this experience.

Going to a wedding

I worried about this for weeks. I was so used to going to weddings, getting wasted, and hooking up with someone and not remembering. This wedding was for one of my good friends, Abby. Building new rituals getting ready is where I realized I was struggling the most with my sobriety. I no longer was taking shots to get loose before heading out. I just had to just breathe through my feelings. Robin always told me to have a plan. So I made one. I knew I had no business staying out late. I told myself I would go to the wedding ceremony and call someone in AA. Then straight to the reception for just about an hour to engage in brief conversation, then go home and call the same person in AA I had called earlier. Robin told me accountability is key, and I wanted to make sure I didn't skip a beat. The wedding was beautiful. I noticed the details of Abby's wedding dress and the décor. I felt the love and all of the emotion. Once I got to the reception and people started to get drunk, that was my cue to leave. I was happy with the outcome. I was noticing how annoying people were getting, and I just kept thinking to myself "That was me! I used to be THAT person." But, did I have nostalgia for not drinking? Of course. I briefly was missing being able to clink a champagne glass with everyone to cheers the bride and groom. I was missing the camaraderie of taking shots with the other women my age. I was missing being able to have someone ask me what I wanted to drink and saying "whiskey-ginger" instead of just "soda water, please." I had to pause and realize that I am in a MUCH better place now.

Telluride Bluegrass Festival

Like the softball game and the wedding, I never thought I could ever attend a Bluegrass Festival without at least drinking beer. Let me tell you, it was interesting. I went with my dad, and we sat up front in the press section, which was nice. This time around at the festival, I noticed every little detail. I noticed how big the stage felt outside in Town Park. I noticed all of the music sounds—the difference between the banjo and the fiddle and the bass. I was actually paying attention to the music. The music was awesome. It could hear how it echoed off the mountains in our beautiful box canyon. I noticed the thousands of people and their bluegrass hippy outfits. Everything was highlighted, it seemed. Before the concert ended, I got hit with a wave of nostalgia. Nostalgia for not dancing and slugging whiskey. Nostalgia for not doing key bumps of cocaine in the disgusting outhouses with friends. I had to allow myself to be okay with that.

All of these things I never thought I could do sober. But I did, and they were even better than I could have ever imagined.

FOMO (Fear Of Missing Out)

FOMO was a big reason I didn't want to get into recovery. The biggest fears I had were missing out on all of the fun during the holidays, not feeling like I was "a part of" during dinner parties, and lastly, just feeling disconnected holding a soda water and not a cold beer or cocktail. I thought I would miss out on so much. Truth be told, I was missing out when I was drinking. I thought I was participating, but I ended up getting so wasted or high that I didn't remember anything. Today, I am not missing out on anything. I actually get to participate in life. But I feared not being accepted. I feared being judged by everyone in town. Truth be told, this was all an inner battle of thoughts within me. Turns out nobody really cared like I thought they would. Robin repeated over and over, "it doesn't matter what anyone else thinks."

My first place of acceptance and new friendships was in the rooms of AA in Telluride. I didn't just go to meetings and leave anymore. People in the rooms invited me to do things such as hike and ski and have dinner and game nights at their houses. All of these people are amazing and are from different walks of life. There were multi-millionaires, chefs, moms, bankers, ski instructors, retired musicians, hotel bellmen, and people who were retired. It was in these moments that I didn't feel alone.

The connections kept coming. When I was two years sober, I felt called to become a health coach and life coach to be able to help people. I signed up with Health Coach Institute for my certifications. As part of my training, I drove down to Phoenix, Arizona, for a coaching conference. As you heard in Scott's story, the trainers asked for volunteers, and I ended up speaking on stage in front of over 800 people. I shared my story of sobriety and why I became a coach. Honestly, I thought after I got up on stage and shared, that I was doomed and everyone would think "stay away from the sober chick." But I was wrong. A woman named Sara came up to me after I spoke and shared my story. She said that she was in recovery as well and wanted to know if I wanted to have a twelve-step meeting with her later. I was thinking to myself, "no way is this incredible, beautiful, high-achieving, smart woman sober, and no way does she really want hang out with me?!" I was taken aback. We connected and have become the best of friends, even though we do not live in the same place.

More and more in recovery, I find that when we are authentic and are true to who we are, the right people will find us and stay, and the others will leave. I want you all to know that when you recover and start your new life, you will not be alone. Sure, some people are always going to judge you, but they will likely be the minutest minority. Sober, you get to live for you and no one else. You will find your tribe.

GIFTS

Everyone in AA said that there would be gifts in sobriety. I didn't exactly know what they meant by that at first. The Big Book couldn't have said it better:

> "If we are painstaking about this phase of our development, we will be amazing before we are half way through. We are going to know a new freedom and a new happiness. We will not regret the past nor wish to shut the door on it. We will comprehend the word serenity and we will know peace. No matter how far down the scale we have gone, we will see how our experience can benefit others. That feeling of uselessness and self-pity will disappear. We will lose interest in selfish things and gain interest in our fellows. Self-seeking will slip away. Our whole attitude and outlook upon life will change. Fear of people and of economic insecurity will leave us. We will intuitively know how to handle situations which used to baffle us. We will suddenly realize that God is doing for us what we could not do for ourselves.
>
> Are these extravagant promises? We think not. They are being fulfilled among us—sometimes quickly, sometimes slowly. They will always materialize if we work for them." (Alcoholics Anonymous Pgs. 83-84).

The biggest gift that I noticed early on was knowing a new freedom and happiness. I can honestly say I can't ever remember a time in my past where I felt truly free. I felt freedom to have a choice in my decisions instead of the bottle of Evan Williams choosing for me. I found a new happiness. This happiness is REAL. I feel it in the core of my being. Just being able to wake up and smile and be happy to live another day. Happy to have a choice.

I absolutely unequivocally know that the Twelve Steps work if you honestly work them.

MY GREATEST ASSET

I'll never forget the first time I heard this: My past is my greatest asset. I was meeting with my sponsor, Robin, and she said this to me to help me get over my shame and guilt for what I had done. I can't change the past. What I can do is accept my past and what I have been through so I can be of service to others. Today, that is what I do. My past has taught me love, compassion, patience, and tolerance. Because of my past I do not judge others. I have love for the people who still struggle because I know what that is like.

I will never forget when I shared my story with a struggling acquaintance. A friend reached out and asked if I would have coffee with a friend of theirs. I agreed, and when I met this person for coffee, I could see the struggle in his eyes. I shared with him the raw, unfiltered, horrendous things that I did before I got sober. I told him how living a secret life could only last for so long before the show would be over. As I shared these moments with him, I saw relief come over him. I think he thought he was alone in the madness, and he was hiding behind so much shame and guilt. He cared WAY TOO MUCH about what people were going to say when they found out. I just said, "So what? Who cares what they will say. Are you willing to risk your life for their opinions?" I told him the right people will stay and the right people will leave his life. He thanked me for my time. He thanked me for my brutal honestly. He said he knew what he needed to do. I simply said "You will never be fully ready. You just have to go for it. You just have to decide right now whether or not you are done wasting time. Time is one resource you will never get back." A few weeks went by, and then I saw him show up in the rooms of AA. The addiction show was over and he was ready to live.

LOVING MYSELF

This has been the biggest revelation for me in my recovery. To finally love myself for exactly who I am. Loving myself fully is about acceptance. I realize that a lot of my drinking and drugging had to do with not being totally comfortable with who I am. Now in sobriety, I have been able to really look at my past, why things happened the way they did, and not beat myself up about it. I have to love myself first before I can love anyone else.

AA/SERVICE

Honestly, it is through AA and the friendships I have made and sponsoring other women and walking them through the steps that makes me such a grateful alcoholic. I mean, c'mon, "normal people" do not have a free place to go to for an hour a day where they can share what they need to and know that they are fully loved and supported. I get to have this in my life. I do not take AA for granted. It has helped me through some of my toughest days and also biggest celebrations in my life.

FRIENDS' DEATHS

Since coming out of Serenity, I have had to witness a lot of deaths from this disease. This disease doesn't care who you are. It will take you if you do not take control of it first. I lost my best friend, Chase, to it. Chase- the friend who packed my bags and helped me get in the car to go to Serenity. Chase went to rehab soon after I did. But he just couldn't get a handle on it. Chase tried. He really did. But he just couldn't get through moments of discomfort in sobriety and would end up drinking instead of feeling his way through it. I was there for him. I took him to the ER when he blacked out and hurt himself and needed stitches in his hand. What I ultimately realized is that I couldn't do more work for Chase's sobriety than Chase was willing to do. Ultimately, Chase drank himself to death alone in his apartment. I was devastated. I have had several other friends in their teens, twenties, and thirties with decades more they could have lived who died from alcoholism or drug addiction. Through these deaths, I did not drink. As sad as I get, I have to be very realistic about it in the sense that you have to want sobriety. You must be all in. If you are not all in, you will lose.

MY SOBRIETY IS and ALWAYS WILL BE #1

Living sober is a daily practice for me. It doesn't matter if you have one day or a lot of years; we are all always one drink away from a drunk. My sobriety comes before everything; my friends, family, loved ones, and they are all supportive. If I don't have my sobriety, then I don't have anything. Sobriety is giving me the beautiful life that I live today. The most amazing part about this acknowledgment is that I am at the place in my life where I can honestly say that today, I am a grateful alcoholic.

ANDREA

At the time of writing, I have three years of uninterrupted sobriety from alcohol. On November 1, 2015, when I said I was DONE with drinking, for the rest of my life, I meant it. The strength of my conviction and the belief that I could do it made abstaining from alcohol easier than it ever had been before. I was not going to let alcohol kill me, and that was finally enough to keep me sober.

I don't remember very much about my first three weeks of sobriety this go-around except that I slept and ate a lot. Unfortunately, because I chose to "go it alone" in my sobriety, I had not learned or developed any positive coping skills. Numbing my emotions was the only way I had ever dealt with them. When I look back, what happened next was incredibly predictable.

I was twenty-six years old and at the heaviest weight of my entire life. My weight had been steadily climbing over the year and a half I spent in the relapse/recovery cycle, but I had ignored it. I had had the more serious problem of alcoholism to deal with, but when my desire to drink left me, it was impossible to continue to ignore my weight. I felt FAT for the first time in years, but the feeling was a familiar one.

The REALITY was that at 150 pounds and 5'2" tall, I was only a little overweight.

For the better part of high school, and into my early twenties, I had struggled with undiagnosed disordered eating. It was something I never sought treatment for, and at twenty-six, it was an enormous part of my past that I had all but forgotten. I was accustomed to recognizing when I was triggered to drink alcohol, but I had allowed time to make me forget about eating disorder triggers.

The day after Thanksgiving, I saw the family photos my boyfriend's sister had posted to Facebook, and I was horrified by my appearance. I did not realize that my face and my body looked as "bad" as they did, and I completely overreacted. I began a very strict but not-quite-disordered diet that same day.

I downloaded my favorite calorie-tracking app, completely overhauled my grocery shopping, and threw out all the junk food in my home. I bought a new bathroom scale, signed up for a gym membership, and took my "before" photos. I started the diet at around 1,200 calories daily, the lowest amount I had ever heard recommended as safe for women.

By New Years, I had lost sixteen pounds in five weeks, or 3.2 pounds a week. That's higher than what is healthy for most people, and I had started at only twelve pounds above the healthy weight range for my height. I was dropping weight fast, but it wasn't fast enough for me. On New Year's Day 2016, I dropped my daily intake to only 942 calories. It took me no time at all to fly back into disordered eating. I weighed 134 pounds. I was no longer dieting for my health.

At the time, and I hate to admit this, but I knew what I was really doing. I was already a Certified Nutritional Therapist and, given my history, I couldn't fool myself once I dropped under 1,000 calories a day. What I did not realize at the time was that I had just *traded* a substance abuse disorder for an eating disorder. It was the same trade I made at twenty-one when I started drinking heavily.

I had never learned how to live without destroying myself in one way or another. Sure, starving doesn't get you drunk—but there's a sort of "high" about restricting at first, and there's the dopamine hits I'd get when the scale went down, when I fit back into my skinny jeans, when I got compliments, etc.

Those "rewards" were addictive, the "control" was addictive, but more than anything else—my disordered thoughts and actions essentially gave me a very similar kind of blanket of numbness that alcohol had given me. It was my constant obsession and the coping mechanism I used to avoid feeling negative emotions or even dealing with my life.

And it simply went downhill from there. By May 2016, I had dropped below 100 pounds and was hardly eating, averaging around 600 calories daily. I had never been what I considered to be thin before, but there was no denying that I was frighteningly skinny at 92 pounds.

I looked and felt like death. It was almost swimsuit season, and I was hiding in as many layers as I could get away with. I was miserable, and I could no longer deny my misery. I needed help. I was not in denial about my behavior being unhealthy and abnormal, but I did not realize that I was also denying myself true healing and true recovery.

In June of 2016, I made another commitment to myself. I was going to get healthy: physically, mentally, and emotionally. I wanted to recover, from everything—from my former life of drinking, from my eating disorder, from my father's suicide, from all the hard things I had gone through.

I did not seek an actual diagnosis for my eating disorder because I didn't have health insurance, and I didn't want it on my medical record. At least, that's what I remember being the reason. But I started going back to therapy, with a new therapist. And because of the reason I was seeking therapy, I was weighed before every appointment, to make sure I was either gaining or maintaining my weight. That was enough accountability for me to cease restricting my calorie intake to any lower than 1,200 at the very minimum.

I got a second opinion on my bipolar diagnosis, and it was overturned. After being on bipolar medications for three years, I was weaned off these medications, and together with my continued sobriety and through therapy, my mind started to finally heal.

I did not work with a dietician, but I knew how to gain weight healthily because of my background in holistic nutrition. What I did do was work with my therapist for an hour every single week to begin to heal all of the wounds I had been covering up in my psyche. My positive behavior changes began immediately because I wanted to be happy and healthy more than I wanted to be skinny. It was never really about my weight anyway; it was about controlling myself and my emotions.

My therapist was *amazing*. Her name was Emily. She was just as short as me, but a few years older, and she always wore her long brown hair up in a messy bun with different brightly colored scrunchies—'90s style. The walls of her office were baby blue when I first started seeing her, then lilac, and later, mint green.

Over the course of the next several months, it felt like Emily and I covered my whole life, session by session, going all the way back to childhood. We dug up all the memories and associated feelings that had given me the beliefs I had lived with for most of my life. All the things I had stuffed deep down inside of myself were finally brought into the light for Emily to help me process.

I was finally opening up and I was finally healing. My self-esteem, which had been garbage since at least middle school, began to rise. I began to believe in myself on a whole new level, way beyond just believing in my willpower. What I had thought were barriers to my happiness and fulfillment were actually stepping stones. I started to realize that my life didn't suck, that I was worth anything, that there were endless possibilities for me and my future.

I began to form a new self-identity, one based on my strengths, talents, and joys. Along with seeing Emily, I dove headfirst into all things related to personal growth/development, self-help, meditation and yoga, and finally—entrepreneurship.

Growing up, I was one of those kids who didn't know what they wanted to be when they grew up, and that was still true for me going into my late twenties. I had a decent paying job, but I wanted a career that reflected my life's purpose. Only, I didn't know what my purpose was. So, I set about doing everything I could to figure that out. I think I went through at least six big ideas before one idea actually stuck with me—and that was becoming a Life Coach.

I had literally no idea what I was going to end up coaching my future clients on when I started coaching school. I knew I wanted to be a coach, and that I would figure it out from there. Over halfway through my coaching certification, I had a really vague idea that I wanted to help women to "empower themselves" and "live on purpose," and even I had no idea what that really meant. I was looking for my coaching niche everywhere outside of myself and my personal story—because I thought coaches were supposed to have perfect lives or something, and mine had been a mess until too recently.

At a conference hosted by my coaching school, I heard Dr. Sean Stephenson speak. I can't remember the exact way he put it, but what I heard was, "Your Mess is Your Message," and that my struggles, particularly alcoholism, were what I most well-equipped to deal with AND most passionate about when it comes to helping other people.

My experiences going through alcoholism and recovery granted me the stories, the tools that work, the knowledge of what does *not* work, the always growing knowledge of what does, and the confidence to grow more vocal about my own recovery so that I can help other people who are still in the thick of it. This journey has been my greatest gift.

SCOTT

So, how did I start allowing myself to talk about my dad's death and the downward spiral I took after? I can tell you this was not an overnight fix. This took a couple years to embrace, and I still work on the growth of this mental muscle to this day. I started by looking for anything and everything that would put my mind in a state of inspiration and empowerment. My first action was scouring YouTube for motivational videos. One of the videos that I stumbled across was Eric Thomas' guru speech. In his speech, the words *"if you want to succeed, as bad as you want to breathe, then you'll be successful!"* struck me to the core. This was my moment of clarity that I needed. In that moment, I knew I wanted more than what my upbringing gave me, and I was willing to work for it.

Another quote that really spoke to me was from the speech that Rocky Balboa gave his son in the last *Rocky* movie. His speech still gives me chills to this day, as I remember putting myself in his son's shoes. Rocky's message to his son covered a few main points:

1. Never stop being you.

2. Take responsibility. Don't place blame elsewhere when things get hard.

3. The world is a tough place to live in sometimes.

4. Life will always punch us harder than we can hit back. Always.

5. It doesn't matter how tough we are or how hard we can hit. True strength lies within the ability to get back up, no matter how hard or how many times life knocks us down. When we realize and practice this concept, we win.

6. We should go get what we are worth without backing down from the challenges it will take to get what we are worth.

7. Only cowards place blame on other people, things, or situations, when they are not in a place in life that they want to be.

I knew at that moment, I was better than that. I was a bigger person than my actions portrayed. As Rocky was scolding his son, I felt that I was the one being scolded. I felt like my dad was in that room with me, scolding me. Telling me to go after what I'm worth and not live like he did. To this day, I get tears in my eyes when I listen to that part of the movie. Now, I welcome the hits because it is a solid belief of mine that the hits make us stronger. The hits build scar tissue over an otherwise penetrable mind. These hits are the challenges that we are supposed to face as individuals on this planet.

After I came to this realization, the deep work began. Before, I was just hanging out in my pit of misery, wondering why nobody wanted to climb down in this hole of darkness with me. That's the easy part. It's actually too easy. That's why people easily get stuck there. The real work started after this realization.

Since I was a criminal investigator in the Marine Corps who was discharged with an "Other Than Honorable" discharge, I had to reinvent myself. I had to dig deep and figure out what really made me tick. I was an adult with no identity, other than overwhelming feelings of shame and guilt. So the first thing I needed to do was to start talking about my dad's death and all that I went through after. It was tough talking about my infidelity during my separation from my wife. It was harsh telling other Marine vets that I had an OTH and not an Honorable. I had a rough time with the shame I felt about coming back to my hometown and seeing some of the Marines I served with in the reserves and telling them that the Sergeant (me) who took everything so seriously and loved the Marine Corps was now a civilian with an OTH.

I would get weird looks from some, judged by others, but to my surprise, most of the people I talked to were understanding and passed no judgment. They were just present and allowed me to talk about what pained me. Although my fear of judgment kept me from speaking too loudly, it was those who were just present when I wanted to talk about it who helped me understand that my voice and my story needed to be shared with others—that we heal and transform each other by hearing about each other's trials and tribulations.

Far too often, people allow tragedy and heartbreak to define who they are, rather than using the tragedy or heartbreak to help them grow as a person. People also tend to bottle up the situations that have caused them pain, instead of talking about it. Talking about it may hurt, but there is ZERO shame in anything you have ever been through. Every person in this life will have scars. Every person who ever existed had good times and hardships. The difference between those who grow from tragedy, hardship, or addiction, and those who don't, starts with talking about it, then comes the action and work.

If you never talk about the things that you are bottling up inside, it's like shaking up a two-liter bottle of soda. Once you pop the top, an explosion ensues. Bottling up the things that are killing us inside is the same. The longer you go without talking about it, the more the bottle is shaken up. It only takes one small trigger to start the explosion. One small comment for the person to do something drastic, such as drug addiction, an act of violence, murder, or suicide.

However, if you talk about it a little at a time, it's just like pouring out the soda a little at a time. Eventually, maybe a trigger does occur, but since you talked about it little by little, there is just a little hiss (a minor reaction, or you've learned how to handle your triggers). Bottom line, if there is anything I can pass to you, from the family member affected by addiction, to the addict or the family member, start talking about what is on your mind and in your heart, and it will help in the long run. There is no better medicine than conversation with those you can trust. In some cases, that medicine might look like taking a bold stance on what is bothering you and going public with it, or even doing what the three of us have done and turn it into a passionate profession!

This year, I received my certification as a certified Health and Life Coach. I share my dad's story frequently in one-on-one conversation, with groups of people, in videos on social media, and, now, through this book.

As I was speaking to a prospective client over the phone about my dad and how all of the events after led me to meeting her, a new realization dawned on me.

"Do you believe everything happens for a reason?" I asked.

"I'm not sure what I think about that. I honestly don't know. I'm not sure I believe that," she responded.

"I'll put it to you this way. Since my dad's passing, I've been through quite the journey that led me to coaching, which led me to you. If my dad didn't pass away in the manner he did, and I did not go through all the struggles I went through, I would not be having this conversation with you."

Then a thought came to mind, and without reflection, it just came out.

"My dad's death is no longer a curse . . . but a gift," I said.

I couldn't believe what I just said. Even more, I couldn't believe how great it felt to say it!

"My dad's death is a gift, not a curse."

I almost got lost in a maze of thoughts until she interrupted my thought process. "How could your dad's death possibly be a gift?!" she interrupted.

"It's simple," I added. "If I didn't take my dad off life-support and watch him die, I would not be having this conversation with you."

At the time of this writing, she experienced amazing breakthroughs in her own personal life.

It was in that moment that I started to understand that I also needed to reach people who have been through similar situations to mine. I needed to coach family and friends of addicts and alcoholics. This was my gift. This was my responsibility. There is a family member somewhere who is currently taking their loved one off of life support and watching them die because of an addiction. I realized that I am the one to reach them with my experience and my message:

Our story is our gift. Our story is our superpower.

Now, I view my dad as a teacher. He has taught me the ways in which not to live. His death is a gift because it led me down this path of enlightenment and transformed me into the person I am today. I had to be open to it, though. If I stayed in my own way, I would not have followed the path that the universe (God, universe, higher power, deity, whichever you choose) led me through.

One thing to keep in mind if you are a loved one who has dealt with a similar situation—the pain will always be there. It is still there for me. I watched a television show just the other night that ended with one of the main characters taking her father off life support and watched him pass. I had tears streaming down my face. I did not see the characters or the set during this part. I saw my own vivid memories playing out on the TV screen. The difference now is, when I feel the pain, it furthers my resolve for the mission I have. That mission is to reach those suffering in addiction or because of a loved one's addiction. To show them that true strength begins in the mind and that they can work through this pain, shame, and guilt.

So I leave you in this chapter with this—there will be work. There will be times you want to give up and go back to your vice (addict), or go back to your self-loathing, shame, and guilt (loved one of the addict). But think about everybody who has ever been in a struggle, whether it is a person in your circle or family, a celebrity, maybe a highly ranked college football team that struggles against an unranked team. In each of these demographics or scenarios, there are always two results, the victim or the victor. One will suffer at their own hand and never see their own true power.

There's a story about two brothers. Their father was a violent man and a drunk. He drank himself into a rage and beat both of the boys and their mother. When they reached adulthood, one brother became an alcoholic- living in and out of rehab, on the streets, in halfway houses. The other brother became an entrepreneur. He started a company that built wells in countries that struggled to access clean water. He started other businesses and became a huge philanthropist. A journalist heard about the family and interviewed the two brothers for a story. The reporter asked the alcoholic brother, "What do you think made you become an addict?"

The brother replied, "My father was an alcoholic. He beat me. He beat my mother. What else could I become?"

The reported asked the CEO brother, "What made you create your companies, help so many people, and become the leader of a global enterprise?"

The CEO brother answered, "My father was an alcoholic. He beat me. He beat my mother. What else could I become?"

Either you or the addiction will be victorious. If you win- if you do whatever you need to do to recover- if you SWIM- that victory will be the sweetest after dealing with such harsh struggles. Which will you be? The victim or the victor? Who cares about how hard you can hit. How much can you get hit and keep moving forward? How much can you take and keep moving forward? THAT, my friends, is how winning is done.

LET'S GET REAL

1. When Michael shares of all of her "firsts" in sobriety, does this help you to know that life really isn't over when you get sober?

2. After reading our stories, can you envision a joyful, sober life for yourself?

3. What will your new life without alcohol or drugs look like? What negative things would go away? What positive things would you be able to add in?

4. Do you really want to quit? Ask yourself deep down. If you still want to answer "No," do you realize the gravity of making that choice?

5. Is your story (or a loved one's) going to be a curse or a superpower?

6. Would you rather suffer in addiction or put the hard work in for recovery and live the life you have always wanted to live?

CHAPTER 11

The Ripple Effect

SCOTT

As we've said, one person's actions, negative or positive, can have a significant impact on not only that person's life, but many others within that person's family, community, state, and country. The ripple effect is not simply a small ripple in a pond from a single rain drop. The ripple effect is actually a tsunami, or seismic tidal wave, of negative consequences pummeling a coastline filled with millions of people! Think of the millions of lives affected during the Japanese tsunami in 2011. The effect that tsunami had on the nation was devastating and catastrophic! Addiction is similar. You see, we tend to think that what we do to ourselves is so insignificant that nobody will ever notice. I'm here to tell you, that is simply not the case. A mere thought in your mind can have drastic implications on the trajectory of your life, positive or negative.

You've heard stories in this book about how an addiction, overdose, or death due to addiction has impacted many families. You've heard of stories about a young fourteen-year old girl being left behind without parents due to drugs and alcohol. You've read stories of a heroin addict brother stealing things from his own brother, including wedding rings, just to get his next fix. You've also heard of the ripple effect my dad's death had on my life.

Fortunately, I view my dad as a teacher now, and that led me to writing this book with Michael and Andrea. In the other examples, the families are thriving. But that's not always the case. A lot of time, these addictions become learned behavior by children. According to www.crchealth.com, approximately twelve percent of children in the United States live with at least one parent who was addicted to drugs or alcohol. This research shows that these children are twice as likely to have an addiction problem or to have an emotional or behavioral problem. That's approximately 8.9 million children, with a population of 74 million children in the US as of 2016, according to www.childtrends.org.

You could roll me into this category if I didn't recognize the increase in my drinking after my dad died. Since it was learned behavior, I figured that drinking would help me cope. However, things just got worse.

If you had the ability to stop your child from wanting to experiment with drugs, would you do it? Or maybe you're the child of the addict—shouldn't it be your goal to do better than your parents did? The cycle can be stopped, but it must start with you. You are the one person who can stop your family's cycle of addiction, prison time, and death.

It's up to the individual to actually make a positive impact on his or her family's life. It's up to the individual to make a positive impact on his or her community, the children of the community, the growth of the community. Maybe you're thinking you just want to have a positive impact on your family, and that's perfectly fine. But that has a ripple effect as well. By virtue of you positively impacting your family, your society becomes stronger as well, due to the growing strength of the nation's future, through children.

Now think of your addiction, or your loved one's addiction, on a global scale. The addiction problems in each country wreak havoc on the nation's economy due to treatment facilities, higher populations in local jails and federal prisons, and millions of first responders needing to be reactive to more than 72,000 cases of drug overdose deaths in 2017 in the U.S. alone (www.drugabuse.gov).

We could look at just one addiction—to one drug—and see ripple effects, such as in the case of crystal methamphetamine, also known as crystal, meth, crank, ice, speed, poor man's coke, redneck cocaine, etc. The impact of addiction to this drug could be severe on people who you may not even know. Meth is made in home meth labs, labs in campers, labs in garages, in the woods, and any other area that one can cook it in. Meth is made with many different types of chemicals and cold medications in pill form. A person simply trying to buy cold medicine for his sick wife may be turned away and have to make her go pick it up due to the tight regulations that states have on cold medicine. This has actually been the case for me on a couple different occasions. I almost felt like I was being interrogated just to pick up cold medicine for my sick wife.

Another problem with meth labs is the highly volatile chemicals that sit in these labs. A quick Google search of meth lab explosions in Indiana showed a laundry list of explosions, injuries from explosions, collateral damage from explosions, investigations into explosions, and the list goes on. These explosions have been known to harm or kill innocent children that were subjected to this environment.

Do you want your children subjected to a bomb scare in their school? I'm guessing that answer is a resounding no. Meth labs are even more dangerous. If the lab is in a house with close-by neighbors, the explosion could take out multiple houses. Even if the house does not explode, most states require a state certification to professionally clean and certify that there is no presence of chemicals left in the house before it can be sold.

So, we ask, what kind of ripple effect do you want to have on your family, community, state, and nation?

MICHAEL

You MUST be IN ACTION

Sobriety and recovery is a daily practice. You must be in action every day with your recovery. Recovering and paving a new, positive, healthy life for yourself requires transformation- not just from your addiction, but in almost every area. Transformation requires work, tending, weeding, and more action. You are either feeding your recovery or your addiction every single day. The newly sober person must ask every day- which will I choose?

We want you to know that recovery is so much more than just reading a book and talking about it with family, friends, or loved ones. Recovery is more than just going to rehab. Just because you go to rehab or read about it- that is not enough. You actually have to put whatever path you choose into action.

Recovery is about taking ownership of your life and choosing to no longer be the victim, but the victor.

The Story of a Man Who Wasn't In Action

Jake was the role model of recovery whom a lot of people looked up to. He had a few years of sobriety under his belt, was very active in AA, and even drove a friend to rehab to get sober. A lot of people looked up to Jake as he seemed to have a solid recovery program. Then something happened. One day, Jake decided to stop going to meetings. He thought he was on solid ground. He didn't think he needed to work on his recovery and sobriety. He thought everything was okay- that he had graduated this chapter, and everything would be okay. Then Jake decided to go on vacation. While on vacation, he decided to have a margarita. It was just one. Well, after vacation, that margarita turned into bottles of wine and vodka. Jake isolated himself from sober friends he'd made, from his support system, from anything positive.

Finally, after about a year of staying back out drinking, Jake was emotionally bankrupt. He was worse off than before. Jake no longer wanted to be back out drinking, so he came back to AA. Jake was brutally honest with his home group about his thought process in thinking that because he had a few years in the rooms that everything was fine until it wasn't.

This happens A LOT. People stop working on their recovery and paying attention to their character defects and their disease tells them they are okay. They are not an alcoholic. They can manage a drink or two- WRONG! So wrong! You have two choices: you are either feeding your recovery or your addiction. Which will it be?

The Story of a Dry Drunk

Travis is a dry drunk. When I say "dry drunk," I'm referring to a person who quits drinking because they know they will die from their disease, BUT they do not work on their recovery- they do not reinvent themselves. They do not do the deeper work of recovery. They fail to really live. They do not thrive in their new life.

Travis is a nice guy. What happened with Travis is that he went away to rehab to get good start on the whole "not drinking" thing. He came back to his home and did nothing else moving forward for his recovery.

- Travis does not do anything to better himself and his life; he just doesn't drink.
- Travis just isolates at home. He goes to work, runs his errands, and then just goes straight home.

Travis has become quite a bitter person. He is quick to snap at people. He moves through life as a victim. He resents other people. He feels deprived. Travis is the perfect example of the iceberg analogy: "Alcoholism is like the tip of an iceberg. It rides atop a submerged mass of other problems."

This is very true. Addiction is truly only a small part to what is really going on with the individual. Addiction is literally the tip of the iceberg, what everyone else sees about that person. What people don't see is what lies below the surface of the water: the bigger part of the iceberg. The bigger part of the iceberg can include trauma, fears, limiting beliefs, resentments, and low self-esteem. A big part of recovery is clearing and transforming all that lay underneath the addiction (i.e., the fears, trauma, resentments, low self-esteem). With all of this stagnating inside of us, we often become blocked in having healthy relationships, pursuing meaningful careers, creating financial prosperity- more importantly, feeling joy and sharing our gifts with others. More importantly, if these underlying factors are not addressed, they can be the reason why you relapse.

Being a dry drunk can be almost as bad as continuing your addiction. When you are a dry drunk, you are actually fighting life every day- swimming upstream .You may not drink, but you will likely not really live.

STAYING IN ACTION:

When you stay in action, amazing things can happen in your life. I knew the minute I stepped foot into Serenity that I was going to take that daily action. I had my motto "I WILL NEVER GO BACK." I took these relapse rates seriously. Relapse rates at the time I got out of rehab were over sixty percent. It was pressed upon me that I could not be complacent, that I would need to take action every day to overcome this addiction.

Every day, I thank my higher power for being able to maintain my commitment. Since choosing to be in recovery, I can honestly say that I live a life beyond my wildest dreams. I live a life that I honestly never thought was possible.

This is all happening for me because I became willing.

I became willing to look at myself and what was not working in my life.

I became willing to quit worrying about what anyone else thought about me and decided to focus on myself.

I became willing to trust.

I became willing to have patience.

I became willing to let go of what no longer was serving me so I could create space for what is and what will serve me.

I became willing to stop being the victim and blaming everyone else for why I was where I was.

I became willing to put my ego in my back pocket and eat a slice of humble pie.

I became willing to let some friends fall away. I had to remove myself from some relationships (like Max).

I became willing to trust that new friends and new healthy relationships would come to me.

What do I do to maintain my sobriety?

- I go to at least four meetings a week.

- I meet with my sponsor once a week.

- I have a morning and evening routine that consists of journaling, meditating, and making gratitude lists.

- I read an excerpt from the big book every day (I also have a travel size big book so I take it with me everywhere I go).

- I sponsor women.

- I pause throughout the day to check myself and my actions: Am I acting in a loving manner or am I being ego-driven and selfish?

- I text people in recovery daily- letting them know how grateful I am to have them in my life.

- I RECOVER OUT LOUD- I have nothing to hide. I am here for anyone to answer questions about my story/recovery/sobriety.

- I don't just carry the message. I AM the message.

I want to assure you that, at first, it may seem like a chore. THAT'S OKAY! Change is uncomfortable at first because you are implementing new ways of acting and thinking on a daily basis. After some time (and this is different for everyone, it took me about six months), you start to feel good because what you are doing is actually good for you, and you'll hopefully desire to stay on this path because it is the better choice.

Recovery has allowed me to meet people and build friendships that are meaningful and have a purpose. I thrive on surrounding myself with people who can be authentic and not fake. My relationships support me, and I support them. Recovery has allowed me to participate in society and to be someone who can contribute in positive manner.

Do I have bad days? Of course I do. It is in those moments that I lean into my recovery and my community for support instead of isolating and not talking. I have absolutely had periods in my sobriety where I get into a funk. I have to ask myself what is going on. This is usually what is happening if I get into a funk:

- I haven't gone to an AA meeting for a few days.

- I am trying to control the outcome of a situation instead of trusting and just letting it be.

- I am being impatient with whatever is going on in my life and not acting from love and tolerance.

- I am being judgmental because I do not want to look inward on what might be going on with me.

- I allow people's opinions to get to me.

- I become ego-driven and not focused on the outcome that will be best for everyone but what will just be best for me.

These are scary places to go. I want to tell you that it is important that if you get into one of these funks, that is when you really need to reach out to someone in sobriety and not isolate. I used to isolate a lot in the beginning because that is what I did towards the end of my addiction. Now, I make sure to reach out. I realize that staying inside of my head is not the best place to be. The best place to be is out of my head and talking with another fellow alcoholic in recovery.

Recovery in action allows me to grow and evolve every day. It is about progress and not perfection. When I am actively working on my recovery, I am creating a ripple effect that people desire to be around. I want to tell you that if you work your recovery, you can exponentially blow up your life!

What has happened for me:

- I have developed incredible friendships with people in recovery all over the world.
- I am finally financially stable.
- I now coach people in recovery and those who are simply using drugs/alcohol to cope with their lives.
- I love myself for all that I am. Seriously- I have never truly loved myself the way I do today and it's beautiful.
- I get to travel all over and connect with people in recovery.
- I have an amazing relationship with my family.

To the future:

I am a hurricane of happiness. My energy is real and genuine. I am passionate about educating, speaking, and inspiring people to see that change is possible. It is my purpose to use my energy, drive, and happiness to inspire, elevate, and bring awareness to people about how beautiful life is in sobriety and that there are so many paths to choose from, as you have read about. You just have to become willing to make a choice and go for it. Don't look back. Recovering out loud has allowed me to live a very honest life- I can only hope that other people choose to do the same. I choose to Make Shift Happen.

ANDREA

Recovery is a choice. I won't tell you that everything is going to be okay, not without some raw truths first. Here's the deal, if you've gotten this far in the book, and you still **make the choice not to commit** to a path of recovery **NOW**, it's unlikely that everything in your life is going to be okay. It's more likely that your addiction will strip you of everything you love (if it hasn't already) before it finally takes your life. Choosing to continue to drink or use when you know it's seriously hurting you is equivalent to hitting your own personal self-destruct button.

If this is you, I beg you to **examine your excuses**. What stories are you telling yourself to justify putting off recovery? We have covered many reasons people delay recovery. Michael and I have shared the exact excuses we each told ourselves (and our loved ones) so that we could keep on drinking despite it nearly killing us. Scott told his father's story because Scott Leeper, Sr., could not.

Are you telling yourself that you can't quit on your own because you might need a medical detox? So **today,** get yourself booked for a medical detox starting tomorrow, and if they can get you in today, go today. Don't let your brain overthink yourself out of that decision. In this case, your life absolutely depends on you getting sober, safely.

Let's look at a less time-sensitive, but perhaps more pervasive, excuse. Are you telling yourself that you will lose all your friends if you quit drinking? Depending on the quality of your friendships and the type of people you hang around, this can be a reasonable fear to have. Here is why that doesn't mean jack: **If your friends won't stick around because you chose living over dying, those people are not your friends.**

What about friends who are strictly drinking buddies? You do not owe them an explanation. This doesn't mean that they don't *matter*, but the path to recovery may mean leaving those types of friendships in the past. It's hard, but this choice can save your life. Best case scenario, your recovery may inspire others to examine their own problematic relationships with alcohol.

On the bright side, most people find that they have at least one and often times many friends who stick by them through their recovery. Hold on to those friends with all your might. For me personally, since it took me a long time to quit for good. I lost those "drinking buddy" types of friends over time. To them, I probably seemed like a flaky friend. To me, being around them was triggering and toxic because all we had in common was binge drinking alcohol.

I have an abundance of real, honest, and true friendships now— some are sober friends who don't drink at all; others drink in a healthy way for them. The old friendships I have kept and the new ones I have cultivated are relationships built to last. In my experience, it is nearly impossible to have relationships grounded in trust and integrity while still in active addiction. Our connections to other people are everything, and you may not know the magnitude of this truth until you experience deep friendships post-sobriety.

To have healthy relationships with other people, we must first have healthy relationships with ourselves. This becomes possible *only* after you make the choice to pursue recovery with everything you have. Getting sober and sticking to your personal version of recovery is much more than simply abstaining from substance abuse. Recovery is a journey of self-discovery, self-love, and forgiveness. Just as we must forgive others to have peace, we must also forgive ourselves to have inner peace.

Giving up the coping mechanism of substance abuse also means that you are opening up room in your life and within yourself. You must fill this place by learning new, positive coping skills and by creating a new way of living for yourself.

Your life is in your hands. Only you have the power to create real change in your life. You are the one you've been waiting for. Recovery is a choice, and there are many different paths and programs to assist you in your recovery—but it's up to you to choose recovery. This isn't something you can put off. This is life or death. Which will you choose?

LET'S GET REAL

1. Which side of the statistics board do you (or your loved one) want to be on—death due to addiction or success story in recovery?

2. What kind of ripple effect do you want to have? What kind of ripple effect would you like to see your loved one have? Inspired or tragic?

3. It takes energy to be in action with drinking and drugging as well as being in action with choosing sobriety. Are you ready to be in action with something that will allow you to live and not die?

4. Ask yourself if the reason you are not in action to be in recovery is because you worry way too much about what other people think.

5. Recovery means freedom from your addiction and a new way of life. Ask yourself, are you afraid of change? Are you more comfortable staying the way you are?

6. What ACTION can you take in the next twenty-four hours?

Sources For The Book

1. https://pubs.niaaa.nih.gov/publications/arh284/252-257.htm

2. https://www.detox.net/first-responders/

3. https://www.militarytimes.com/2013/03/29/medicating-the-military-use-of-psychiatric-drugs-has-spiked-concerns-surface-about-suicide-other-dangers/

4. https://www.therecoveryvillage.com/alcohol-abuse/related-topics/facts-alcoholism-police-officers/#gref

5. https://www.addictioncenter.com/college/drinking-drug-abuse-greek-life/

6. https://www.alcohol.org/professions/first-responders/

7. https://www.firerescue1.com/fire-chief/articles/2150808-Firefighters-and-alcohol-what-the-data-says/

8. https://www.therecoveryvillage.com/heroin-addiction/how-much-is-heroin/#gref

9. https://streetrx.com/

10. https://www.marchofdimes.org/pregnancy/street-drugs-and-pregnancy.aspx

11. https://www.psychiatryadvisor.com/ptsd-trauma-and-stressor-related/ptsd-can-be-predicted-following-the-death-of-a-loved-one/article/579576/

12. https://adaa.org/understanding-anxiety/posttraumatic-stress-disorder-ptsd/symptoms

13. https://www.menshealth.com/health/a19538285/ptsd-causes-sexual-dysfunction/

14. https://www.drugabuse.gov/related-topics/trends-statistics/overdose-death-rates

15. www.childtrends.org/indicators/number-of-children